Gilles Deleuze

Modern European Thinkers

Series Editor: Professor Keith Reader,
University of Newcastle upon Tyne

The Modern European Thinkers series offers low-priced introductions for students and other readers to the ideas and work of key cultural and political thinkers of the postwar era.

Edgar Morin
Myron Kofman

André Gorz
Conrad Lodziak and Jeremy Tatman

Guy Hocquenghem
Bill Marshall

Régis Debray
Keith Reader

Julia Kristeva
Anne-Marie Smith

Gilles Deleuze

Vitalism and Multiplicity

John Marks

Pluto Press

LONDON • STERLING, VIRGINIA

First published 1998 by Pluto Press
345 Archway Road, London N6 5AA
and 22883 Quicksilver Drive,
Sterling, VA 21066–2012, USA

British Library Cataloguing in Publication Data
A catalogue record for this book is available from the British Library

ISBN 0 7453 0873 2 hbk

Library of Congress Cataloging in Publication Data
Marks, John, 1964–
Gilles Deleuze: vitalism and multiplicity/John Marks.
p. cm. — (Modern European thinkers)
Includes bibliographical references.
ISBN 0–7453–0873–2
1. Deleuze, Gilles. I. Title. II. Series.
B2430.D454M35 1998
194—dc21 97–50567
CIP

Designed and produced for Pluto Press by
Chase Production Services, Chadlington, OX7 3LN
Typeset by Stanford DTP Services, Northampton
Printed in the EC by Redwood Books, Trowbridge

Contents

Abbreviations

Abbreviations used in the text for major works by Gilles Deleuze

A Thousand Plateaus (TP)
Anti-Oedipus (AO)
Bergsonism (B)
Cinema 1: The Movement-Image (C1)
Cinema 2: The Time-Image (C2)
Critique et clinique (CC)
Dialogues (D)
Difference and Repetition (DR)
Empiricism and Subjectivity (ES)
Expressionism in Philosophy: Spinoza (EP)
Foucault (F)
Francis Bacon: logique de la sensation (FB)
Kafka: Toward a Minor Literature (K)
Kant's Critical Philosophy (KCP)
Masochism (M)
Negotiations (N)
Nietzsche (Nietzsche)
Nietzsche and Philosophy (NP)
Proust and Signs (PS)
Spinoza: Practical Philosophy (S:PP)
The Fold: Leibniz and the Baroque (LB)
The Logic of Sense (LS)
What is Philosophy? (WP)

Preface

Gilles Deleuze, who died in 1995, was one of the most important philosophers in the postwar era in France. His work has not, up until now, received the same attention as that of his contemporaries Michel Foucault and Jacques Derrida. However, at the time of writing Deleuze's reputation is growing, with international conferences and Internet sites devoted to discussing his work. Deleuze is often identified as a proponent of 'Continental' theory, which has had an important cultural influence in the English-speaking world in the past twenty-five years. This body of work, which seeks to call into question some of the dominant assumptions of modern thought, has sometimes been accused of being unsystematic and relativist. These are both accusations which it would be difficult to level at Deleuze. For him, relativism is a poor relation to the much more subtle question of perspectivism, and he is always careful to present philosophy as a rigorous discipline.

We do not have the space here to discuss at length the criticisms that the work of French thinkers such as Foucault, Derrida and Deleuze has attracted. However, it is worth pointing out that the difference between 'analytic' English-speaking and 'Continental' theory is at least in part a difference of approach. Analytic philosophers are usually concerned with a particular problem, and the arguments which derive from this problem. In order to approach a problem, an analytic philosopher will often take as a starting point the intuitions offered by common sense, and will attempt to organise in as precise language as possible the arguments advanced by other philosophers. A Continental philosopher, on the other hand, will also tend to work on a problem, but in terms of a specific author, or a particular historical era. The language used by a Continental philosopher is therefore often more synthetic and syncretic.[1]

In many ways, Deleuze corresponds to this model of the Continental philosopher. The foundation of his work is the subtle reading of other philosophers, and he places the problems raised by these philosophers in a historical context. Leibniz, for example, develops his perspectivism in a Baroque world that has lost its centre. Similarly, Bergson's work must be viewed in the context of technological developments such as the early cinema. Deleuze felt that by engaging with the work of Leibniz or Bergson he could bring the problems that they work with into contact with current philosophical problems. In this way, Bergson helps Deleuze to explore a contemporary 'philosophy' of cinema. Deleuze is always aware of philosophy as a discipline which is historically conditioned.

For Deleuze, then, the creation of concepts which refer back to concrete problems is at the heart of the history of philosophy. So, Plato creates the concept of the Idea which corresponds to the problem of democratic rivalry. Bergson creates the concept of intuition in response to the problem of badly analysed composites. Deleuze, in his turn, takes up Bergson's concept of the movement-image in response to the problems of movement and time posed by cinema. Throughout his career Deleuze looks back at somewhat 'neglected' or unconventional figures such as Bergson and Nietzsche in order to reactivate some of the concepts and problems that they produced. Ultimately, they point in different ways to one important concept; 'becoming'. Being and matter are never stable: they are always caught in a process of variation, becoming. For example, we have talked so far of the 'history' of philosophy. However, although Deleuze often has a historical perspective, he does not consider philosophy to be the history of errors which are gradually overturned. In fact, philosophy is not, strictly speaking, a matter of history. It is rather a matter of 'becoming':

> Philosophical time is thus a grandiose time of coexistence that does not exclude the before and after but *superimposes* them in a stratigraphic order. It is an infinite becoming of philosophy that crosscuts its history without being confused with it. The life of philosophers, and what is most external to their work, conforms to the ordinary laws of sucession; but their proper names coexist and shine either as luminous points that take us through the components of a concept once more or as the cardinal points of a stratum or layer that continually come back to us, like dead stars whose light is brighter than ever. (WP, 59)

Any study of Gilles Deleuze faces an obvious question of authorship, since a significant proportion of his work was written in close collaboration with Félix Guattari. I have attempted to be consistent in indicating within the text publications which are attributed to Deleuze and Guattari.

I would like to thank the following people, who have generously helped me in a variety of ways: Alex Edwards, Mariam Fraser, Mike Gane, Philip Goodchild, Ruth Kinna, John and Gill Marks, Keith Reader, and Georges Salemohamed. In December 1996 I attended the 'Deleuze: a symposium' conference, organised by Ian Buchanan, at the University of Western Australia, which provided me with an important impetus to complete this project. My thanks also to Anne Beech and Robert Webb at Pluto Press for their encouragement and patience.

CHAPTER 1

Gilles Deleuze: A Life in Philosophy

> It cannot be regarded as a *fact* that thinking is the natural exercise of a faculty, and that this faculty is possessed of a good nature and a good will. 'Everybody' knows very well that in fact men think rarely, and more often under the impulse of a shock than in the excitement of a taste for thinking. (DR, 132)

> People will readily agree that intense physical pursuits are dangerous, but thought too is an intense and wayward pursuit. Once you start thinking, you're bound to enter a line of thought where life and death, reason and madness, are at stake, and the line draws you on. (N, 103)

Gilles Deleuze was a philosopher who posed the question of what it is to think, questioning the conventional mechanisms – the 'images' – that constitute thought. In short, thinking for Deleuze is a matter of experimentation and problematisation, of becoming something different. We tend to rely upon the fact that we speak and think as a coherent and relatively transparent 'subject', but Deleuze calls this assumption into question. Speaking 'for yourself' is not quite as self-evident as we might assume:

> It's a strange business, speaking for yourself, in your own name, because it doesn't at all come with seeing yourself as an ego or a person or a subject. Individuals find a real name for themselves, rather, only through the harshest exercises in depersonalization, by opening themselves up to the multplicities everywhere within them, to the intensities running through them. (N, 6)

For these reasons, there is also an element of vitalism in Deleuze's work. He is interested in the force of life which passes through us as individuals: individuals are in fact multiplicities. Subjectivity is not a stable given; it is rather a 'collective' subjectivity which is to be produced.[1] Deleuze admires the theme of 'subjectification' in the later work of Michel Foucault. Subjectification is not about returning to the subject, but rather the Nietzschean preoccupation with inventing new possibilities of life, '[...] a vitalism rooted in aesthetics' (N, 91). The production of a new way of existing is not the production of a subject, but of a 'specific or collective individuation' which is divested of interiority or identity: 'It's a mode of intensity, not a personal subject' (N, 99).

Deleuze committed suicide in November 1995 by jumping from the window of his Paris apartment. He had been afflicted by serious respiratory problems for many years and had become increasingly unwell as he entered old age. His death elicited a number of admiring obituaries in the world's press and in academic journals.[2] These assessments of his work and influence speak frequently of the patient construction of a serious and challenging philosophical project. The glimpses of Deleuze that appear in pieces by friends and colleagues tend to reveal a modest, elusive character who seemed to share at least some of the ascetic tendencies of Spinoza, whom he so admired. Jean-François Lyotard, for example, recalls a solitary figure, in his '[...] modest student den, an armchair under a lamp for reading, a nondescript table for writing'.[3] Deleuze's death was also seen in some quarters as yet another indication of the general decadence, or even madness, which has afflicted postwar French intellectuals. A certain received wisdom circulates: those – like Foucault, Althusser, Barthes and Debord – who have engaged in deliberately 'difficult' and inaccessible work, have paid the price with their own sanity, and even their lives. Far better, as Hume reminds us, to live a life of routine and order, only briefly and occasionally entering the dangerous and tiring domain of philosophy. There may be some wisdom in Hume's observations, but, as a general point, the reader who wishes to understand the importance of the particular period of the history of European ideas in which Deleuze took such an important part should bear the following points in mind.

Firstly, it would be simplistic to suppose that thinkers who actively introduce a principle of disorder into our habitual perceptions of the world should necessarily suffer a consequent measure of disorder in their everyday lives. Any life is characterised by order *and* disorder. Hume and Deleuze may not have been so different after all. As James Miller has pointed out, Deleuze did in fact, just like Hume, have a domestic life – married with two children – which was outwardly 'conventional' and, for both thinkers, this apparent conformity contrasted with their bold, unconventional intellectual lives.[4] Secondly, Deleuze would most probably reject such a clear distinction between public and private, domestic and academic, life. He sometimes suggested that his intellectual life was a way of obtaining the extreme effects of experiments with drugs, sexuality and personality 'by different means' (N, 11). Thirdly, thinkers such as Deleuze in some ways reverse Hume's formula for philosophical work. Hume shared the general Enlightenment faith in the civilising processes of illumination, education and order. Deleuze, on the other hand, points out that just as we pay a price for disorder, we also pay a price for order. Finally, we must ask whether the privileged and unusual conditions that French intellectuals experienced – particularly in terms of their intensive philosophical training – might not have placed them in an equally privileged and unique position in their experiments with thought. Although some of the insights of intellectuals such as Deleuze and Foucault might now appear to be a product of the times, there is also something vital in them which perhaps anticipates things to come.[5] There may be ways in which their ideas cannot be reduced to a historical context: something about them is 'untimely'. We should bear in mind Foucault's prediction that one day the century will be 'Deleuzian'.[6] It is in this spirit that Deleuze's work will be approached. That is to say, there is always just a little more energy in the history of philosophy than we might think. Deleuze reminds us that real thinking is a rare activity, and that we are perhaps too often tempted to see order where it does not exist. Ultimately, we take what we need from an author; a book can be treated as if it were a box of tools. However, in order to find what we need, it is necessary to be open-minded, take on the work of an author as a whole (see N, 85–6).

Deleuze was born in 1925, studied philosophy at the Sorbonne in the 1940s and published his first important work in the 1950s. Just as it is difficult to identify discrete strands in Deleuze's work – characterised as it is by a series of intersecting 'planes' of thought – so it is equally difficult to divide this work into periods. In part at least this is because Deleuze constantly returns to earlier themes, creating difference out of repetition. However, in an interview from 1988 Deleuze does agree to a provisional overview of his work as falling into three periods (N, 135). The first period concentrates on the history of philosophy, mainly by means of concise studies of individual authors. This period culminates with two books, *Difference and Repetition* (*Différence et répétition* 1968) and *The Logic of Sense* (*Logique du sens* 1969), which attempt to synthesise this work onto a philosophy of difference. He then moved on to a period of intense collaboration with Félix Guattari, producing the two volumes of *Capitalism* and *Schizophrenia* (*Capitalisme et schizophrénie tome 1*: 1972 *L'Anti-Oedipe* and *Capitalisme et schizophrenie tome 2: Mille plateaux* 1980). This collaboration aims at producing the outline of a materialist, 'universal' history which acknowledges, but also attempts to go beyond, Marx and particularly Freud. However, this collaboration is also theoretically interesting in its own right. The project of writing 'as two' is a practical experiment into the possibility of escaping from the confines of the 'subject'. Finally, in the third period, Deleuze is preoccupied with aesthetic themes, with books on Francis Bacon and two very important books on cinema. In this period he becomes concerned with the definition of philosophy itself. In his final work Deleuze evinces confidence and optimism with regard to the vitality of philosophy. Philosophy may have its rivals, in the form of advertising and information technology, but it retains a unique role in the world:

> Philosophy is always a matter of inventing concepts. I've never been worried about going beyond metaphysics or any death of philosophy. The function of philosophy, still thoroughly relevant, is to create concepts. Nobody else can take over that function. (N, 136)

Of course Deleuze's work has formed an important part of one of the most creative and unusual periods in European, and particularly French, thought. That is to say, the growth of 'structuralist' and 'poststructuralist', and 'deconstructionist' theory in postwar France. However, movements and trends in areas such as art and ideas rarely demonstrate the coherence attributed to them in retrospect, and although Deleuze's work is closely linked to that of other French theorists, particularly Michel Foucault, it would be wrong to think in terms of these thinkers as constituting anything like a school. Deleuze's work is a singular contribution which combines notions of multiplicity and difference with a commitment to a certain vitalism; a belief that 'life' is frequently imprisoned and that it could be freed. However, it is crucial to understand that he did share with his contemporaries the fact of having come from a highly competitive and intensive education, which exposed them at an early age to the history of philosophy. In the early 1970s Deleuze reflected, with more than a touch of humour, upon this training: 'I belong to a generation, one of the last generations, that was more or less bludgeoned to death with the history of philosophy' (N, 5). Deleuze belonged to a generation of French thinkers who, by virtue of their education, were steeped in conventional philosophy. Several of them, like Foucault and Deleuze, attempted to take this training, which represented amongst other things a *lingua franca* of shared knowledge, and invent a 'new approach' which would bring philosophy into contact with important social and political questions.

Life and Work

> Nietzsche had at his disposal a method of his own invention. We should not be satisfied with either biography or bibliography; we must reach a secret point where the anecdote of life and the aphorism of thought amount to one and the same thing. (LS, 128)

> Actually, there is only one term, Life, that encompasses thought, but conversely this term is encompassed only by thought. (S:PP, 14)

In a recent article, the novelist Michel Tournier recalls the young Deleuze as a student in Paris in the 1940s, and writing *Empiricism and Subjectivity* (*Empirisme et subjectivité: Essai sur la Nature humaine selon Hume* 1953) in the 1950s. Tournier talks of attending a performance of Sartre's *Les Mouches* with Deleuze one Sunday afternoon in 1943.[7] The performance was interrupted by an air-raid warning, and most of the audience sought shelter. However, Deleuze and Tournier strolled around a deserted Paris, observing at close quarters the mushroom-like explosions of German anti-aircraft fire. Talking to Claire Parnet, Deleuze talks at some length about his childhood and adolescence in the 1930s and 1940s.[8] He was born into what he describes as an 'uncultivated' ['inculte'] bourgeois Parisian family, who lived in the seventeenth *arrondissement*. He remarks with some amusement that his current apartment in rue Bizerte is in a somewhat more downmarket part of the same *arrondissement*. He claims to have few memories of his childhood, but he was struck by the atmosphere of tension that prevailed in the 1930s, with the general economic crisis which followed the Wall Street Crash, and the increasingly inevitable onset of war in the late 1930s. At this time, he began to understand the world in what might broadly be called 'political' terms, becoming aware of a deep-seated anti-Semitism in French society, which was often directed at Léon Blum, the leader of the Front Populaire. He was also struck by the antipathy of the bourgeoisie to the social advances – a reduction in the working week and annual paid holidays – introduced by the Front Populaire, which came to power in 1936. In the period of the 'phoney war' ['drôle de guerre'] just before France was invaded, Deleuze and his brother were sent to a makeshift lycée in Deauville. It was here that Deleuze, a mediocre student up to that point, encountered an inspirational teacher – Pierre Halwachs – who introduced him to Anatole France, Gide and Baudelaire, igniting a lifelong interest in literature. Deleuze returned to Paris for the duration of the war, and was a pupil at the Lycée Carnot. Here, he knew from his very first philosophy classes that he had found a subject that he wished to pursue. (He was not actually taught by Merleau-Ponty, the celebrated French phenomenologist, but recalls the latter's melancholy demeanour as he surveyed the daily throng of raucous pupils.) Deleuze's remarks on the political affiliations of his classmates, which ran the gamut from Vichy sympathisers to members of the French resistance, illustrate some of the extraordinary everyday tensions which characterised life under occupation. In some ways these memories appear to be the conventional coordinates of biography. However, on closer inspection, Deleuze's memories of his childhood seem to be deliberately chosen and presented in such a way as to show that childhood is not at all interesting if it is merely a question of 'intimate' autobiography ['sa petite histoire à soi']. One's own story is interesting in that it has something to do with a life that 'passes through' the individual: we are all collective beings.

This brings us on to the properly philosophical quesion of life and work. For some time now the notion of a 'psychoanalytic' reading of life and work – 'His work was motivated by an unresolved relationship with his mother', for example – has been seen as reductive. Deleuze himself rejects such a psychoanalytic approach to literature. However, this does not mean that the intriguing notion of authorship cannot be problematised. What are the relationships between life and work? What do we mean by life and work? What does it mean to speak in one's own name? These questions become much more interesting and productive when the notion of 'life' is as rich and as unusual as it is in the work of Deleuze. The problem is tackled in a characteristically bold way when Deleuze and Guattari propose a provocative reading of Kafka. Coventionally, Kafka's work is frequently seen as an allegorical expression of his own tortured isolation, but Deleuze and Guattari present him as a 'collective' writer, who is 'plugged into' the huge bureaucratic and military machines which will dominate the world in the twentieth century (see K, 70–1 and 83–4). The 'conventional' psychoanalytic reading is unsatisfactory, since Kafka deliberately exaggerates the Oedipalisation of his father to a global scale. The father is only a cog in the machine:

> Thus, the too well-formed family triangle is really only a conduit for investments of an entirely different sort that the child endlessly discovers underneath his father, inside his mother, in himself. The judges, commissioners, bureaucrats, and so on, are not substitutes for the father; rather it is the father who is a condensation of all these forces that he submits to and that he tries to get his son to submit to. The family opens onto doors [...]. (K, 11–12)

Great writers are literally overwhelmed by social and political forces which they translate into fictional form. Consequently, the idea of writing a biography of such a writer is fraught with difficulties: 'All writers, all creators, are shadows. How can anyone write a biography of Proust or Kafka? Once you start writing, shadows are more substantial than bodies' (N, 134).

My Life: A Hole I Fell Into...

Several recent biographies of Deleuze's contemporary Michel Foucault have tackled some of these problems, and have succeeded in opening up new and complex ways of thinking about the relationship between life and work.[9] Writing can be the expression of a life which is itself an experiment with difference, with becoming something other. Writing can be imbued with the disparate elements which constitute the life of the author. Like Foucault, Deleuze must be seen as one who tries to write 'without a face'. In an interview from 1988 he initially attempts to avoid the question of an obvious relation between, as the interviewer puts it, 'bibliography and biography', by claiming that the life of 'teacher' is rarely interesting, and that he cannot be considered to be an intellectual since he has no general cultural reserve at his fingertips. It should be borne in mind that the French intellectual, from Zola to Sartre, was traditionally willing to pronounce judgement on any given subject, but Deleuze does not consider himself to be a 'universal' intellectual: 'We don't suffer these days from any lack of communication, but rather from all the forces making us say things when we've nothing much to say' (N, 137). However, the few comments that he does venture on the subject of 'bibliographie-biographie' suggest something of the ascetic approach to writing and thinking that Deleuze shared with Foucault. For Deleuze, to think is, like Foucault, to seize that which is nomadic, which escapes conventional categories. The interesting parts of our life are the points at which identity breaks down. There may be a point where we 'fall into a hole', or as Scott Fitzgerald puts it, we become a 'cracked plate'. For this reason, in discussing his biography, Deleuze chooses to dwell upon the period of eight years which elapsed between his first and second major publications. He retains only an 'abstract' knowledge of this period, as if the memories belonged to somebody else:

> That's what I find interesting in people's lives, the holes, the gaps, sometimes dramatic, but sometimes not dramatic at all. There are catalepsies, or a kind of sleepwalking through a number of years, in most lives. Maybe it's in these holes that movement takes place. (N, 138)

An individual can experience these holes or, conversely, an 'excess' of memory, floating memories that do not appear to belong to that individual: it is a question of amnesias and 'hyperamnesias'.

Deleuze shares this commitment to 'thinking differently' with Michel Foucault. The object of philosophical work, and writing in particular, is to transform the self, to think differently from the way one thought previously. In this way, the identity of the self, and what Deleuze calls the 'image' of thought is brought into question. Thought is constantly changing, constantly encountering new problems. We are understandably disturbed by the chaos that is endemic to thinking: 'Nothing is more distressing than a thought that escapes itself, than ideas that fly off [...]' (WP, 201). For this reason, we tend to prefer 'fixed opinions' to the potentially infinite variability of thought.[10] Deleuze and Guattari suggest that we should cultivate the habit on not relying on what we were previously; the habit of becoming something other. In a short piece published shortly after Deleuze's death Paul Patton highlights this attempt to free oneself from what one was and thought previously:

> If, as he and Guattari suggested, Spinoza was the Christ of philosophers, then Deleuze was surely one of the saints. Nietzsche suggests that what distinguished the saints was their extraordinary strength of will and capacity to overcome their former selves. Deleuze exhibited all these qualities in his work and in his life, to the very end.[11]

My Work: An 'Intimate' Confession

In this way, philosophy can become intertwined with the thinker's life to constitute a relationship of 'consistency'; thought can become something vital (see S:PP, 13). The following chapter will discuss the way in which Deleuze writes about Spinoza's life and thought. For the moment, it is worth considering briefly the way in which Deleuze tackles this theme with regard to Nietzsche. Apart from *Nietzsche and Philosophy* (*Nietzsche et la philosophie* 1962), Deleuze also published a collection of extracts translated into French in the P.U.F. 'Philosophes' collection, intended as an introductory guide for students. In his introduction to these extracts Deleuze attempts to make some connections between Nietzsche's work and his life. The facts of illness and madness are obviously important for any discussion of this kind. However, Deleuze rejects the idea that Nietzsche's philosophy is in any way a 'mad' philosophy, or that illness was an external event that Nietzsche the 'thinking subject' managed to overcome. He suggests rather that Nietzsche strives to invent illness as a privileged perspective upon health. In keeping with Nietzsche's refusal to believe in a unified self, he attempts to create a sort of 'intersubjectivity' between different selves (conceptual personae), in this case represented by health and illness (Nietzsche, 10). Ultimately, Deleuze admits, Nietzsche does succumb to a form of madness which causes his final work to lapse into incoherence. However, up to this point, Nietzsche manages to treat illness as yet another 'mask' in his work. For Deleuze, Nietzsche proposes '[...] a new image of the thinker and thought' (Nietzsche, 17).[12] Nietzsche actually returns to an ancient concept of the philosopher: a presocratic notion of the philosopher as an artist, interpreter and evaluator of the world; a presocratic unity of life and work. He concludes that, since he does not believe the 'drive to knowledge' to be at the origin of philosophy, the work of the philosopher is in fact a sort of 'confession': 'It has gradually become clear to me what every great philosophy has hitherto been: a confession on the part of its author and a kind of involuntary and unconscious memoir [...].'[13] In this way Nietzsche seeks to forge new links between philosophy and life, rather than a philosopher such as Kant who allows philosophy to stunt his life:

> A complex unity: one step for life, one step for thought. Ways of living inspire ways of thinking, modes of thinking create ways of thinking. Life *activates* thought, and thought in turn *affirms* life. We no longer have any notion of this presocratic unity. (Nietzsche, 18)

One way of understanding this presocratic unity is to define 'life' in wider terms than the individual, personal life of the writer. It is also necessary to conceive of philosophy as a 'force'. Forces may appear without having to mask themselves in the forms of previous forces, whereas life is bound to the form of matter. It is in being forced to take on the mask of previous forms – that of a priest, for example – that philosophy has been separated from its true force. In this sense, philosophy must strive to be 'untimely', to arrive, as it were, from nowhere, and in a totally new form. Philosophy and art seek to free life from everything that imprisons it.

Deleuze invokes his desire to experiment with identity when he is faced with criticism concerning the 'discrepancy' between his ideas and his domestic life. In 'Letter to a Harsh Critic', published originally as the preface to Michel Cressole's *Deleuze* (1973), he responds vigorously to these criticims.[14] Deleuze rejects Cressole's allegation that he has always 'just tagged along', using others' marginal experiences. Identity, marginal or not, can easily become a ghetto; and arguments which are based upon privileged experience of marginal activity are, Deleuze says, 'reactionary'. Rather than claiming an identity, it is a question of becoming and experimenting (see N, 3–12). We do not have to become alcoholic like Fitzgerald, or succumb to mental breakdown like Nietzsche. However, nor should it be a question of 'professionalising' our interest in the alcoholism and madness of famous writers. There is a third way: becoming 'a little alcoholic, a little crazy', just enough to create a meaningful imaginative experience of these states (LS, 157–8). Deleuze travelled little, and, although illness may have often prevented him, this also appears to have been a deliberate strategy.[15] He explains his unwillingness to travel by referring to Arnold Toynbee's claim that true nomads are those who refuse to move from one stable identity to another: they refuse to move on, since they are so attached to their particular territory. Too much travel can stifle 'becomings' (see N, 77–8 and 137–8). There is more than one way to travel: 'If I stick where I am, if I don't travel around, like anyone else I make my inner journeys, that I can only measure by my emotions, and express very obliquely and circuitously in what I write' (N, 11). In his own portrait of Spinoza's life, Deleuze argues that the 'nomadic' lifestyle of this 'Christ' of philosophers had less to do with the distances he covered, and more to do with his ascetic renunciation of property and attachments, 'an inclination to stay in boarding houses' (S:PP, 8–9).

The ABC of Gilles Deleuze

In 1988 Deleuze recorded a series of interviews with Claire Parnet. The interviews, which were originally intended for posthumous release, were broadcast on French television shortly before Deleuze's death.[16] The eight hours of interviews constitute a remarkable document, a sort of Deleuze 'primer'. In his Paris apartment Deleuze talks on diverse subjects from A to Z, taking in 'A as in animal', 'C as in culture', 'L as in literature', 'O as in opera', and 'T as in tennis': literally an 'ABC of Gilles Deleuze'. He talks equally seriously, and equally humorously, about subjects as diverse as Kant and John McEnroe, showing that philosophy is always a matter of the 'concrete' ['le concret']. By way of introducing his work, it is worth considering at some length the picture of Deleuze and his thought that emerges from these interviews.

Firstly, it is obvious that Deleuze was, at the age of sixty-four, a frail individual. It is clear that his breathing is difficult and his movements appear slow. He addresses the subject directly in 'M as in malady/illness', where Claire Parnet begins by stating that in 1968 he suffered from a severe case of tuberculosis, and suffered from fragile health from that point onwards. Deleuze maintains that this particular illness was in some ways a 'privilege'. It was fairly readily cured with antibiotics and was 'without pain', and it allowed him to come into contact with 'life', to perceive a wider sense of life that went beyond his own particular illness. Illness sharpens one's perceptions, and provides a privileged perspective on life. Even though illness is literally debilitating, it still offers possibilities for realising one's 'forces' ['la puissance']. For one thing, it allowed Deleuze to free himself from onerous social chores, and to decline offers to travel; a situation which suited him well.

Deleuze certainly has eccentric views on some subjects. For example, he claims to find eating a chore, which can only be made bearable by the presence of companions. He particularly dislikes cheese, considering its consumption to be tantamount to 'cannibalism', and expresses a preference for three types of 'nourishing' foods: brain, tongue and marrow. He also refers to Björn Borg as a 'Christlike' figure, who introduced a 'proletarian' form of tennis, whereas John McEnroe is 'aristocratic' in style, 'half-

Egyptian, half-Russian'. When Claire Parnet asks him about an amusing incident from his childhood when he was photographed by *Le Figaro* asking the King of Sweden for an autograph, having mistaken him for a famous Swedish tennis player, Deleuze replies with a straight face that he knew that it was the King of Sweden all along. It is striking that Deleuze switches rapidly from moments of humour – ideas seem to suddenly strike him as humorous and he breaks out into a grin full of complicity, spluttering with laughter – to 'serious' philosophical points. He can be scrupulously discreet, refusing to name the chairman of the jury which examined his thesis, but he appears at ease discussing his own preferences and idiosyncracies ['phobies']. Perhaps this is because, as he argues, the charm of an individual is only grasped in that part of the individual that is a little crazy, a little 'unhinged'.

The interview functions as a sort of philosophical 'portrait' of Deleuze, in which two dimensions emerge. Firstly, it is obvious that his philosophy is systematic, in that he is able to provide concise summaries of key concepts, and has no difficulty in illustrating these concepts with examples. For example, he shows that the concept of the 'assemblage' has four components, which he outlines rapidly and with great clarity. In other words, Deleuze's philosophy is held together by a sort of conceptual scaffolding. However, it is also striking to note the way in which Deleuze moves through this conceptual framework by means of imaginative leaps, frequently invoking physical images. Everything is a question of encounters ['rencontres'], of desire which flows through individuals and assemblages, of friendship as the perception of a gesture. Thought is a matter of gesture, shape, movement; and this movement is accomplished by the emission of signs.

The notion of 'life' which goes beyond one's own personal preoccupations recurs throughout these interviews. Literature is not a question of recounting one's interesting personal experiences, of rooting about in the family archives, but of coming into contact with the impersonality and singularity of life: 'To write is not to recount one's memories and voyages, one's loves and griefs, one's dreams and phantasms.'[17] Personal memories of childhood are only interesting insofar as they help to locate the richness of the indefinite article: *a* child, rather than *the* child. In this way, writing is a universal affair. Deleuze seems to be saying that there is always something collective in the best art, and it is not therefore surprising that, although he admires the operas of Berg, he also has a great interest in popular song, and in particular Edith Piaf. For one thing, Piaf expressed this sense of a life which was overwhelming for her: her song is literally a 'cry'. In general, popular song is a very basic form: what Deleuze calls a 'ritornello', literally a 'little tune'. We sing a little tune to accompany our household chores, as we patrol our territory, when we are not home by nightfall in order to lift our spirits, and when we leave home we sing a song to say 'farewell, I will carry you with me in my heart'. The popular song, the 'lied', is intimately connected to our sense of territory. Even a great classical musician such as Mahler can make use of the ritornello in 'Das Lied von der Erde'. It as if Mahler combines the most basic elements of folk music – the ritornellos of the shepherd and the tavern – into a great 'song of the earth'. This conviction that art is, in its most basic and 'pure' expression, a matter of territory is one of the most curious and productive features of Deleuze's work.

Throughout the interview Deleuze constantly dismisses certain modes of thought as stupid, 'feeble' ['débile']. His target is often the banality, infantilism and 'cruelty' of the media. Philosophy poses questions and problems, unlike media culture which constantly interrogates people on their 'opinions', seeking to extract a confession. We might look at two examples of the way in which philosophy is, for Deleuze, a vital activity which concerns us all in our daily lives. As an example of the way in which real problems are avoided, Deleuze proposes that question: 'Do you believe in God?' For philosophy the straightforward statement of faith involves neither question nor problem. The real question is what one means by 'God'. Does it mean, for example, that you will be judged after your death? The second example of philosophy as an 'everyday' activity occurs when Deleuze talks of a theme that he sees as one of the great themes in art and thought in general: what he calls a certain shame of being human. He finds Primo Lévi's overriding sense of a shame following his return from the Nazi death camps to be one of the most beautiful expressions of this motif. However, this does not mean that 'we are all guilty', which is, for Deleuze, a banal and stupid thing to say. It would be unjust to confuse victim and executioner. Instead, it is important to understand that Primo Lévi is expressing a complex, 'composite' idea, which is made up of disparate elements. It has something to do with asking how humans could do such things, and also something to do with a guilt at having reached certain compromises in order to survive. Deleuze maintains that we may experience this shame in belonging to humanity on a miniscule, apparently trivial everyday level. We may witness a scene in which somebody behaves badly, in a 'vulgar' way, but we don't want to make a fuss, and we turn away. This leaves us troubled, and we experience pangs of shame for the person wronged, and as a result of the way in which we have compromised ourselves. Of course, such an incident cannot be compared with the horrors of Auschwitz, but the feelings of shame are related. For Deleuze, these feelings of shame constitute one of the primary motivations for art.

Philosophy and Non-philosophy

> The non-philosophical is perhaps closer to the heart of philosophy than philosophy itself, and this means that philosophy cannot be content to be understood only philosophically or conceptually, but is addressed essentially to non-philosophers as well. (WP, 41)

All worthwhile philosophy, Deleuze says, must lend itself to a sort of double reading: philosophical and non-philosophical. It is not the case that the non-philosophical reading is simpler, just as Beethoven's music does not have to be simplified in order to have an effect on non-musicians. Deleuze gives as an example the work of Spinoza, claiming that anybody can read Spinoza and be caught up in the profound movement of the text. Of course, the work of some philosophers lends itself to a non-philosophical reading more than others. For example, Spinoza and Nietzsche, pervasive influences on French postwar thought, would be examples of this kind of philosophy. Deleuze's constant aim is to push philosophy to its limits, often attempting to explore the borderline at which that which pertains to philosophy meets that which becomes 'non-philosophy'. To think is to encounter and to question limits. 'Non-philosophy' constitutes philosophy's continual confrontations with chaos (see WP, Conclusion). For these reasons, he is particularly interested in philosophers who advance our philosophical knowledge of the body. For example, Spinoza proposes a doctrine of 'parallelism', a non-hierarchical relationship between the soul and the body; Nietzsche reminds us that the violence of 'civilised' society is imprinted upon the history of the body, and Leibniz considers the relationship between the body and the soul to be a form of 'fold'. Assessing the final shift towards a calm, austere style in Michel Foucault's later work, Deleuze reminds us that thinking is quite simply a part of life: 'It wasn't all just theory, you see. Thinking's never just a theoretical matter. It was to do with vital problems. To do with life itself' (N, 105).

Talking to Claire Parnet, Deleuze speaks enthusiastically of his years teaching at the new University of Vincennes in Paris.[18] He apparently enjoyed the fact that his audience was so varied ['bigarré'], made up as it was from painters, psychiatric patients, musicians, addicts, architects, etc. For Deleuze, he was able to address something that was completely philosophical to non-philosophers.

A Theatre of Movement

One of Deleuze's key themes is highlighted in the first line of his obituary in *Le Monde*, which chooses one word to sum up his work: *movement*.[19] At the beginning of *Difference and Repetition* Deleuze places his own project alongside that of Nietzsche and Kierkegaard, who seek to introduce movement into thought:

> They want to put metaphysics in motion, in action. They want to make it act, and make it carry out immediate acts. It is not enough, therefore, for them to propose a new representation of movement; representation is always mediation. Rather, it is a question of producing within the work a movement capable of affecting the mind outside of all representation; it is a question of making movement itself a work, without interposition; of substituting direct signs for mediate representations; of inventing vibrations, rotations, whirlings, gravitations, dances or leaps which directly touch the mind. (DR, 8)

We tend to be disturbed by movement because it undermines our reassuring perception of the world as static and stable: 'There's nothing more unsettling than the continual movement of something that seems fixed. In Leibniz's words: a dance of particles folding back on themselves' (N, 157). However, as thinkers, we must learn to leap like Kierkegaard, dance like Nietzsche, and dive like Melville (WP, 71). In order to create these movements, Deleuze seeks the help of philosophers like Nietzsche and Kierkegaard in setting up a sort of 'philosophical theatre'. Anybody who has enjoyed a performance at the theatre knows that it is often the very physicality of the theatrical experience which touches the spectator. Even if a play does not contain a great deal of dynamic physical movement, it is still an art of *gesture*. The spectators are struck by the words and movements, the gestures, of the actors. This is the 'theatrical'[20] effect that philosophy must seek, in the same way that it should develop the feeling for movement that music has (N, 163). Thought has its own distinctive movements, which constitute a style. For example, Deleuze describes Spinoza's *Ethics* in terms of three forms of movement: a calm stream of definitions, proofs, corollaries, etc.; volcanic parentheses which break this stream; and finally a line of fire which moves 'elliptically', in 'rending flashes'. This is Spinoza's 'style':

> Style in philosophy strains towards three different poles: concepts, or new ways of thinking; percepts, or new ways of seeing and construing; and affects, or new ways of feeling. They're the philosophical trinity, philosophy as opera: you need all three to *get things moving*. (N, 164–5)

In an interview from 1985, reprinted in *Negotiations* as 'Mediators' (*Negotiations 1972–1990* 1995), Deleuze offers what amounts to a general description of the dimension of movement in thought. Philosophy, politics and art all need 'mediators', who will get things moving (see N, 121–34). He suggests that we are at the moment in a 'weak phase' of thought, a period which has returned to abstractions and the search for origins, instead of looking at things in terms of movement: 'Any analysis in terms of movements, vectors, is blocked' (N, 121). With the revelation of the Soviet Gulag in the 1970s and the end of the Cold War, much has been made of the return to 'eternal' values, such as universal human rights. If we are oppressed, looking to human rights and the 'constitutional state' will not help us. On the contary, such frameworks will only restrict movment further (N, 122). Mediators are necessary to get subjectivity moving, to explore the multiplicity of subjectivity: 'I need my mediators to express myself, and they'd never express themselves without me: you're always working with a group, even when you seem to be on your own' (N, 125). Like a surfer, it is a question of inserting oneself into an already existing movement:

> There's no longer an origin as starting point, but a sort of putting-into-orbit. The key thing is how to get taken up in the motion of a big wave, a column of rising air, to 'get into something' instead of being the origin of an effort. (N, 121)

Hegel

> We will misunderstand the whole of Nietzsche's work if we do not see 'against whom' its principal concepts are directed. Hegelian themes are present in this work as the enemy against which it fights. (NP, 27)

Deleuze's anti-Hegelianism is at the heart of his attempt to put movement into thought, since Hegel is for Deleuze the thinker of 'false' movement: 'What I most detested was Hegelianism and dialectics' (N, 6). He maintains this anti-Hegelianism throughout his career (see WP, 94–5).[21] When Deleuze studied philosophy at the Sorbonne in the late 1940s Hegel was considered to be a major philosopher who, perhaps surprisingly, was in the process of being rediscovered. In the version of his thought transmitted to the French academic institution by Kojève, which influenced thinkers as different as Raymond Aron and Jean-Paul Sartre, history would inevitably move towards a final synthesis which is its telos.[22] In this reading, Hegel predicted that human consciousness would proceed, via a dialectical process of negation, towards a state of perfected human consciousness that would effectively be the 'end of history'. The principle of negation is crucial here, if somewhat elusive. Stated simply, it means that consciousness will develop by negating the errors of past consciousness, but also that reason and rationality will emerge from the tension between the rational and the irrational. Kojève's reading of Hegel forces philosophy to consider the fact that reason might have 'unreasonable' origins.[23] As human reason encounters and overcomes the category of the negative, so the accepted division between Subject (humankind) and Object (the natural world) will be overcome. According to this perspective, History is constantly moving towards the accomplishment of a final identity and synthesis. According to Hegel, the properly philosophical method is dialectical, moving towards the final transcendence of Spirit. Deleuze and his contemporaries reject this method, preferring instead a 'poststructuralist' philosophy of difference.[24] Michael Hardt argues that the unifying theme of poststructuralism is in opposition to the Hegelian tradition: 'For the generation of Continental thinkers that came to maturity in the 1960s, Hegel was the figure of order and authority that served as the focus of antagonism.'[25] Jacques Derrida, for example, sees his 'deconstructive' approach as a philosophical strategy which works at the 'margins' of the philosophical territory staked out by Hegel.[26] This 'false humility', as it were, is the starting point of the deconstructionist approach which has gained so much momentum in the past twenty years. Hardt shows that Deleuze, however, sought to confront Hegel 'head on', to construct a 'total critique' which would clear the ground for further work by achieving a theoretical separation from Hegel. In this way, Hardt claims, Deleuze carried out the most focused and precise attack on Hegelianism.[27] Deleuze actively seeks out an alternative tradition from which he can draw support aginst the line which runs through Plato, Hegel and Heidegger.[28]

Deleuze outlines his attack on Hegel in *Difference and Repetition*. Here, he concedes that Hegel has attempted to make representation 'infinite', to cause '[...] a little of Dionysus' blood to flow in the organic veins of Apollo' (DR, 262), but he argues that the attempt is ultimately fraudulent:

> Thus, Hegelian contradiction appears to push difference to the limit, but this path is a dead end which brings it back to identity, making identity the sufficient condition for difference to exist and be thought. It is only in relation to the identical, as a function of the identical, that contradiction is the *greatest* difference. The intoxications and giddinesses are feigned, the obscure is already clarified from the outset. (DR, 263)

Deleuze seeks the aid of thinkers such as Nietzsche in his attack on Hegel. Nietzsche seeks to create real movement in philosophy, as opposed to the 'false movement' of Hegel (DR, 8). In his book on Nietzsche, Deleuze goes so far as to present the dialectic as a plebeian form of thought. The dialectic is an abstract notion of contradiction and negation, rather than the affirmative idea of difference. The positive movement of the dialectic in Hegel is only achieved by means of a negation. In Deleuze's reading, Nietzsche sees Hegel's concepts of development and synthesis in the history of philosophy as being based on a hierarchical model of master and slave. The pleb or the slave accepts this hierarchical model and compensates for this situation by relying on the fact that the current contradiction will eventually be overcome. Against this, Nietzsche proposes a philosophy of forces which affirm only their difference (NP, 10–11). Difference is obviously one of the important concepts in Deleuze's work. It is through difference that he can attack and possibly undermine the Platonic tradition of the ideal. Difference allows him to break out of the tradition of representation in philosophy.

A rejection of Hegel is obviously fraught with difficulties. For one thing, Hegel's theory of history apparently acknowledges in advance any objections. That which is irrational, which stands outside reason, will always be recuperated into an ever-expanding category of reason. In one way, then, Hegel anticipates the post-structuralist challenge to rationality by acknowledging, as we have seen, the potentially 'irrational' roots of reason.[29] This is the theme developed by Michel Foucault in his inaugural lecture at the Collège de France. Foucault acknowledges this debt which contemporary 'anti-Hegelian' philosophy owes to Hegel:

> But any real escape from Hegel presupposes that we have an accurate understanding of what it will cost us to detach ourselves from him; it presupposes that we know the extent to which Hegel, perhaps insidiously, has approached us; it presupposes that we know what is still Hegelian in that which allows us to think against Hegel; and that we can assess the extent to which our appeal against him is perhaps one more of the ruses he uses against us and at the end of which he is waiting for us, immobile and elsewhere.[30]

Similarly, Michael Hardt has also recently emphasised the idea that Hegelianism represents an extremely difficult adversary for post-structuralists, since it has a sort of inbuilt capacity to recuperate opposition. How can we 'break with' Hegel if he makes the concept of 'breaking with' part of the dialectic itself?[31]

Catherine Malabou has suggested that Deleuze underestimates Hegel, and that this represents a sort of blind spot, as it were, in his work.[32] Malabou claims that Deleuze might himself be guilty of that which he condemns in Freud, that is to say, of reducing Hegel's multiplicity and complexity to an unjustified unity: 'Hegel benefits from no extenuating circumstances that might be brought to bear in order to vary the intensity of his name, conferring on it the rich and extensive register of semantic variegation.'[33] Other thinkers, even 'enemies' such as Kant, are permitted to exist as an envelope of conceptual personae, a 'pack'. Hegel, however, becomes a signifier for that which is 'unalterable and univocal'.[34] In short, she presents a *deconstructive* reading of Deleuze's reading of Hegel. Hegel becomes Deleuze's anomalous figure; the 'white whale' to Deleuze's Captain Ahab.[35] Malabou argues – a classic deconstructive tactic – that she does not wish to attack Deleuze, but rather do justice to his work by emphasising the important place that Hegel has in it. Hegel is, she suggests, much more a thinker of becoming than Deleuze claims.

Ultimately, however, Deleuze cannot be regarded as anything else but anti-Hegelian. As Michael Hardt shows, his is perhaps the boldest attempt to clear the ground for a vital and concrete philosophy of immanence which rejects the abstraction of transcendence.

CHAPTER 2

The Philosophy of Deleuze

The Question Posed at Midnight

> The history of philosophy isn't a particularly reflective discipline. It's rather like portraiture in painting. Producing mental, conceptual portraits. (N, 135)

In what turned out to be their last publication together Deleuze and Guattari permitted themselves the luxury of defining philosophy and its role. *What is Philosophy?* (*Qu'est-ce que la philosophie?* 1991) contains a discussion of many of Deleuze and Guattari's favoured themes: immanence, concepts, conceptual personae and 'friendship', becoming, the image of thought, philosophy and non-philosophy, indiscernibility, empiricism. It is a remarkable book, at times highly abstract and perplexing, and yet also direct and full of wit. As Jean-Jacques Lecercle argues, it is at once a primer in philosophy, and a complex continuation of the ideas that Deleuze and Guattari worked on for many years.[1] Just as Nietzsche allows himself a brief self-reflexive moment of grace in the shadowless noon of his life, so Deleuze and Guattari reflect on philosophy in 'a moment of grace between life and death', something like a last burst of creative energy which points forwards as much as it looks backwards (WP, 1–2). As always, their answer is at once straightforward and yet also complex and at times perplexing. Philosophy is, they claim, the creation of concepts. In Nietzschean terms, *What is Philosophy?* is a set of arrows launched out into the world.[2] In a discussion between Foucault and Deleuze in the early 1970s, they had argued similarly that their work might be treated as a 'tool-kit' for general use.[3] One question we must ask as readers is whether *What is Philosophy?* offers us what Deleuze and Guattari see in other thinkers and artists, but are too modest to claim for themselves. That is to say, the gift of a 'third age'. Do they offer something new, something which might take their work in a new direction, just as Kant's *Critique of Judgement* is an 'unrestrained work of old age', which continues to pose new questions? (WP, 2) It is perhaps too early to tell, but Lecercle does point out that the fourth, and central chapter 'Geophilosophy', lies outside the otherwise systematic construction of the book.[4] Deleuze and Guattari had planned to work on a book about the philosophy of nature, a project which was perhaps beginning to take shape in this chapter (see N, 155).

Not Communication, but Philosophy

> Ours is the age of communication, but every noble soul flees and crawls far away whenever a little discussion, a colloquium, or a simple conversation is suggested. (WP, 146)

In his study of signs in Proust's *A la recherche du temps perdu* Deleuze compares Proust's essences to Leibniz's monads. Both express uniquely *different* viewpoints upon the world. This element of difference undermines the privileged value normally associated with conversation, communication and friendship:

> This is why friendship never establishes anything but false communications, based on misunderstandings, and frames only false windows. This is why love, more lucid, makes it a principle to renounce all communication. Our only windows, our only doors are entirely spiritual: there is no intersubjectivity except an artistic one. Only art gives us what we vainly sought from a friend, what we would have vainly expected from the beloved. (PS, 42)

In the same way, in *What is Philosophy?* Deleuze and Guattari insist upon the antipathy of philosophy to debate and communication. Philosophy must follow a more solitary path. Contemporary notions of 'democratic' discussion and debate are really an unjustified appropriation of the Greek concept of the *agora*. Received wisdom tells us that Socrates instituted the practice of philosophy as a conversation between free men. But Deleuze and Guattari are uncompromising. Socrates was actually the enemy of discussion, preferring instead the model of the contest (WP, 29). Debate and communication are often founded on *ressentiment*, hiding the desire to achieve victory over another behind a veil of disinterested debate.

Deleuze and Guattari are particularly scathing on the subject of a consensual and communicative model of philosophy.[5] In *Untimely Meditations*, Nietzsche attacks the cosiness of an academic culture of 'public opinion'.[6] He sees his own age as a dark age of public opinion and 'private laziness', dominated by 'pseudo-men'. This culture of public opinion, perpetuated by academics who do little but commentate on the work of others, diverts attention from what should be the ultimate aim of philosophy, to be 'simple and honest' in both thought and life.[7] In the recent *What is Philosophy?* Deleuze and Guattari argue along similar lines. They are scornful of the culture of opinions, which provides us with the popular idea of '[...] philosophy as providing pleasant or aggressive dinner conversations at Mr. Rorty's' (WP, 144). (They refer here to the 'neo-pragmatism' of the American thinker Richard Rorty.[8]) The function of the philosopher is *not* to engage in debate and discussion. It is rather to produce concepts, which are launched into the world like Nietzsche's arrows. Discussions, on the other hand, are not creative, they 'take things no farther', since the participants are simply not talking about the same thing (see WP, 28). In short, when philosophers criticise and discuss, they are often talking at cross-purposes. Debate and discussion often only serve to debase the intensity of the concepts which are presented and examined:

> Of what concern is it to philosophy that someone has such a view, and thinks this or that, if the problems at stake are not stated? And when they are stated, it is no longer a matter of discussing but rather one of creating concepts for the undiscussable problem posed. Communication always comes too early or too late, and when it comes to creating, conversation is always superfluous. (WP, 28)

In *What is Philosophy?* Deleuze and Guattari attempt to define the role that philosophy can and must play in the contemporary world. In part, they present a heartfelt rejection of what philosophy is *not*. Quite apart from eschewing communication, neither is philosophy a matter of reflection or contemplation, despite the fact that it may sometimes present itself as such. Contemplation and reflection can only produce Universals, such as the Self, and as such are the enemies of a philosophy which is seeking to create concepts. For Deleuze and Guattari, Universals explain nothing, and must rather be explained themselves (WP, 6–7). Philosophy is not a prerequisite for reflection: no artist, for example, needs philosophy in order to reflect meaningfully upon the world. Deleuze and Guattari reserve their greatest hostility for the pretensions of '[...] computer science, marketing, design, and advertising, all the disciplines of communication' (WP, 10). These disciplines have attempted to pass themselves off as domains in which thought occurs as a sort of 'event', as something new. They consciously present themselves as fields of activity which are 'creative'. However, real thinking, which actually gives rise to a sort of 'general indifference' is an inherently dangerous exercise which draws its power from potentially dark sources, creating intoxicating and excessive effects: 'To think is always to follow the witch's flight' (WP, 41).

Philosophy is also distinguished from science, logic and art. Science is not driven by concepts, but rather 'functions' that work as propositions in discursive systems (WP, 117). Science and philosophy work on different sides of the Stoic distinction between bodies and states of affairs, and incorporeal events. (The Stoic conception of the event is discussed later in the chapter.) Science is concerned with states of affairs, things, and bodies. So, whereas philosophy uses concepts to extract events from states of affairs, science uses functions to actualise the event in states of affairs. Philosophy is concerned with the 'smile without the cat', the incorporeal event (WP, 126). In this way, the history of science is a question of the construction of axes: 'States of affairs refer to geometrical coordinates of supposedly closed systems, things refer to energetic coordinates of coupled systems, and bodies refer to the informational coordinates of separated, unconnected systems' (WP, 123). In general terms, philosophy works with a plane of immanence and is a matter of infinite speed, whereas science works on a plane of reference. Science is referential, and is concerned with finite movements of thought. Therefore for science it is a question of 'slowing things down'.

> In the case of science it is like a freeze-frame. It is a fantastic *slowing down*, and it is by slowing down that matter, as well as the scientific thought able to penetrate it with propositions, is actualized. A function is a Slow-motion. (WP, 118)

It is also the case that science is, as Kuhn argues, paradigmatic, whereas philosophy is syntagmatic. The two disciplines also operate according to different rhythms, different frameworks of time. Science operates according to a 'serial' time, in which the proper names of scientists indicate points of rupture and reconnection. Philosophy, on the other hand, operates according to a 'stratigraphic' time, whereby what comes after is always superimposed on what came before (WP, 124–5).

Logic is another of philosophy's rivals, in that it wants to turn the concept into a function (WP, 135). Deleuze and Guattari are ultimately dismissive of logic, seeing its claims to be a 'language game' as amounting to nothing more than a 'television quiz game' (WP, 139). They accuse logic of being locked within an image of thought which is based upon the model of recognition. Ultimately, it undermines itself by the insignificance of the cases upon which it is founded. Rather than the language games of logic, which reduce language to a set of rules like a game of chess, Deleuze and Guattari propose an analysis of 'interior monologue'. This would be a way of introducing *movement* into thought, a way of thinking movement:

> Instead of a string of linked propositions, it would be better to isolate the flow of interior monologue, or the strange forkings of the most ordinary conversation. By separating them from their psychological, as well as their sociological adhesions, we would be able to show how thought as such produces something

> *interesting* when it accedes to the infinite movement that frees it from truth as supposed paradigm and reconquers an immanent power of creation. (WP, 139–40)

Problematisation

One of the guiding themes in Deleuze's work is the conviction that philosophy is a matter of posing questions, rather than proposing solutions. In *L'Abécédaire de Gilles Deleuze* (1997) he argues that the history of philosophy is a history of problems. There can be no critique of solutions, only a critique of problems. It is an error to respond to great philosophers by saying 'things are not like that': '[...] it is a matter of knowing *whether the question which presents things in such a light is good or not, rigorous or not*' (ES, 106). It is not sufficient to say that a philosophy is in error. It is rather necessary to formulate a new question, and it is wrong to believe that the categories of true and false only come into play at the stage of solutions. This conception of truth and falsity is inherently bureaucratic, based as it is on a particularly narrow view of education. (It should be remembered that Deleuze did spend some time teaching in a Lycée.) According to this model, the schoolteacher poses problems and the pupil must discover the solutions (B, 15). However, there are two main drawbacks with this way of dealing with problems and solutions. Firstly, it leaves the pupil with very little freedom: 'In this way we are kept in a kind of slavery. True freedom lies in the power to decide, to constitute problems themselves' (B, 15). Secondly, anybody who has marked an essay knows that they do not always produce identifiable errors or falsehoods. It is more frequently a case of '[...] nonsensical sentences, remarks without interest or importance, banalities mistaken for profundities, ordinary "points" confused with singular points, badly posed or distorted problems' (DR, 153). In short, the problem has the solution that it deserves. This is not to say that solutions are not important, but rather that we must begin with a well-stated problem:

> In this sense, the history of man, from the theoretical as much as from the practical point of view is that of the construction of problems. It is here that humanity makes its own history, and the becoming conscious of that activity is like the conquest of freedom. (B, 16)

In a recent article, Arnaud Villani emphasises the fact that Deleuze draws inspiration from Bergson's 'problematology'.[9] Philosophy must locate well posed questions, and reject false problems. If 'error' exists, it is in terms of badly posed problems. Villani quotes from a letter in which Deleuze claims that any worthwhile book on philosophy must fulfil three criteria. Firstly, it must address itself to a sort of general 'error' which other books on the subject commit. Secondly, it must attempt to reinstate something essential which has been forgotten on the given subject. Thirdly, it should create a new concept: error, neglect, concept. Villani goes on to show how several of Deleuze's books might be summarised in terms of the 'problematological' method. For example, in *Proust and Signs* (*Marcel Proust et les signes* 1964) Deleuze points to the error of concentrating on memory as being at the heart of Proust's work, shows that the theme of signs has been forgotten, and creates the concept of the coexistence of the three dimensions of time. In *Bergsonism* (*Le Bergsonisme* 1966) the general 'error' concerns problems themselves; multiplicity, *la durée*, and coexistence have been forgotten, and the new concept is the badly analysed composite.

Deconstruction and Indirect Discourse

> Even the history of philosophy is completely without interest if it does not undertake to awaken the dormant concept and to play it on a new stage, even if this comes at the price of turning it against itself. (WP, 83)

> Instead of denouncing the fundamental omission that is thought to have inaugurated Western culture, Deleuze, with the patience of the Nietzschean genealogist, points to the variety of small impurities and paltry compromises.[10]

In recent times the term 'deconstruction' has become highly problematic. It is often used to indicate an attempt to break down or critically examine a belief or a 'construct' such as 'masculinity'. It would be somewhat pedantic to reject such uses of the word completely, but 'deconstruction' does have a more specific, philosophical sense, which generally refers to a way of reading texts 'against themselves'.[11] In simple terms, then, 'deconstructing' means looking for contradictions, gaps, ellisions, revealing metaphors. Although Deleuze has never used the word 'deconstruction', he is, in the most general sense of the term, a deconstructive author, as Paul Patton argues:

> [...] he detailed the perverse procedure by which he fabricated monstrous versions of Bergson, Nietzsche, Spinoza or Kant: the crucial rule was to say nothing that the author in question had not in fact said, but to do so in a manner which produced unrecognizable fascimiles. Deleuze was a pioneer of the deconstructive technique of reading philosophical texts against themselves. He employed it to produce among others a systematic Nietzsche, an anti-Platonist Plato and Kantian foundations for a transcendental empiricism.[12]

Deleuze's 'deconstructive' method is best considered as a project of 'free indirect discourse'. Deleuze seeks to work with other thinkers and artists so that his own voice and the voice of the author become indistinct. In this way, he institutes a zone of indiscernibility between himself and the authors with whom he works. According to Michel Tournier, Deleuze demonstrated this power of 'translation', the ability to transform another's work, at a young age.[13] It is a matter of picking up another's arrows and relaunching them. This technique provides much of the charge of Deleuze's work. Alain Badiou argues that this 'indirect' approach is a method which conveys a commitment to perspectivism: we can never be sure who is speaking.[14] The form of enunciation, the 'discourse', that results from this mixing of voices is – although it bears Deleuze's proper name as the author – indirect, impersonal. In fact, Deleuze argues that language exists in its 'natural' state in this impersonal form: 'Language is a huge "there is", in the third person [...]' (N, 115). The attribution of defined subject-positions is merely a convention; interesting things only take place when the subject is erased and a sort of indefinite third person takes precedence. This was the effect that Deleuze sought in the courses that he taught at Vincennes, comparing the desired result to a version of *Sprechgesang*: 'It was like an echo chamber, a feedback loop, in which an idea reappeared after going, as it were, through various filters' (N, 139). Similarly, he describes the style that develops in his work, finding its most complex form in the 'zones of continuous variation' of *A Thousand Plateaus* (1987) as a sort of 'polytonality' (N, 142). For Deleuze, the only way to come into contact with this impersonal, indirect discourse is, paradoxically enough, to experience fully one's own solitude. This is the duty of the teacher whose students demand a little 'communication', who complain of being so alone.[15] The American novelist Paul Auster has explored the same paradox in his autobiographical work *The Invention of Solitude*:

> I felt as though I were looking down to the bottom of myself, and what I found there was more than just myself – I found the world. That's why that book is filled with so many references and quotations, in order to pay homage to all the others inside me. On the one hand, it's a work about being alone; on the other hand, it's about community. That book has dozens of authors, and I wanted them all to speak through me.[16]

If, as Deleuze shows, truth is complex, it can only be approached indirectly. The concept of free indirect discourse is an extremely important component of Deleuze's work on cinema. The readings of cinematic texts in *Cinema 1* (*Cinéma-1: L'Image-mouvement* 1983) and *Cinema 2* (*Cinéma 2: L'Image-temps* 1985) are at first perplexing, illusive, often idiosyncratic. Yet, after reading these books, it is difficult not to look at cinema in a new light, not to feel the experimental and philosophical potential that film can have. Firstly, it has the potential – even if it is rarely realised – to experiment with free indirect discourse. Secondly, Deleuze comes close to creating a form of discourse in which the cinematic and philosophical 'voices' become indistinct.

Similarly, Deleuze proposes audacious readings of literary texts. Kafka, as we have seen, becomes a prescient 'political' writer, a sort of social realist, and Zola a Stoic philosopher. These are not merely wilfully contrary readings; they rather find something new in already existing texts. It will hopefully be shown throughout this study that the importance of indirect discourse in Deleuze's work cannot be overestimated. Much of his thought seeks to gain access to an impersonal world of singularities, a sort of empirical 'reality' which does not lie behind, but rather 'between' conventional perceptions.

Aesthetics

We have already seen that Deleuze considers that the third period of his work is preoccupied with aesthetic themes. Art, in the form of literature, painting, music and cinema, plays an important part in his work. For one thing, artistic production offers a route into the impersonality of free indirect discourse. Deleuze also attempts to bring philosophy into contact with the related fields of science and art. For example, one of the objectives of his books on cinema is to illustrate some of the potential affinities between cinema and philosophy, without suggesting that they are both in some way 'philosophical'. Cinema, like philosophy, but by deploying different means, may act as an exploration of consciousness. Art in general is capable of thought, but through 'percepts' and 'affects' rather than 'concepts' (WP, 66). Great artists are also thinkers, but they think in terms of sensations or 'sensory aggregates' rather than in terms of concepts, like philosophers, or in terms of functions like scientists (N, 123). In this way, science, art and philosophy are all equally creative fields (WP, 5). In an interview, Deleuze proposes the example of Riemannian mathematics to illustrate the links between philosophy, art and science. Bresson creates a cinematic form of space, in which neighbourhoods are joined through infinite possibilities, which echoes Riemannian space. Similarly, Resnais' film *Je t'aime, je t'aime* echoes the 'baker's transformation' that Prigogine and Stengers have developed in relation to probabilistic physics (N, 124). It is just as hard for the artist to create new 'visual or aural combinations' as it is for the philosopher to create concepts. However, as is always the case for Deleuze, it is a question of a parallel evolution between two disciplines rather than '[...] a matter of one monitoring or reflecting another' (N, 125). It is striking that the objects of Deleuze's interest are frequently taken from the canon of high modernism. He favours writers such as Kafka, film-makers such as Godard and Antonioni, and painters such as Francis Bacon. As Daniel W. Smith points out, Deleuze is interested in art which seeks to gain access to forces or sensations. So, Cézanne paints the forces which allow mountains to exist, Van Gogh invents the force of the sunflower and Proust discovered invisible structures of time.[17] The painter renders visible forces that are not visible, the musician renders audible forces that are not audible, and the philosopher renders thinkable forces that are not thinkable.[18]

Anti-Humanism

> It's not a question of being this or that sort of human, but of becoming inhuman, of a universal animal becoming – not seeing yourself as some dumb animal, but unraveling your body's organization, exploring this or that zone of bodily intensity, with everyone discovering their own particular zones, and the groups, populations, species that inhabit them. (N, 11)

Deleuze and his contemporary Michel Foucault are sometimes accused of anti-humanism (see N, 84 and 94). It is easy to see why: Deleuze talks of 'non-human' becomings, and in the 1960s Foucault announced the 'death of man'.[19] However, it seems that much of the criticism that has been directed at this 'anti-humanism' stems from a misunderstanding of the problem. There can be no doubt that Deleuze develops a mode of thought which calls into question what it means to be 'human', but this does not necessarily make him an 'anti-humanist'. It is simply that the category 'human' is too abstract, constituting a universal.[20]

In an interview from 1986, discussing his book on Michel Foucault, who died in 1984, Deleuze sets out what he considers to be the misunderstandings surrounding Foucault's alleged anti-humanism (See N, 83–93). Foucault was neither talking about the death of real, existing men, nor was he remarking upon a change in the concept of man. It is, according to Deleuze, a more abstract question of forms and forces. In the 1960s Foucault showed how, in the nineteenth century, a form called 'Man' is born from the combination of human forces with new 'finitary' forces discovered in life, labour and language. Contemporary forces lead to a new form: 'These days it's often said that man is confronting new forces: silicon and no longer carbon, the cosmos rather than the world ...' (N, 90). The human form is neither eternal nor universal; it will inevitably come into contact with new forces.

Similarly, for Deleuze the idea of 'universal human rights' is a meaningless abstraction. He considers the idea of the respect for the 'rights of man' ['les droits de l'homme'] to be an example of weak thinking ['la pensée molle'].[21] Rather than abstract notions of justice, it is necessary to concentrate on jurisprudence, which has a historical dimension, and which acknowledges the particularity of situations. In *What is Philosophy?* Deleuze and Guattari expand upon the questions of the democratic State and human rights in relation to global capitalism:

> Human rights will not make us bless capitalism. A great deal of innocence or cunning is needed by a philosophy of communication that claims to restore the society of friends, or even of wise men, by forming a universal opinion as 'consensus' able to moralize nations, States and the market. Human rights say nothing about the immanent modes of existence of people provided with rights. (WP, 107)

There is no universal State, precisely because States are only the 'trading floors' of the universal market. In the same way, there can be no universal democratic State, since the bottom line is the world market. Therefore, by virtue of the fact that they both must refer back to the global capitalist axiomatic, democratic and dictatorial States are bound up with each other (WP, 106 and N, 152). Although the market is universal, it is not *universalising*, but rather a creator of wealth and misery (N, 172). In short, Deleuze and Guattari express a deep suspicion of the way in which a defence of human rights is necessarily complicit with, and compromised by, the inequalities and brutalities of the global capitalist order: 'There's no democratic state that's not compromised to the very core by its part in generating human misery' (N, 173). The attempt to establish new universal rights, along with the production of intersubjective 'consensus' so scorned in *What is Philosophy?*, is nothing less than a sort of 'philosophy-as-marketing' (N, 152). It is not that human rights should be dismissed out of hand, but a defence of these rights should not be confused with a defence of the benefits of liberal capitalism. We should not forget the ignominy and poverty of the possibilities for life that are offered to the vast majority of people in these democracies. Deleuze is unequivocal: the cultural consequences of liberal capitalism are, as the film-maker Rossellini points out, frequently infantile and pointlessly cruel (N, 129).

As we have seen already, Deleuze also perceives a certain general shame at being human, which is something more than a rejection of the complacency of Western 'social democratic' values. Philosophy, particularly in Europe, must now always be haunted by the spectre of Auschwitz: 'It is not only our States, but each of us, every democrat, who finds him or herself not responsible for Nazism but sullied by it' (WP, 107). In the face of this shame, thought must experiment with non-human becomings:

> This feeling of shame is one of philosophy's most powerful motifs. We are not responsible for the victims but responsible before them. And there is no way to escape the ignoble but to play the part of the animal (to growl, burrow, snigger, distort ourselves): thought itself is sometimes closer to an animal that dies than to a living, even democratic, human being. (WP, 108)

Philosophy and art are frequently motivated by a certain 'becoming-animal'. On the one hand this is because, as mentioned already, art in its most basic state is linked to the notion of territory (see WP, 184–5). On the other hand, art entails a special sort of 'athleticism' which expresses the 'breakdown' of the organic body. Writing, in particular, is a way of becoming non-human: 'Literature begins with a porcupine's death according to Lawrence or with the death of a mole in Kafka.'[22] Similarly, Bacon shows that every man who suffers is a 'piece of meat', and that meat is a zone of indiscernibility between man and animals. Bacon's 'Anglo-Irish pity' means that he is moved by the image of the slaughterhouse: he is seized with the idea that he could be there rather than the animals (see FB, 20–1).

Four Dimensions: Vitalism, Becoming, Empiricism, the Untimely

Vitalism

> It's organisms that die, not life. Any work of art points a way through for life, finds a way through the cracks. Everything I've written is vitalistic, at least I hope it is, and amounts to a theory of signs and events. (N, 143)

In the final piece of work published before his death, a short article entitled 'Immanence: a life ...'[23] Deleuze presents a concise statement of his philosophical concerns. Although he does not use the word 'vitalism', the ideas presented here are undoubtedly vitalist in inspiration. The article begins by defining a transcendental field. That is to say the field which constitutes the basis of his philsophy: transcendental empiricism. This field is defined as '[...] a pure a-subjective current of consciousness, an impersonal prereflexive consciousness, a qualitative duration of consciousness without self'.[24] Obviously, this 'pure' current of consciousness has links with the notions of impersonal, indefinite discourse dealt with above. Pure immanence exists in opposition to the world represented and mediated through the framework of the subject and the object. The notion of immanence goes to the heart of Deleuze's transcendental empiricism which embraces both vitalism and multiplicity:

> Pure immanence is A LIFE, and nothing else. It is not immanence to life, but the immanence which is in nothing is itself a life. A life is the immanence of immanence, absolute immanence: it is sheer power, utter beatitude. Insofar as he overcomes the aporias of the subject and the object Fichte, in his later philosophy, presents the transcendental field as *a life* which does not depend on a Being and is not subjected to an Act: an absolute immediate consciousness whose very activity no longer refers back to a being but ceaselessly posits itself in a life.[25]

To illustrate what he means by this use of the definite article, *a life*, Deleuze describes a scene in Dickens' *Our Mutual Friend*, in which 'a universally scorned rogue' is brought back to life. Those working to bring him out of his coma respond not to the individual, but to a pre-individual power of life which is 'impersonal but singular nevertheless'. Deleuze also perceives the pre-individual nature of life in young children:

> Very young children, for example, all resemble each other and have barely any individuality; but they have singularities, a smile, a gesture, a grimace – events which are not subjective characteristics. They are traversed by an immanent life that is pure power and even beatitude through the sufferings and weaknesses.[26]

Deleuze's problematising approach to the question of life and work derives in part from his vitalist perspective. The act of writing itself is an attempt to make of life something more than personal, '[...] to free life from what imprisons it' (N, 143). One of the aims of philosophy and art is to render visible the forces that have captured life. Artists and philosophers may be frail individuals, but they are literally 'vital' personalities by virtue of the excess of life that they have seen, experienced or thought about: 'There's a profound link between signs, events, life and vitalism: the power of nonorganic life that can be found in a line that's drawn, a line of writing, a line of music. It's organisms that die, not life' (N, 143). The writer comes into contact with things that threaten to overwhelm the individual:

> [...] he possesses irresistible and delicate health that stems from what he has seen and heard of things too big for him, too strong for him, suffocating things whose passage exhausts him while nonetheless giving him the becomings that dominant and substantial health would render impossible. The writer

returns from what he has seen and heard with red eyes and pierced eardrums.[27]

Deleuze's vitalism is in this way linked to his 'anti-humanism'. A sign is created when thought encounters 'non-organic life', the 'outside' as Deleuze sometimes calls it. Signs are also an expression of the flux and indeterminacy of life. The sign is an expression of the pre-individual, of the flux of life where the constraints of identity have yet to be applied. Philip Goodchild has argued that Deleuze's project represents a 'practical vitalism', which enables thought to come into contact with the power of life.[28]

The theme of vitalism in Deleuze's work has also been taken up in some detail recently by Mireille Buydens in *Sahara: l'esthétique de Gilles Deleuze* (1990).[29] Buydens argues that Deleuze's 'transcendental' field is constituted by a 'swarm' of pre-individual singularities. This fluid structure is that of the rhizome or the multiplicity. Vitalism is a way of connecting with, of being in the *presence* of, this pre-individual world of flux and becoming. Deleuze's vitalism is expressed in his preference for verbs, particularly in the infinitive form, over nouns: 'Infinitives express becomings or events that transcend mood and tense' (N, 34). For Buydens, the theme of vitalism comes first and foremost from Bergson. She draws attention in particular to Bergson's *Creative Evolution* (1911), where the 'élan vital' is described as a form of becoming, which eludes analysis and the material forms in which it can be perceived.[30] Buydens also points to Nietzsche and Spinoza as thinkers who influence Deleuze in his development of vitalism.

Of course, the theme of vitalism requires a discussion of Deleuze's reading of Bergson, and this will be dealt with in the following chapter. However, it is important to understand that other thinkers, such as Nietzsche and Spinoza, help Deleuze to develop the question of vitalism. For example, Petra Perry claims that Deleuze's innovative reading of Nietzsche in the 1960s enabled Deleuze, in his subsequent work, to reactivate some of the debates generated by turn-of-the-century vitalism in France.[31] Also, in the introductory chapter,'The Life of Spinoza', in *Spinoza: Practical Philosophy* (*Spinoza: Philosophie pratique* 1981) Deleuze presents a portrait of a frail individual whose very individuality is the product of powerful lines of force. Spinoza's life was on one level startlingly ascetic, undermined as it was by illness and characterised by a nomadic, propertyless existence. However, Spinoza was able to embrace an affirmative, joyous conception of life. He pre-empts Nietzsche's distaste for resentment and bad conscience, the tendency to turn against life and to fight for one's own enslavement. It is this latter tendency that marks Spinoza out as pre-empting the 'modern' question of fascism. In his *Theological Treatise* Spinoza is preoccupied with the question of why people are apparently so willing to be separated from the positive force of life. Why do they submit so willingly to the forces that imprison life?

> Why are the people so deeply irrational? Why are they proud of their own enslavement? Why do they fight 'for' their bondage as if it were their freedom? Why is it so difficult not to win but to bear freedom? Why does a religion that invokes love and joy inspire war, intolerance, hatred, malevolence, and remorse? (S:PP, 10)

Ultimately, as Todd May claims, this is the question which makes all of Deleuze's work political.[32] Theories of ideology and false consciousness only recognise the injustices and oppressions we suffer against our will or because we are somehow duped into believing that they are good for us. Deleuze, however, poses a question which is both much more direct and more subtle: why do we desire what oppresses us? This is one of the aspects of *Anti-Oedipus* that Foucault so admires, when he talks of Deleuze and Guattari's attempt to tackle the problem of fascism: '[...] the fascism in us all, in our heads and in our everyday behavior, the fascism that causes us to love power, to desire the very thing that dominates and exploits us' (AO, xiii).

Becoming: Starting in the Middle

> One never commences; one never has a *tabula rasa*; one slips in, enters in the middle; one takes up or lays down rhythms. (S:PP, 123)
>
> It is never the beginning or the end which are interesting; the beginning and end are points. What is interesting is the middle. (D, 39)

The 'indefinite life' that Deleuze talks of in his very last article 'Immanence: a life ...' takes place 'in the middle': 'This indefinite life does not have moments, however close they might be, but only meantimes [*des entretemps*], between-moments.'[33] Starting in the middle, becoming, constitutes a guiding principle in Deleuze's work: 'being is becoming'. As Bergson points out, the intellect tends to spatialise, to immobilise the flux of life which is being. In this way, perception of being is reduced and impoverished. For this reason, Bergson promotes the development of a philosophical intuition. This is a *problematising* method which attempts to come to terms with the irreducible flux of being. In developing this Bergsonian perspective Deleuze goes some way to creating an image of thought which is subtle enough to seize the flow of life.[34] This is also a question of the indirect, impersonal 'style' that

Deleuze develops : 'Your writing has to be liquid or gaseous simply because normal perception and opinion are solid, geometric' (N, 133). Deleuze also admits that the middle is the most comfortable place for him to be. It corresponds to his 'habit' of thinking of things in terms of lines rather than points (N, 161). For Deleuze, the 'English' have a particular tendency to begin in the middle, whereas the 'French' are obsessed with roots, beginnings and foundations:

> The English zero is always in the middle. Bottlenecks are always in the middle. Being in the middle of a line is the most uncomfortable position. One begins again through the middle. The French think in terms of trees too much: the tree of knowledge, points of aborescence, the alpha and omega, the roots and the pinnacle. (D, 39)

In the later part of his career Deleuze continued to develop the question of that which is in the middle with his work on Leibniz and the Baroque concept of the fold. Leibniz's 'monadic' conception of matter undermines distinctions between organic and inorganic matter, interior and exterior, and bodies and souls. If matter is continuous and endlessly folded, it must express a concept of movement which is always in the middle:

> Everything moves as if the pleats of matter possessed no reason in themselves. It is because the Fold is always between two folds, and because the between-two-folds seems to move about everywhere: Is it between inorganic bodies and organisms, between organisms and animal souls, between animal souls and reasonable souls, between bodies and souls in general? (LB, 13)

The conjunction 'and' helps us to think in terms of the middle, to escape the way is which thought is conventionally modelled on the verb 'to be'. 'And' is a tool for producing a sort of 'stammering' in thought and language: it is the possibility of diversity and the destruction of identity. Multiplicity is not the sum of its terms, but is contained in the 'and':

> AND is neither one thing nor the other, it's always in between, between two things; it's the borderline, there's always a border, a line of flight or flow, only we don't see it, because it's the least perceptible of things. And yet it's along this line of flight that things come to pass, becomings evolve, revolutions take shape. (N, 45)

Becoming, a question of being in the middle rather than at the beginning or the end, is often discussed by Deleuze and Guattari in terms of 'becoming-animal', an activity shared by children and novelists. Similarly, they talk of 'becoming-woman' (see TP,

122–6). It is a matter of metamorphosis and not metaphor: rather than being 'like', it is a matter of entering into a zone of indiscernibility *with*. *Moby Dick* is the novel of Captain Ahab's 'becoming-whale'. Deleuze and Guattari give as an example Robert De Niro in what we must assume is Scorsese's *Taxi Driver*. De Niro walks 'like' a crab, '[...] but, he says, it is not a question of his imitating a crab; it is a question of making something that has to do with the crab enter into composition with the image [...]' (TP, 274). Becoming is 'molecular', a matter of emitting particles which enter into proximity with animal- or woman-particles: 'You become animal only molecularly' (TP, 275). The activity of becoming defines 'minor' literature; a literature which is in the middle, which rejects the 'molar' dualisms that define and constrain identity. In this way, Virginia Woolf is a 'minor' writer: 'The only way to get outside the dualisms is to be-between, to pass between, the intermezzo – that is what Virginia Woolf lived with all her energies, in all of her work, never ceasing to become' (TP, 277).

Empiricism

Deleuze conceives of empiricism as a form of pluralism: abstract universals such as Totality, Unity and the Subject are rejected. Rather than an analysis of that which is universal and eternal, it is a question of discovering the conditions under which something new might be produced (see D, vii and N, 88–9). Empiricism assumes that things exist only as 'multiplicities'. For the empiricist, every 'thing' is made up of a series of elements – referred to by Deleuze as 'lines' or 'dimensions' rather than points – which are 'irreducible to one another' (D, vii). Another way of stating this principle of heterogeneity is the idea that relations are external to their terms. Again, it is a question of the middle: something happens 'between' two terms, which leaves two terms intact in their singularity:

> And even if there are only two terms, there is an AND between the two, which is neither the one nor the other, nor the one which becomes the other, but which constitutes the multiplicity. This is why it is always possible to undo dualisms from the inside, by tracing the line of flight which passes between the two terms or the two sets, the narrow stream which belongs neither to one nor the other, but draws both into a non-parallel evolution, into a heterochronous becoming. (D, 34–5)

Deleuze's approach to empiricism is something more than the conventional attachment of empiricists to experience as opposed to abstract reason. It is a 'transcendental' form of empiricism which seeks to gain some sort of purchase on the 'given', the chaotic flux of the sensible. The transcendental field revealed by Deleuze's version of empiricism is directly opposed to the system of the subject and the object. Rather than a conventional distinction between 'raw' experience and the mind that represents and interprets, he looks at the ways in which the mind, by means of certain tendencies, constructs itself from the flux of the 'given'. Empiricism is, in this way, a sort of 'absolute consciousness':

> There is something wild and powerful in such a transcendental empiricism. This is clearly not the element of sensation (simple empiricism) since sensation is only a break in the current of absolute consciousness; it is rather, however close together two sensations might be, the passage from one to the other as becoming [...].[35]

Transcendental does not mean 'transcendent': it refers instead to a plane of immanence which is populated only by 'events' (WP, 48). Empiricism takes up the challenge laid down to philosophy by 'non-philosophy'. It does not allow itself the assumption that the world conforms to the principles of identity and representation, and rejects transcendence in favour of immanence. Hume, for example, brings into question the relatively stable identity which is frequently attributed to the self by emphasising the principles of habit and contingency. Deleuze also makes much of Hume's idea that relations are external to their terms. This simple formula is the motor behind Deleuze's own principle of heterogeneity. A relation between two elements does not transcend those elements. It rather leaves them intact and discrete. The relation itself is therefore external to the elements which remain discrete and separate from it. The notion that empiricism is an 'English' form is found throughout Deleuze's work. For example, in his books on cinema he emphasises that empiricism is a way of thinking which pervades English-speaking culture by presenting Hitchcock's films as a way of experimenting with thought, and in particular the empirical question of relations and conjunctions. According to Deleuze, Hitchcock is 'one of the greatest English film-makers' because he develops a narrative style which is particularly suited to exploring images of 'mental relations' (C1, x). For example, Hitchcock considers what happens when an apparently straightforward relation, a marriage, is dissolved when a man and a woman discover that they are not, in fact, married. In *What is Philosophy?* Deleuze and Guattari point out that the English empiricist tradition is reflected in the fact that English law is based largely on convention (WP, 106).

Geophilosophy and the Untimely

> There are dimensions here, times and places, glacial or torrid zones never moderated, the entire exotic geography which characterizes a mode of thought as well as a style of life. (LS, 128)

> In the trinity Founding-Building-Inhabiting, the French build and the Germans lay foundations, but the English inhabit. For them a tent is all that is needed. They develop an extraordinary conception of habit: habits are taken on by contemplating and by contracting that which is contemplated. (WP, 105)

The theme of 'geophilosophy' is dealt with at some length in *What is Philosophy?* In order to introduce this idea, they refer to Fernand Braudel's innovative historical approach which had an important influence on so-called 'structuralist' work.[36] In seeking to move historical studies away from a narrative approach which concentrated on great men and great events, Braudel sought to shift some of the emphasis of history to two rather different dimensions: the 'minor' events of everyday life, and the historical trends of the *longue durée*, which are frequently linked to geography and landscape. By insisting upon the plurality of time Braudel introduces the neglected questions of space and geography into history. This emphasis on geographical questions allows Braudel to treat history as 'a web of problems', forming an open system.

Deleuze and Guattari propose 'geophilosophy' as a way of emphasising the role of contingency in philosophy. Just as Braudel asks why capitalism emerges as it does in certain places and not, for example, in China, we need to ask why philosophy emerges in Greece when it does:

> Philosophy appears in Greece as a result of contingency rather than necessity, as a result of an ambience or milieu rather than an origin, of a becoming rather than a history, of a geography rather than a historiography, of a grace rather than a nature. (WP, 96–7)

How, Deleuze and Guattari ask, could anything come from history? History is dominated by two models which are in many ways contradictory: agency and necessity. Geography offers two productive ways of thinking about history: becoming and contingency. Geophilosophy seeks out the 'moment of grace' which escapes the necessity of history; what Nietzsche calls the 'untimely'.[37] The becoming of an event lies outside the scope of history. For example, May 1968 can be interpreted as a set of events which are actualised in particular circumstances. But it can also be seen as a moment of grace, 'a becoming in its pure state' (N, 171). Geophilosophy also aims to bring philosophy down to earth; to show that, rather than it being a question of the relationship between the subject and the object, it is a question of a milieu – a territory, and of the relationship between that territory and the earth (WP, 85–6). Human life, even in its smallest details, involves a recurring triple movement: the search for a territory, deterritorialisation, and reterritorialisation. (WP, 67–8). Philosophy should always seek out the possibility of the event by means of deterritorialisation: 'Revolution is absolute deterritorialization even to the point where this calls for a new earth, a new people' (WP, 101).

Tools for Thinking

Signs

> We are wrong to believe in facts; there are only signs. We are wrong to believe in truth; there are only interpretations. The sign is an ever-equivocal, implicit, and implicated meaning. (PS, 90)

> What forces us to think is the sign. (PS, 162)

Deleuze conceives of the sign in a way which departs from what might be called the structuralist view, which considers the sign to be essentially a result of the arbitrary relation between the signifier and the signified. A sign comes into being when thought is thrown into crisis because the reassuring world of representation has broken down. The signifier and the signified constitute a 'dreary world', whereas signs indicate the deterritorialisation and reterritorialisation of thought (TP, 67). The sign itself entails heterogeneity in three ways: it 'flashes' between the two realities of the sign itself and the object which carries it; the sign also 'envelops' another object within the object that bears it; and the sign does not produce resemblance in someone perceiving the sign, but rather perception as a sort of aparallel evolution (DR, 22–3). Deleuze uses as an example the process of learning to swim:

> The movement of the swimmer does not resemble that of the wave, in particular, the movements of the swimming instructor which we reproduce on the sand bear no relation to the movements of the wave, which we learn to deal with only by grasping the former in practice as signs. [...] Our only teachers are those who tell us 'do with me', and are able to emit signs to be developed in heterogeneity rather than propose gestures for us to reproduce. (DR, 23)

The sign is an expression of the way in which order has been *created* rather than discovered. Rather than being linked to language, signs are linked to thought. In his books on cinema he reinforces his non-linguistic approach to the world of signs by adopting the categories of 'Firstness', 'Secondness' and 'Thirdness' set out by the American pragmatist Peirce. In simple terms, this schema places signs within an empirical framework. Firstness is the world as it is in itself, what might be called the 'haecceity' of the world. The experience of Firstness is an experience of immediate and unreflected consciousness. Secondness is the initial opposition of consciousness to undifferentiated Firstness. And Thirdness is the extraction of a law of regularity from the first two. In his pragmatic version of the self Peirce shows that even our own thoughts must be interpreted as signs. When thought experiences a violent shock which shakes it out of its natural stupor, signs are created. In Deleuze's reading of Proust, the hero of *A la recherche du temps perdu* undergoes an apprenticeship in signs. The ultimate world of signs in this apprenticeship is the world of art, since its signs are immaterial. Through the interpretation of signs we learn that truth itself is a matter of interpretation.

The sign conforms to an image of thought that is not dogmatic. As Daniel W. Smith points out, Deleuze frequently refers to Plato's *Republic* in his discussions of aesthetics.[38] Deleuze takes Plato's distinction between sensations which leave the mind tranquil and those which force us to think, and labels the first *recognition* and the second *signs*. Sensations of recognition correspond to the Kantian notion of a harmonious use of the faculties, and signs correspond to an 'involuntary discord'.[39] The sign is an encounter rather than an act of recognition, and it can only be felt or sensed: signs act directly upon the nervous system.[40]

Friendship is, for Deleuze, a question of the emission of signs. We all know that we 'click' with some individuals and not with others. There are people with whom one cannot speak even about the simplest things, and yet there are also people with whom one might disagree, but with whom one establishes a profound understanding about even quite abstract subjects.[41] Deleuze believes that this is because we are all susceptible to a certain way of perceiving 'charm'. This sensitivity to the signs of friendship functions at a level of perception which occurs prior to signification. One of the reasons that Deleuze so admires and enjoys the work of Proust is that it is preoccupied with the world of signs. Similarly, he is fascinated by the 'empty' signs of 'sophisticated' society, which are similar to the signs created by animals.[42]

Events

> I have, it's true, spent a lot of time writing about this notion of the event: you see, I don't believe in things. (N, 160)

> I've tried in all my books to discover the nature of events; it's a philosophical concept, the only one capable of ousting the verb 'to be' and attributes. (N, 141)

Deleuze remains faithful throughout his career to the Stoic logic of events: 'A life contains only virtuals. It is made of virtualities, events, singularities.'[43] In *The Logic of Sense* (*Logique du sens* 1969) he points out that the Stoics distinguish between two kinds of things: bodies and 'states of affairs', which are determined by mixtures of bodies, and 'incorporeal' entities (LS, 4). The latter are 'events'; incorporeal singularities which must be extracted from the situations in which they take place.[44] The event is a 'hecceity' (sometimes spelt 'haecceity'): '[...] a draft, a wind, a day, a time of day, a stream, a place, a battle, an illness' (N, 141). The Stoics introduce a new distinction, contrasting the 'thickness of bodies' with the incorporeal events which operate on the surface of bodies like a 'mist over the prairie' (LS, 5). At the beginning of *The Logic of Sense* Deleuze points to the recurrence of the theme of the event in the history of philosophy, dealt with by the Stoics, Ockham's school in the fourteenth century, and Meinong in his attack on Hegelian logic in the nineteenth century (LS, 19). All three moments in philosophy pose the same question:

> The question is as follows: is there something, *aliquid*, which merges [...] neither with the 'lived', or representation or the mental activity of the person who expresses herself in the proposition, nor with concepts or even signified essences? If there is, sense, or that which is expressed by the proposition, would be irreducible to individual states of affairs, particular images, personal beliefs, and universal or general concepts. (LS, 19)

There is a general consensus that three distinct relations can generally be found in a proposition. Firstly, a relation of denotation which is the relation of the proposition to some external state of affairs (LS, 12). Secondly, the proposition contains a relation of manifestation to the person who is speaking: this person expresses beliefs and desires (LS, 13). The third dimension of the proposition is that of signification, of the relation to universal or general concepts. However, there is a fourth, 'aliquid' dimension of the proposition, which is also the most difficult to locate. In fact, Deleuze argues that the attempt to bring this dimension to evidence is a task comparable to Lewis Carroll's hunt for the illusory Snark. The difficulty stems from the fact that the dimension of sense exists neither in things nor in the mind, and does not appear to be of practical use. The hunt for the 'logic of sense' is actually the task of empiricism, looking for '[...] a phantom at the limit of a lengthened or unfolded experience' (LS, 20). To illustrate this particular dimension of 'sense' further Deleuze turns to Husserl, who distinguishes the 'sense of perception', or the 'perceptual noema' from the physical or mental existence of the object (LS, 20). The real tree can burn, be cut down, or made into a cabin. However, the 'noema' tree has a different status, since the noema does not exist apart from the proposition which expresses it (LS, 21). Sense as 'event' is a dimension of becoming, best described linguistically by a verb in the infinitive. In this way, events '[...] are not living presents, but infinitives: the unlimited Aion, the becoming which divides itself infinitely in past and future and always eludes the present' (LS, 5). So, for example, Deleuze shows that we must distinguish between green as a quality of the tree and 'to green' as an attribute or 'noematic colour' (LS, 21). According to Deleuze, this Stoic distinction between bodies or states of affairs and incorporeal events represents a challenge to philosophy. Rather than relying upon a philosophy of Being, the Stoics introduce a dimension of 'extra-Being' (LS, 7).

The concept of the event is linked to two other themes in Deleuze's work. Firstly, it is an ethical theme, which recalls Nietzsche's dual commitment to the eternal return and to a life lived free of *ressentiment*. In *The Logic of Sense* Deleuze makes a passionate plea for a revival of the Stoic ethic of the event. In fact, the contemporary common usage of the term 'stoic' in English is derived from the idea that the event has its own singularity which must be separated from the person to whom the event occurs. The ethic that Deleuze recommends involves making oneself worthy of the event:

> It is a question of attaining this will that the event creates in us; of becoming the quasi-cause of what is produced within us, the Operator; of producing surfaces and linings in which the event is reflected, finds itself again as incorporeal and manifests in us the neutral splendor which it possesses in itself in its impersonal and pre-individual nature, beyond the general and the particular, the collective and the private. (LS, 148)

In short, it is a question of being worthy of what happens to us; a question of *amor fati*, of being able to say 'My wound existed before me ...'.[45] Every event has what we might call a double structure: there is the event as it is actualised in bodies or a state of affairs, and there is also the dimension of the event which sidesteps the present, being neither general nor particular, divided between past and future (LS, 151). It is as if we can only establish a perspective on the event if we accept that the event is something which is completely separate from us as individuals. Of course, the event which puts this ethic into the starkest relief is death, and Deleuze turns to Blanchot's analysis of death:

> Death has an extreme and definite relation to me and my body and is grounded in me, but it also has no relation to me at all – it is incorporeal and infinitive, impersonal, grounded only in itself. [...] Every event is like death, double and impersonal in its double. (LS, 151–2)

Deleuze suggests that Foucault's attitude towards suicide had something to do with this Stoic ethic of accepting the impersonality of the event, and yet trying to make oneself entirely worthy of the event. In this way, Foucault produces subjectivity in the absence of the subject (see N, 113–14).

The second theme which is connected to the event in Deleuze's work is that of indirect discourse. The event gives us access to a 'fourth' person; a genuinely impersonal dimension where everything is both collective and private:

> How different this 'they' is from that which we encounter in everyday banality. It is the 'they' of impersonal and pre-individual singularities, the 'they' of the pure event wherein *it* dies in the same way that *it* rains. The splendour of the 'they' is the splendour of the event itself or of the fourth person. (LS, 152)

Humour, rather than irony, is the 'savoir-faire of the pure event', the art of the 'fourth person singular' (LS, 141). As we have already seen, the fact that every event is both collective and private is extremely important to Deleuze's literary work. For Deleuze, literature often seems to celebrate the impersonal 'they'. We will also see, particularly in the conclusion, that Deleuze's drive to make contact with the impersonality of the event – his own particular version of 'empirical' reality – has been the focus of some recent criticism.

It can hopefully be seen, then, why Deleuze should be so dissatisfied with the capacity of the contemporary media to grasp the 'event'. (Similarly, the media seems often unable to grasp the full complexity – the composite nature – of questions and problems.) All too often the media concentrates merely on a beginning or an end, or something merely 'spectacular' (N, 159–60). The event cannot be separated from empty periods in which nothing happens: these periods are part of the event. In postwar cinema Ozu and Antonioni deal frequently with these 'empty' periods and their relation to the event. In this way, Deleuze suggests, both are inherently political directors, in that they constitute viewers as 'visionaries', allowing us to participate in the event in a genuinely 'problematic' way. The mass media, on the other hand, tends to turn its audience into passive spectators, or even voyeurs.

Concepts

Concepts are composites, amalgams of lines, curves. (N, 147)

We have seen already that, right at the end of his life in *What is Philosophy?*, Deleuze defended the specificity of philosophy as an activity which consists of the creation of concepts. This was an idea that he had already stated quite clearly in his book on Spinoza, *Expressionism in Philosophy* (*Spinoza et le problème de l'expression* 1968):

> A philosophy's power is measured by the concepts it creates, or whose meaning it alters, concepts that impose a new set of divisions on things and actions. It sometimes happens that those concepts are called forth at a certain time, charged with a collective meaning corresponding to the requirements of a given period, and discovered, created or recreated by several authors at once. (EP, 321)

Philosophers do not contemplate 'universals' such as Authority, Politics, the State, in a timeless vacuum. On the contrary, philosophy always arises out of concrete historical problems. As an example, Deleuze considers Plato's concept of the Idea. The 'Idea' is the concept of something that is pure, that is itself and nothing else: only the Idea of justice is nothing else but just.[46] Deleuze argues that the problem to which Plato's concept corresponds is in fact a concrete historical problem. Plato is concerned with the need to distinguish amongst the rivals in Athenian democracy who claim a 'political' role. The concept of the Idea will help to 'put things in order', to distinguish between 'suitors'. In this way, Plato's concept is a typically Greek problem, since Athenian society was based upon the rivalry of candidates.

Concepts are 'signed', which, in simple terms, means that a concept represents the major, innovative contribution that an individual philosopher has made to philosophy. So, we talk of Aristotle's substance, Descartes's cogito, and Leibniz's monad (WP, 7). The concept is, Deleuze and Guattari tell us, a 'fragmentary whole' (WP, 16). All concepts are made up of components which remain distinct, whilst allowing something to pass between them. These components may also come from other concepts (WP, 20). In terms of the dualism between bodies and incorporeal events, the concept is an event: 'The concept speaks the event, not the essence or the thing – pure Event, a hecceity, an entity: [...] It is like the bird as event' (WP, 21). However, this is all very abstract. Fortunately, Deleuze and Guattari illustrate some of the features of the concept by examining one of the most famous 'signed' philosophical concepts: the Cartesian cogito. This concept – *cogito ergo sum* – has three components: doubting, thinking, and being:

> As intensive ordinates the components are arranged in zones of neighbourhood or indiscernibility that produce passages from one to the other and constitute their inseparability. The first zone is between doubting and thinking (myself who doubts, I cannot doubt that I think), and the second is between thinking and being (in order to think it is necessary to be). (WP, 25)

If a new component is added to the concept, then it reconfigures itself as a new assemblage. To illustrate this, Deleuze and Guattari propose the example of the Kantian cogito. Kant adds the new component of time to the Cartesian cogito (WP, 31). Kant's concept of the cogito is taken up in turn by Deleuze, when he emphasises, on Kant's behalf as it were, the component of the Other to which the self must refer. Kant's cogito is, in this way, a preparation for Rimbaud's formula 'I is another' (WP, 32).

Conceptual Personae

> For most philosophers their philosophy's like a personality they haven't chosen, a third person. (N, 96)

Works of philosophy are populated by figures who are, Deleuze and Guattari seem to say, 'paraconceptual'. A philosopher's style is the philsopher in the 'third person'. For Descartes, for instance, it is the Idiot who effectively poses questions about the cogito (WP, 61–2). Nietzsche works with a range of conceptual personae who are both sympathetic and antithetic: Dionysus, Zarathustra, Christ, the Priest, the Higher Men (WP, 65). Rather than being pseudonyms for the philosopher, conceptual personae are philosophical activations of the multiple potentials for subjectivity which traverse the author's name. Everybody, not only philosophers, is a collection of individuals:

> The conceptual persona is not the philosopher's representative but, rather, the reverse: the philosopher is only the envelope of his principal conceptual persona and of all the other personae who are the intercessors [*intercesseurs*], the real subjects of his philosophy. Conceptual personae are the philosopher's 'heteronyms', and the philosopher's name is the simple pseudonym of his personae. (WP, 64)

There is sometimes a lineage of conceptual personae which helps us to establish a history of thought. Deleuze takes as an example the concept of the priest, which is pursued in turn by Spinoza,

Nietzsche, and then Foucault.[47] In all three cases, the priest is shown to have invented the idea that human beings live in infinite debt. Before the priest, in 'primitive' societies, debt existed in finite blocks. Foucault, particularly in his later work, investigated what he called a 'pastoral' power. This is a new concept, different from Nietzsche's priest, but inspired by it. For Foucault, it is often a question of emphasising the normative, perhaps violent, and even irrational elements of power which claims to be, and thinks of itself as, 'caring'. In this way, Deleuze, Guattari and Foucault supplement the figure of the priest with that of the psychoanalyst.

New Image(s) of Thought

Deleuze argues that there is a dominant 'image of thought' which has been formed throughout history, and that this image of thought stops people from thinking. (see D, 13). The idea of an image of thought is in some ways similar to Foucault's notion of the 'archaeology' of knowledge. It is a 'system of coordinates, dynamics, orientations' which define what it means to think at a certain time (N, 148). For Deleuze, the dominant image is intimately linked to the development of the modern State:

> Hence the importance of notions such as universality, method, question and answer, judgement, or recognition, of just correct, always having correct ideas. Hence the importance of themes like those of a republic of spirits, an enquiry of the understanding, a court of reason, a pure 'right' of thought, with ministers of the Interior and bureaucrats of pure thought. Philosophy is shot through with the project of becoming the official language of a Pure State. (D, 13)

In *Difference and Repetition* a thought 'without Image' is set against the dominant image (see DR, 132). This dominant image is defined as that of 'recognition', a sort of philosophical 'common sense'. The vocation of philosophy in the contemporary world must now be similar to that of modern art; to divest itself of the drive for representation. In *Negotiations* Deleuze refers to the study of images of thought, 'noology', as a theme which runs throughout his work. Apart from *Difference and Repetition*, he points to *The Logic of Sense* which looks at the image of thought in terms of coordinates: height, depth and surface, and *Proust and Signs*, where he shows how Proust questions the Greek image of thought by invoking the power of the sign. *A Thousand Plateaus*, on the other hand, confronts the tree image with the rhizome (see N, 149).

The Rhizome

In the introduction to *What is Philosophy?* Deleuze and Guattari claim that, despite rumours to the contrary, there is no end to history or metaphysics, and that systems are not bankrupt. It is rather the case that the concept of the system has changed (WP, 9). Deleuze and Guattari's contribution to this re-evaluation of the concept of the system is the figure of the 'rhizome'. The rhizome is a figure borrowed from biology, opposed to the principle of foundation and origin which is embodied in the figure of the tree. The model of the tree is hierarchical and centralised, whereas the rhizome is proliferating and serial, functioning by means of the principles of connection and heterogeneity. In simple terms, any line can be connected to any other line. However, these lines do not converge to form an organic whole. In short, the rhizome is another step in Deleuze's project of creating a new image of thought. The rhizome is a multiplicity, and as such seeks to move away from the the binary subject/object structure of Western thought. An example of a rhizomatic structure or system would be the generalised use of any particular language. In such a diverse field there can be no homogeneous linguistic community. Any language must be seen as a heterogeneous entity. In general terms, it is essential to understand that the rhizome is multiple; there can be no points or positions within a rhizome, only a mobile and bifurcating series of lines. Deleuze and Guattari also propose the example of their own book as a rhizome, a multiplicity of 'planes of intensity' or 'plateaus', rather than chapters. 'Each plateau can be read starting anywhere and related to any other plateau' (TP, 22). Deleuze and Guattari argue that the book has been linked traditionally to the model of the tree, in that the book has been seen as an organic unit, which is both hermetically sealed, but also as a reflection of the world. In contrast, the rhizome is neither mimetic nor organic. It only ever *maps* the real, since the act of mapping is a method of experimenting with the real: and it is always an open system, with multiple exits and entrances. In short, the rhizome is an 'acentred' system; the map of a mode of thought which is always 'in the middle'.

As an acentred system of communication, the rhizome allows for none of the comforting certainties of an organising system of memory and a hierarchical system of knowledge. Rather than organisation and rigidity of structure, the strength of thought is its potential for collapse. Recently, Jean-Jacques Lecercle, in *Philosophy of Nonsense* (*The Philosophy of Nonsense: The Intuitions of Victorian Nonsense Literature* 1994), has drawn attention to the importance of the schema of the rhizome as an alternative to the logic of representation. As with Foucault's concept of heterotopia, the rhizome brings together fragments and elements which defy the logic of representation, functioning as an outrage to common sense:

> This logic turns the logic of representation on its head: it works not through separation but through contiguity (the scandalous contiguity of heterogeneous elements or fields); not through replacement but through coexistence (the various elements are co-present, so that no one element is abstracted from the rest to represent them); not through hierarchy but through conjunction.[48]

The Plane of Immanence: Plane of Consistency

> In the end, does not every great philsosopher lay out a new plane of immanence, introduce a new substance of being and draw up a new image of thought, so that there could not be two great philosophers on the same plane? It is true that we cannot imagine a great philosopher of whom it could not be said that he has changed what it means to think; he has 'thought differently' (as Foucault put it). (WP, 51)

Immanence is the driving force of Deleuze's philosophy, and the plane of immanence contains events, singularities and concepts: 'Concepts are like multiple waves, rising and falling, but the plane of immanence is the single wave that rolls them up and unrolls them' (WP, 36). The plane of immanence is like a desert, populated by concepts. Immanence constitutes a logic of multiplicities, allowing the movement which the transcendent arrests:

> Immanence does not relate to a Something that is a unity superior to everything, nor to a subject that is an act operating the synthesis of things: it is when immanence is no longer immanence to anything other than itself that we can talk of a plane of immanence.[49]

Spinoza lays out a plane of immanence which is composed of 'speeds', which are capacities for affecting and being affected. In *Expressionism and Philosophy* Deleuze describes Spinoza's concept of nature as containing everything whilst at the same time being 'explicated and implicated' in everything (EP, 17). This differential plane of immanence is therefore the basis of Spinoza's ethics. We do not know what we are capable of in terms of good or bad, or what a body and mind can do: it is a question of encounters (S:PP, 125). Everything is a matter of velocity:

> There are only relations of movement and rest, speed and slowness between unformed elements, or at least between elements that are relatively unformed, molecules and particles

> of all kinds. There are only haecceities, affects, subjectless individuations that constitute collective assemblages. Nothing develops, but things arrive late or early, and form this or that assemblage depending upon their compositions of speed. Nothing subjectifies, but haecceities form according to compositions of nonsubjectified powers or affects. We call this plane, which knows only longitudes and latitudes, speeds and haecceities, the plane of consistency or composition (as opposed to the plan(e) of organization or development). It is necessarily a plane of immanence and univocality. (TP, 266)

The plane of immanence is also referred to as a plane of 'consistency'. As Philip Goodchild points out, consistency implies the possibility of interaction between heterogeneous elements (see also TP, 327–37). He describes Deleuze and Guattari's thought as a sort of 'garbage tip' in which everything is thrown together in the form of a multiplicity. For something interesting to happen, these heterogeneous terms need to acquire some 'consistency' so that immanent, machinic relations can be constructed.[50] In this plane of consistency/immanence organisation is constantly dismantled, but connections can still be made. As examples, Deleuze and Guattari propose certain forms of modern music, such as Steve Reich and Philip Glass, which '[...] carries only differential speeds and slownesses in a kind of molecular lapping [...]' (TP, 267). They also refer to Nathalie Sarraute, who perceives two planes of writing; a transcendent plane which organises forms and develops characters; and a plane that '[...] liberates the particles of an anonymous matter [...]' (TP, 267). In this way the plane of immanence is in continuous variation.[51] In fact, the plane of consistency is, paradoxically, also a plane of 'nonconsistency', a plane of 'proliferation, peopling, contagion', which is opposed to the dominant plane of organisation (TP, 267).

Machinic Materialism: A 'World with Subject'

The concepts produced by Deleuze (and Guattari) constantly address the indiscernibility between the organic and the non-organic, and the natural and the artificial. Just as philosophy is informed by the category of non-philosophy, so that which is human is pervaded by the non-human, an idea which is derived from Spinoza's notion of the unity of being (see Robert Hurley's introduction to S:PP). Some recent work has tended to link Deleuze and Guattari's attack on the dominant biological metaphor of the organic body to contemporary theory which is attempting to accommodate materialism to the rapidly advancing technological world.[52] In short, Deleuze is seen as a theorist of 'cybertheory'.

Cybertheory is particularly concerned with the way in which the boundaries between the human body and machines are being broken down. One of the most prominent exponents of 'cybertheory', which she pursues as a form of feminist theory, is Donna Haraway.[53] Essentially, Haraway takes the insights of poststructuralist theory – the radical interrogation of the subject – and looks at the ways in which this theory is beginning to take on a real material existence in the contemporary world. In a recent article on the relevance of Deleuze's work for contemporary feminism Rosi Braidotti sums up Haraway's recent work thus:

> More than ever, therefore, the question then becomes: What counts as human in the posthuman world? How do we rethink the unity of the human subject, without reference to humanistic beliefs, without dualistic oppositions, linking instead body and mind in a new flux of self? What is the view of the self that is operational in the world of the 'informatics of domination'.[54]

Paul Virilio has also speculated on the consequences of a world in which our accepted notions of human and non-human are called into question. Virilio talks in terms of three technological revolutions that the world has experienced: the industrial revolution; the revolution of electronic communications; and finally, the technological revolution of 'transplants'.[55] Rather than seeking to colonise the body of the earth, like railways and motorways, these new transplants are designed to colonise the body. The body is nourished by technology in the same way that it is nourished by chemical products.

It is certainly justified to use Deleuze's work in order to think about the questions which arise out of 'cybertheory'. However, he is not himself a 'cybertheorist'. Despite the fact the Deleuze seeks to call into question the notion that the organic and the inorganic are in strict opposition, the materialist analysis he proposes is concerned with questions of a different order. We stand to learn more, he argues, from the brain than we do from computers, and it is thought which will have a material effect on the brain, opening up new synapses and pathways (see N, 149).

The questions posed by cybertheory, then, should be clearly disnguished from the theme of the 'machine', and the 'machinic' which run throughout this work. We might start with the definition of machine proposed in the useful glossary of terms Philip Goodchild provides in his study of Deleuze and Guattari:'[...] an assemblage of parts that works and produces'.[56] Machinic materialism is initially discussed at some length in *Anti-Oedipus*. Although, as we have seen, Deleuze sees his work as vitalist, it is important to understand that the 'machinic' vitalism that interests him is distinguished from the term as it appears in the traditional polemic between vitalism and mechanism (see AO, 283–7). Deleuze and

Guattari draw on Samuel Butler who, they argue, goes beyond the vitalist model of the 'personal unity of the organism' and the mechanistic model of the machine as a 'structural unity' (AO, 284). The distinction between the organism and the mechanism is redundant: both are machines. The concept of the machine is first dealt with at length in *Anti-Oedipus*. Here, the image of the machine is opposed to that of the theatre. The individual and social body are constructed from a series of 'desiring machines', through which there are material flows. The unconscious itself is a desiring machine which 'produces' desire rather than being a theatre where desire is contained and represented upon a stage. The term 'desiring machine' is designed to disrupt the generally accepted idea that a machine is an instrument to be used by a subject. It is rather the case that the subject itself is a machine that produces desire.[57] Why not, they ask, have a machinic view of the unconscious? Why not have a machinic view of the individual and the social body? 'Everything is a machine.' In *A Thousand Plateaus* the concept of the machine or the machinic is shown to be the principle of the rhizome. A book, for example, is an assemblage that works in relation to other assemblages: a book is a machine which needs to be 'plugged into' other machines.

In *A Thousand Plateaus* the 'plane of consistency' calls into question all conventional forms of ordering the world into categories such as organic, non-organic, linguistic, technological, etc. It offers continual possibilities for the machinic assemblages: '[...] a semiotic fragment rubs shoulders with a chemical interaction, an electron crashes into a language, a black hole captures a genetic message, a crystallization produces a passion [...]' (TP, 69).

Ultimately, Deleuze develops what we might call a *materialist metaphysics*. We have seen already that he is concerned with the expression of those forces which cannot be seen, heard, or thought. As these forces emerge from their silence, we can understand that the world is made up from a series of machines which are 'plugged into' one another. For example, Deleuze argues that art, particularly cinema or painting, can act directly upon the nervous system. Art is capable of materially affecting the brain, of producing new pathways in the brain. In *Cinema 1: The Movement-Image* Deleuze completes a train of thought that Bergson suggested but never completed. Bergson talks of a 'cinematographic illusion', but in fact also created the concept of the 'movement-image' which was inherently cinematic. This concept, to which cinema makes a unique contribution, entails nothing less than a 'new metaphysics'. The movement-image as a concept is concerned with the equivalence of three components: matter=image=movement. Whereas phenomenology is organised around the idea that all consciousness is consciousness *of* something, the problem of the cinematographic illusion suggests to Bergson the idea that all consciousness *is* something (C1, 56). At first sight, this is a peculiar and particularly inaccessible idea. However, considered in terms of the concrete problem of cinema, it begins to make sense. Phenomenology depends upon a certain idea of 'natural' perception, which involves a certain 'anchoring' of the subject in the world. In this way, phenomenology conceives of consciousness as a sort of searchlight which picks out objects in the world. However, cinema quickly dismantles this notion of natural perception: 'The cinema can, with impunity, bring us close to things or take us away from them and revolve around them, it suppresses both the anchoring of the subject and the horizon of the world' (C1, 57). What cinema offered Bergson – if only he had followed it through – was an alternative model of perception in which no point of anchorage or centre of reference would be possible: perception as constant variation. Bergson needs the model of perception to complete his new metaphysics which conceives of the world as 'flowing-matter' in a constant process of change:

> My eye, my brain, are images, parts of my body. How could my brain contain images since it is one image among others? External images act on me, transmit movement to me, and I return movement: how could images be in my consciousness, since I am myself image, that is, movement? And can I even, at this level, speak of 'ego', of eye, of brain and of body? Only for simple convenience; for nothing can yet be identified in this way. It is rather a gaseous state. Me, my body, are rather a set of molecules and atoms which are constantly renewed. [...] It is a state of matter too hot for one to be able to distinguish solid bodies in it. It is a world of universal variation, of universal undulation, universal rippling: there are neither axes, nor centre, nor left, nor right, nor high, nor low ... . (C1, 58)

Bergson prepares a metaphysics for a world in which the light of consciousness is already *in* things themselves, where the 'movement-image' and 'flowing-matter' are the same thing. In this way, Bergson imagines the universe as a form of 'metacinema'; a machinic rather than mechanistic universe (C1, 59). This machinic universe is a plane of immanence which requires no subject, since it is made entirely from 'Light'. It is a universe without eyes, in which light has not yet been reflected or stopped: 'In other words, the eye is in things, in luminous images in themselves' (C1, 60). Bergson and Deleuze are machinic materialists, who consider consciousness as immanent to matter. In Bergson, philosophy is at last able to provide us with 'a world without subject' ['un monde sans sujet']. In *Matter and Memory* Bergson produces something quite extraordinary, a marriage of 'pure spiritualism and radical materialism' (N, 48).

CHAPTER 3

Untimely Philosophies

> Following Nietzsche we discover, as more profound than time and eternity, the untimely: philosophy is neither a philosophy of history, nor a philosophy of the eternal, but untimely, always and only untimely – that is to say, 'acting counter to our time and thereby acting on our time and, let us hope, for the benefit of a time to come'. (DR, xxi)

In the early part of his career Deleuze published a series of works on individual philosophers – Hume, Nietzsche, Kant, Bergson, and Spinoza – along with an influential study on Proust and an introduction to Sacher-Masoch. In a recent interview Deleuze identifies this as the first of three distinct periods in his work:

> Three periods, not bad going. Yes, I did begin with books on the history of philosophy, but all the authors I dealt with had for me something in common. And it all tended toward the great Spinoza–Nietzsche equation. (N, 135)[1]

In a letter which was published as the preface to Michel Cressole's *Deleuze*, published in 1973, Deleuze sets out his own view of this first phase of his work (see N, 4–7). He acknowledges that his work was in some ways conventional, in that he was 'doing' the history of philosophy. However, he tried to make his own particular history of the subject innovative in two ways. Firstly, he chooses philosophers, or reads them in such a way that they stand outside the rationalist tradition. Thinkers like Hume, Spinoza, Nietzsche and Bergson share a 'secret link', in that they seek to explore the limits of reason.[2] More than this, they also attempt to look beyond reason, to explore the irrational. In this way they are 'joyful' philosophers, unencumbered by the weight of reason, interiority and negativity. Secondly, Deleuze looks to produce the 'monstrous' offspring of these philosophers, to produce a reading which is entirely faithful and yet which activates their thought in a new way. Alain Badiou, confirming what we have already seen in the introduction, speaks of a 'constant use of free indirect discourse', whereby Deleuze creates a zone of indiscernibility between his ideas and the ideas of the thinkers that he writes about.[3] In short, these thinkers become something different in Deleuze's hands:

'There is a philosophy-becoming which has nothing to do with the history of philosophy and which happens through those whom the history of philosophy does not manage to classify' (D, 2).

Few thinkers, Deleuze claims, avoid the temptation of becoming 'professors of their own discoveries', of professionalising their private insights (S:PP, 8). However, Deleuze is more interested in philsophers, such as Spinoza, who form an underground tradition of 'private thinkers', rather than 'public professors'. The latter do nothing to undermine the existing order of 'established sentiments' (S:PP, 11). In simple terms, Deleuze is interested in philosophers who do not feel entirely at home. The true philosopher is nomadic, seeking a genuine freedom of thought:

> [...] he never confuses his purposes with those of a state, or with the aims of a milieu, since he solicits forces in thought that elude obedience as well as blame, and fashions the image of a life beyond good and evil, a rigorous innocence without merit or culpability. The philosopher can reside in various states, he can frequent various milieus, but he does so in the manner of a hermit, a shadow, a traveler or boarding house lodger. (S:PP, 4)

In one way this disparate group of thinkers have few obvious links between them. However, as well as entering into a zone of indiscernibility with each one individually, Deleuze also attempts to recreate a sort of indirect discourse, an 'interstellar conversation' which takes place between them in a sort of 'ideal space', to turn their separate voices into a multivocal 'becoming' (see D, 16).

Michael Hardt argues that there is within this early work a progression from Bergson, through Nietzsche, to Spinoza.[4]

Hume

> Why write, why have written about empiricism, and about Hume in particular? Because empiricism is like the English novel. It is a case of philosophizing as a novelist, of being a novelist in philosophy. (D, 54)

If Deleuze's work is to be understood in its entirety, it is important to consider his first major publication on the Scottish philosopher Hume. His discussion of Hume's *Treatise of Human Nature* indicates a general approach to the question of identity. Deleuze emphasises Hume's striking idea that the mind is a sort of theatre which constantly 'stages' new movements and perceptions:

> The mind is a kind of theatre, where several perceptions successively make their appearance; pass, re-pass, glide away, and mingle in an infinite variety of postures and situations. There is properly no *simplicity* in it at any one time, nor *identity* in

different; whatever natural propension we may have to imagine that simplicity and identity.[5]

Hume is preoccupied with the problem of human subjectivity. More specifically, he is concerned with the question of how the mind is constituted from the 'given', which is initially no more than a bundle of heterogeneous perceptions. Deleuze emphasises Hume's conviction that the mind is not prior to the given, although it does go beyond the given. The 'given' is:

> [...] the flux of the sensible, a collection of impressions and images, or a set of perceptions. It is the totality of that which appears, being which equals appearance; it is also movement and change without identity or law. (ES, 87)

By emphasising that ideas are connected in the mind, and not by the mind (ES, 24), Deleuze's Hume addresses the central problem of consciousness. Philip Goodchild argues convincingly that Deleuze uses Hume in order to escape from the three dominant traditions of Continental philosophy: dialectical history, phenomenology, and fundamental ontology.[6] All three traditions depend upon the notion that we build upon a sort of pre-existent, baseline consciousness. History is, for example, itself a form of consciousness. However, as Goodchild emphasises, Deleuze is concerned throughout his work with a level of reality which precedes any particular form of consciousness.

The importance of the question of consciousness can be illustrated by considering current debates on the problem of artificial intelligence. Advocates of artificial intelligence do not only argue that human 'intelligence' can be in some way replicated, they also claim that the human mind is more 'robotic', more machine-like, than we commonly think. The phenomenon we know as 'consciousness' is not an expression of a deep-rooted selfhood, but rather the consequence of complexity in the mind, of the 'society of the mind'. The notion of a core of subjectivity which is individual consciousness is merely a useful fiction.[7] Those who are sceptical concerning the possibility of genuinely artificial intelligence necessarily have recourse to the transcendent nature of consciousness. In commonsense terms they argue that a machine cannot achieve self-consciousness.

We must locate Deleuze's Hume alongside those who argue that the mind is a complex 'society' rather than an organising consciousness. In short, Hume offers a materialist explanation of the mind. Although Freud is now acknowledged to have explicitly undermined the fiction of consciousness by theorising the unconscious, Deleuze shows how 'nomad' thinkers such as Hume had suggested previously that the subject does not predate the 'given'.

Deleuze emphasises Hume's belief that an identity is always a work of fiction: fiction becomes a principle of human nature (ES, 80). What we think of as our individual subjecthood or identity is really only a habit of saying 'I' (WP, 105).

Hume's dismantling of consciousness also has important consequences for his views on reason. Firstly, reason is displaced from the dominant position that it held in philosophy before the Enlightenment. In Hume's reckoning, reason must be considered in the context of custom, convention, and habit. In this way Hume attacks rationalism:

> Rationalism has transferred mental determinations to external objects, taking away thereby from philosophy the meaning and the intelligibility of practice and of the subject. The fact is, though, that the mind is not reason; reason is an affection of the mind. In this sense, reason will be called instinct, habit, or nature. (ES, 30)

Secondly, the division between reason and madness established by rationalism is shown to be arbitrary. We cannot separate madness from delirium within the mind (ES, 83). Reason always holds the potential for being *unreasonable*: as Hume shows – and for Deleuze this is the most important statement of the *Treatise* – it is not unreasonable, i.e. contrary to the principles of reason, to prefer the destruction of the whole world to a scratch upon one's finger (ES, 33).

Essentially, Hume poses two questions. Firstly, as an empiricist, he asks how the mind, which is initially in a state of virtual chaos – like a theatre without a stage – can become a subject. Secondly, again from an empirical point of view, he asks, given the partial nature of human beings, how society and culture can be organised in any meaningful way. As for the first question, he argues that the mind becomes a subject under the impetus of a minimal human nature, which is guided by a complex relationship between the principles of association – based on relations of resemblance, contiguity and causality – and passion (ES, 32). We construct beliefs by means of association and passions lend an inclination, or disposition. The basis of knowledge for Hume, therefore, is a secular form of *belief* (see WP, 53). However, this leaves Hume with a problem with regard to his second question; the subject thus constituted by human nature would be partial and narrow. The construction of an ethical subject must, therefore, be guaranteed by artificial, cultural rules. Just as Hume has faith in a minimal form of human nature in as far as knowledge is concerned – the capacity to develop knowledge from basic sense impressions – so he has faith in the ability of human society to extend and extrapolate from individual passions, through customs, to useful social institutions: 'The social is profoundly creative, inventive, and positive' (ES, 46). Society is a matter of convention, institution and artifice, rather than obligation and contract:

> The fault of contractual theories is that they present us with a society whose essence is the law, that is, with a society which has no other objective than to guarantee certain pre-existing natural rights and no other origin than the contract. Thus, anything positive is taken away from the social, and instead the social is saddled with negativity, limitation, and alienation. (ES, 45)

In this way, Hume promotes utility rather than contract, institution rather than law: '[...] not a limitation but rather a model of actions, a veritable enterprise, an invented system of positive means or a positive invention of indirect means' (ES, 45–6).

It is initially surprising to encounter such enthusiastic discussion of custom and convention in Deleuze's work. After all, as he points out, Hume espouses the importance of private property and shared, perhaps even 'traditional' values (ES, 41–2). However, Deleuze shows how Hume mobilises 'conservative' notions of custom and habit in order to call into question the assumption of stable human identity. For example, Hume dismisses 'egoism' as a theory of human nature, since it neglects the equally 'natural' phenomenon of sympathy. In this way, Hume is also a philosopher of difference:

> If by 'egoism' we understand the fact that all drives pursue their own satisfaction, we posit only the principle of identity, A=A, that is, the formal and empty principle of a science of humanity – moreover, of an uncultivated and abstract humanity without history and without difference. More specifically, egoism can designate *some* means only that humanity organizes in order to satisfy drives, but not all possible means. (ES, 44–5)

In summary, then, Hume allows Deleuze to develop a theory of subjectivity which is thoroughly materialist. He also suggests that invention and creativity are important in both individual and collective human affairs, a Nietzschean theme which recurs throughout Deleuze's work. And, as a consequence of the idea that fiction becomes a principle of the human mind, Deleuze introduces a theme which will reappear throughout his work; the intimate connections between sense and nonsense. Since there can be no coherent identity without the artificial intervention of fiction, so that which is reason is intimately linked to that which is madness or delirium (ES, 83–4).

Nietzsche

After his book on Hume Deleuze published no major work for eight years, until 1962, when *Nietzsche and Philosophy* appeared. The figure of Nietzsche is undoubtedly central to French thought in the postwar period, particularly in the 1960s and 1970s. Deleuze's reading of Nietzsche was an extremely influential component of this re-reading, and was to be central to his own philosophical project. The salient features of Nietzsche's thought as it is read by Deleuze are flux, movement and creation: in short, a philosophy of 'becoming'. In this way, Nietzsche provides Deleuze with a way out of Hegelianism and, more generally, the rationalist tradition of philosophy, a tradition which meant that even a thinker like Bergson was in many ways unwelcome within the French university system:

> It was Nietzsche, who I read only later, who extricated me from all this. Because you just can't deal with him in the same sort of way. He gets up to all sorts of things behind *your* back. He gives you a perverse taste – certainly something neither Marx nor Freud ever gave anyone – for saying simple things in your own way, in affects, intensities, experiences, experiments. (N, 6)

In other words, Nietzsche's work lends itself perfectly to the sort of non-philosophical reading that Deleuze talks of in *L'Abécédaire de Gilles Deleuze*. It is not necessary to have an understanding of the history of philosophy in order to understand Nietzsche, since it is possible to be swept along with the force of his ideas.

In assessing 'Nietzsche's French Legacy', Alan D. Schrift shows how important Deleuze's reading is to the 'Nietzschean' strand of French thought which he labels as 'poststructuralism'.[8] In general terms, Schrift defines poststructuralism intellectually as a move away from 'three H's' – Hegel, Husserl and Heidegger – towards a new triumvirate of Nietzsche, Freud and Marx, the 'masters of suspicion'.[9] Schrift locates Deleuze, along with Derrida, Foucault and Lyotard, in an influential group of thinkers who try to carry Nietzsche's work forward, to use Nietzsche as a particularly important reference point in their own thinking. For example, in the same way that Nietzsche inverts the traditional hierarchy of truth over falsity, showing that error can be more valuable than truth, so Derrida questions hierarchical oppositions between speech and writing and presence and absence. Nietzsche shows that the world is much more complex than these oppositions would suggest. It is a world which is caught in the plural and frequently contingent processes of becoming. As Schrift points out: 'Both Foucault and Deleuze engage in projects that reformulate traditional binary oppositions between given alternatives in terms of a pluralistic continuum, in which choices are always local and relative rather than global and absolute.'[10] In this way, Deleuze elaborates upon Nietzsche's concept of the 'will to power' as a qualitative difference between forces rather than a quantitative difference between power. Rather than concentrating on individuals, selves and substances we should look for relations and difference without exclusion. Petra Perry also points to the importance of Deleuze's contribution to the introduction of Nietzsche into French intellectual life in the 1960s and 1970s.[11] She considers *Nietzsche and Philosophy* to have been Deleuze's first really important philosophical work in terms of its effect on intellectual debate.[12] For Perry, Deleuze is innovative in his reading of Nietzsche as an *affirmative* thinker, attacking the system of negation and opposition set up by Hegel, and she traces the way in which this Nietzschean influence develops in Deleuze's work. According to Perry, the final genuine transformation of Nietzsche's affirmative philosophy emerges in the form of the concept of 'intensity', which is proposed in *Difference and Repetition*. In subsequent works, Nietzsche still appears, but this time '[...] it is a Nietzsche by way of allusion and not a new application'.[13]

Nietzsche and Philosophy was the first major work on Nietzsche in France to follow Heidegger's influential two-volume study in 1961. Interest in Nietzsche was growing, and major international conferences on Nietzsche were held at Royaumont in 1964,[14] and at Cérisy-la-Salle in 1972.[15] Several of the most influential essays on Nietzsche written by European thinkers, including Deleuze, Heidegger and Blanchot, appear in English translation in *The New Nietzsche*.[16] Even though each one of these writers invents his or her own Nietzsche, the continuity of themes in this collection is striking. The dominant theme is Nietzsche's attempt to undermine the principle of unitary identity. The notion of the self is shown to be a 'grammatical fiction' and, linking Nietzsche to Freud, the individual consciousness is seen as the surface 'symptom' of unconscious drives and forces. Further to this, French 'Nietzscheanism' is characterised by a critique of humanism, and the conviction that truth and language is 'always already' metaphorical. According to Nietzsche's formulation, truth is a 'mobile army of metaphors, metonymies, and anthropomorphisms'. Often, things that we accept as self-evident truths are simply 'congealed' metaphors. Nietzsche's particular use of aphorism and metaphor constitutes a strategy employed against such 'congealed' thought. Both are incomplete, active forms, expressing a thought which is always in motion. As David Allison remarks in his introduction to the collection, the aphorism '[...] is essentially metaphorical: it gathers, culls, collects, compares, and assembles – however briefly – this movement of thought'.[17] The essays in this collection also refer repeatedly to the notion of becoming, expressed in Nietzsche's concept of the Eternal Return. Alphonso Lingis, for example, sees this doctrine as a Dionysian shattering of identity:

> Metaphysical reiteration of the ideal is founded on the death of God and on the dissolution of the ego. Recurrence in the Dionysian world must not be understood as the return of *something* that is, that is one, or that is the same. What recurs is not being, but becoming; not identity, ideality, but difference.[18]

One of the most important ways in which Deleuze is influenced by Nietzsche is in the development of a 'relational' form of thinking. Meaning cannot be a straightforward question of the relationship between the signifier and the signified. Since the use of language to signify is a matter of convention, language offers us a shifting sign system rather than a fixed system of transcendent meaning. As David Allison points out, Nietzsche provides what is essentially a semiotic analysis, whereby what is immediately apparent to perception is only a sign or symptom of 'nonapparent and differential forces'.[19] Allison perceives two strands in Nietzsche's 'semiotics': a differential analysis and a genealogical analysis.[20] Both are crucial for Deleuze's reading of Nietzsche. For example, as Alan Schrift has claimed in a more recent paper, *Anti-Oedipus* often reads as a sort of genealogy of psychoanalysis.[21]

Deleuze's paper from the Cérisy-la-Salle conference appears in translation in *The New Nietzsche* as 'Nomad Thought'.[22] Deleuze argues that if the dawn of modern culture can be identified with the trinity Nietzsche-Marx-Freud, as Foucault claims, then Nietzsche has a special place within the trinity. He represents not only the birth of a culture, but also the birth of a *counter*-culture. In some ways, Marx and Freud actually misunderstand modern society, in that they wish to 'recodify' the errors of the state and the family. Nietzsche, on the other hand, is not concerned with the recodification of everything that has been decodified:

> His task lies elsewhere: beyond all the codes of past, present and future, to transmit something that does not and will not allow itself to be codified. To transmit it to a new body, to invent a body that can receive it and spill it forth; a body that would be our own, the earth's, or even something written ... .[23]

Deleuze here points towards the theme of deterritorialisation which will become so important in later work. To accept Nietzsche's invitation to embark on a period of 'drifting', or 'deterritorialisation', is to experiment with an escape from the framework of contract, law and institution. Rather than attempting to reverse the tendency for modern societies to become progressively decodified and unregulated, Nietzsche suggests that this process has not yet gone far enough. Nietzsche can be compared to Kafka in his desire to use language to express something which cannot be codified. In the same way that Kafka decodifies the German language by dint of 'a certain indeterminacy and sobriety' that he finds in the language of Prague Jews, so Nietzsche felt himself to be 'Polish' in his use of German.[24] Nietzsche uses this style in order to create a form of thought which is characterised by a drive towards absolute exteriority. This exteriority, a relation with the outside, as Blanchot calls it, is expressed in Nietzsche's work by the aphorism. This form resists the constraints of totalisation and, consequently, identity and interiority:

> An aphorism is a play of forces, the most recent of which – the latest, the newest, and provisionally the final force – is always *the most exterior*. Nietzsche puts this very clearly: if you want to know what I mean, then find the force which gives a new sense to what I say, and hang the text upon it.[25]

In his 'Preface to the English Translation' of *Nietzsche and Philosophy* Deleuze talks of 'Nietzsche's very special empiricism and pragmatism' (NP, ix). He also claims that Nietzsche managed to introduce a 'new image' into philosophy. This 'new image' is based upon the idea of movement. Nietzsche's thought is inseparable from movement:

> It is a thought-movement, not merely in the sense that Nietzsche wants to reconcile thought and concrete movement, but in the sense that thought itself must produce movements, bursts of extraordinary speed and slowness [...]. As a result philosophy has a new relationship to the arts of movement: theatre, dance and music. (NP, xiii)

In this preface, Deleuze singles out two main axes in Nietzsche's work: force and power. In Deleuze's reading of Nietzsche, the world of 'things, organisms, societies, consciousness and spirits' are only really 'signs' which are related to the world of forces. In this way, philosophy should aspire to be a method for reading signs. It should be a 'symptomatology'; Deleuze discovers a 'semiotic' Nietzsche. If Nietzsche's thought is primarily pluralist, and Deleuze believes it is, then it is the element of force which is irreducibly plural. In this way, Nietzsche presents a critique of atomism. Atomism sees matter as plural, whereas only forces can be plural (NP, 6). In a crudely atomistic conception of the world each atom can only be one thing, it has an identity. Whereas in Nietzsche's pluralism each thing can be 'this and then that' (NP, 4). This non-atomistic model of pluralism is the basis of Deleuze's project of a philosophy which would be a 'transcendental' empiricism, and has also been developed as a model of social theory by Michel Foucault. The second axis of Nietzsche's thought, which has proved equally important to the social theory of Michel Foucault, is that of power. Nietzsche's particular conception of power is the notion of the 'will to power'. To read the will to power as a desire for power in the sense of domination is to misread the concept. It is certainly possible, for example, that those who dominate a given society will be, in terms of the will to power, weak. Deleuze calls the will to power the 'genetic element of force' (NP, 51), since he sees the will to power as a sort of internal motor in force. More important than the drive to dominate, is the capacity of the will to power to be affected:

> It follows that the will to power is manifested as a capacity for being affected. This capacity is not an abstract possibility, it is necessarily fulfilled and actualised at each moment by the other forces to which a given force relates. [...] In the first place, therefore, the will to power is manifested as the capacity for being affected, as the determinate capacity of force for being affected. (NP, 62)

Forces provide one aspect of this philosophy of movement, and the Eternal Return provides another. In Deleuze's hands, Nietzsche's concept of the Eternal Return is an expression of the philosophy of becoming. The Eternal Return has little to do with a cyclical view of history. It is rather yet another way in which Nietzsche provides a philosophy of movement. It is precisely in avoiding any notion of a return of that which is the same that Nietzsche elaborates a critique of identity (NP, xi). Nietzsche wishes to show that the world constantly returns to a moment of becoming. In this way, the Eternal Return expresses the synthetic nature of the present moment in all its rich possibilities for life. In short the principle rests upon difference, and not identity:

> It is not being that returns but rather the returning itself that constitutes being insofar as it is affirmed of becoming and of that which passes. [...] returning itself is the one thing which is affirmed of diversity or multiplicity. In other words, identity in the eternal return does not describe the nature of that which returns but, on the contrary, the fact of returning for that which differs. (NP, 48)

In *Difference and Repetition* Deleuze emphasises the opposition between a philosophy of Eternal Return as difference and a philosophy of identity. According to the concept of identity, the world must either be finite or infinite, whereas the principle of difference encounters a world which is 'completed and unlimited' (DR, 57). Deleuze perceives in the Eternal Return an ethical rule 'as vigorous as any Kantian one' (NP, 68). That is to say, whatever one wills, one should be comfortable with willing its eternal return.

This is an ethical doctrine which would require the individual to live each moment in its full sense of becoming. It is perhaps fair to say that, taken literally, this doctrine would entail a manic and even unliveable approach to life. However, the force of Nietzsche's ethical consideration – an attack on the sorts of petty consolations and generally lazy thinking which detract from the power of life – is undeniable.

As for Nietzsche's concept of the will to power, Deleuze is adamant that to interpret it as a straightforward desire for power or domination is to misinterpret Nietzsche's thought. Deleuze instead comes up with the rather enigmatic statement that '[...] power designates the element, or rather the differential relationship, of forces which directly confront one another' (NP, xi). Force is not conceived of in personal terms. It is rather an 'event', in that forces are always in relation to other forces. To emphasise that the will to power is nothing to do with domination, Deleuze points out that even a 'reactive' force, such as an illness, which apparently separates us from our power, can give another form of power, another way of being affected (NP, 66). (This is, of course, the point that Deleuze makes in *L'Abécédaire de Gilles Deleuze* when talking about his own long-standing respiratory problems.) As we have seen, Nietzsche considers that those who dominate may be slaves just as much as those who are dominated. The will to power is concerned with a certain integrity of the will, which has more to do with the potential to be affected than the ability or desire to dominate others. The 'weak' or 'slavish' do not suffer from a lack of strength, but are rather separated from what they can do. For this reason the being who is the least strong may actually attain power ['puissance'] by deploying, for example, '[...] the cunning, the subtlety, the wit and even the charm by which he makes up for his lesser strength' (NP, 61).

In general terms Deleuze takes from Nietzsche, as does Michel Foucault, a thoroughly sceptical approach to the question of truth. The motives of the 'truthful man' should always be treated with suspicion, since the real motive of such an individual will usually be to judge life. Deleuze admires the way in which Foucault, in his final work, showed how forces might be 'bent', made to impinge upon themselves. In this way, the will to power will create new possibilities for life, rather than judging life (see N, 98).

In his second book on cinema, *The Time-Image*, Deleuze shows how Nietzsche's concept of the will to power might be used to investigate the notion of 'truth' in film. In the postwar period cinema tends to confront problems of truth and falsity. It is a cinema of *seers* rather than *actors*, in which time is no longer subordinated to movement. Cinema in the earlier part of the twentieth century had correponded in abstract terms to a Euclidean space consisting of a defined field of tensions and oppositions, based upon the spatial distribution of centres of forces. The 'crystalline' narration of postwar cinema, on the other hand, corresponds to a new, disconnected space. Consequently, time is no longer subordinated to movement in film, and cinema – or rather 'cinema thought' as Deleuze calls it – becomes able to deal with what Leibniz calls the 'incompossibility' of truth in time. In fact, postwar cinema manages to go even further than this crystalline narration towards a 'falsifying' narration. The concept of the will to power anticipates a world in which straightforward notions of truth and falsity collapse in favour of perspectivism:

> Crystalline description was already reaching the indiscernibility of the real and the imaginary, but the falsifying narration which corresponds to it goes a step further and poses inexplicable differences to the present and alternatives which are undecidable between true and false to the past. The truthful man dies, every model of truth collapses, in favour of the new narration. We have not mentioned the author who is essential in this regard: it is Nietzsche, who, under the name of 'will to power', substitutes the power of the false for the form of the true [...]. (C2, 131)

Spinoza

> Who is a Spinozist? Sometimes, certainly, the individual who works 'on' Spinoza, on Spinoza's concepts, provided this is done with enough gratitude and admiration. But also the individual who, without being a philosopher, receives from Spinoza an affect, a set of affects, a kinetic determination, an impulse, and makes Spinoza an impulse, a passion. (S:PP, 130)

There can be no doubting the importance of Spinoza in Deleuze's work. In *What is Philosophy?* Deleuze and Guattari claim that he is the 'Christ' of philosophers, having been incarnated just once to suggest the 'possibility of the impossible': all subsequent philosophers are merely apostles. For Deleuze, Spinoza is *the* thinker of immanence:

> Spinoza, the infinite becoming-philosopher: he showed, drew up, and thought the 'best' plane of immanence – that is, the purest, the one that does not hand itself over to the transcendent or restore any transcendent, the one that inspires the fewest illusions, bad feelings, and erroneous perceptions. (WP, 60)

Spinoza provides Deleuze with a conceptual persona who will act out several important themes: immanence, a 'joyful' philosophy, a philosophy of the body, ethics as opposed to morals, the value of a nomadic existence, the importance of the affect. All of these themes are to some extent shared with Nietzsche: Nietzsche-Spinoza, a new conceptual persona.[26] There are also themes with which Deleuze was still grappling, still developing, towards the end of his life: relations of speed and slowness, and the importance of non-philosophy for the philosopher. Bergson and Nietzsche may form the building blocks of Deleuze's thought, but Spinoza is a 'wind' that constantly blows at Deleuze's back: sometimes a 'great calm wind', and sometimes a whirlwind (S:PP, 130).

Deleuze published two books on Spinoza: *Expressionism in Philosophy: Spinoza* appeared in 1968, and formed part of his doctoral thesis; and in 1970 he published a shorter introduction to Spinoza called *Spinoza: Practical Philosophy*, which was intended as an introductory guide for students (*Spinoza: textes choisis* 1970 and *Spinoza: Philosophie pratique* 1981). We shall concentrate here mainly on the second book, in which Deleuze starts by using a discussion of Spinoza's life as a way of approaching his thought. Spinoza was a genuine outsider. As a Jew who incurred the wrath of the Jewish Church he led a nomadic life: propertyless, often in flight, and plagued by ill health. Deleuze links this fugitive life to a nomadic form of thinking which refuses the comfort of an attachment to fixed identities:

> Spinoza, the man of encounters and becoming, the philosopher with the tick, Spinoza the imperceptible, always in the middle, always in flight although he does not shift much, a flight from the Jewish community, a flight from the Powers, a flight from the sick and malignant. (D, 62)

In a similar way, Deleuze also claims that Spinoza's thought and his profession of polishing lenses should be treated as a whole. This profession is an expression of the desire for a 'third eye' which will have a clear and free vision of '[...] life beyond all false appearances, passions, and deaths' (S:PP, 14).

In presenting Spinoza's 'joyful' philosophy, Deleuze explicitly states his aim to 'start in the middle', as it were. Spinoza's main thesis, that Nature is a single substance with an infinity of attributes, is well known. However, according to Deleuze, we should rather concentrate on Spinoza's denunciation of 'consciousness', 'values' and 'sad passions' (S:PP, 17). This triple denunciation highlights three main areas of resemblance between Spinoza and Nietzsche. It also leads to a triple accusation directed at Spinoza: he is 'guilty' of materialism, moralism, and atheism (S:PP, 17). In his denunciation of consciousness, Spinoza acts in some ways as a forerunner of Freud. Like Nietzsche (and Foucault), Spinoza proposes a philosophy of the body. This philosophy stems from the relatively straightforward thesis of 'parallelism'; the idea that neither the body nor the mind holds primacy one over the other. Nor is there a real relation of causality between the two. This does not mean that Spinoza writes a history of the body – although a blueprint for such a history could certainly be deduced from future philosophers of the body such as Nietzsche and Foucault – but rather that he uses the body as a model for philosophy. The motto of such a philosophy is, 'We do not know what a body can do.' In the same way, we do not know what a mind can do: 'It is a matter of showing that the body surpasses the knowledge that we have of it, *and that thought likewise surpasses the consciousness that we have of it*' (S:PP, 18). There are forces of thought which may not be immediately apparent to consciousness and, for Spinoza, consciousness is a sort of waking dream, since our mind and body are simply the effects of encounters with other bodies. In this way, consciousness is an illusion, a misunderstanding of cause and effect. It can register the effect of an encounter between bodies, but knows nothing of the cause. Our ideas are therefore only ever inadequate, '[...] effects separated from their real causes' (S:PP, 19). In attacking consciousness, Spinoza courts controversy by implicitly attacking religion. Adam is not innocent or perfect, he is merely ignorant of causes, and so he eats the apple. Spinoza shows that the anguish of this ignorance is calmed by three illusions on the part of consciousness: taking effects for causes, invoking itself as a primary cause, and, if this fails, invoking a God as a final cause (S:PP, 20).

In his renunciation of 'values', Spinoza develops a philosophy which is concerned with ethics rather than morals: a philosophy of immanence which rejects transcendent moral values:

> Morality is the judgement of God, the system of Judgment. But Ethics overthrows the system of judgement. The opposition of values (Good-Evil) is supplanted by the qualitative difference of modes of existence (good-bad). The illusion of values is indistinguishable from the illusion of consciousness. (S:PP, 23)

In one way, Spinoza is quite simply denouncing superstition. Those things that we think of as 'evil' are really much more prosaic, in that they are the result of unhealthy relations: '[...] bad encounters, poisoning, intoxication, relational decomposition' (S:PP, 22). Everything comes back to the question of the relations between bodies:

> The good is when a body directly compounds its relations with ours, and, with all or part of its power, increases ours. A food, for example. For us, the bad is when a body decomposes our body's relation, although it still combines with our parts, but in ways that do not correspond to our essence, as when a poison breaks down the blood. (S:PP, 22)

Similarly, a 'good' individual is someone who endeavours to create good encounters, whereas a 'bad' individual is content to be the passive victim of encounters but complains when these encounters are not 'good' (S:PP, 23).

Ultimately, Spinoza defends life against sad passions and the values which detract from its power: he despises all that imprisons life. Nietzsche and Spinoza are both thinkers who denounce '[...] all that separates us from life, all these transcendent values that are turned against life' (S:PP, 26). For example, law is value as institution, and Spinoza attacks it as negative and unproductive, since it demands only obedience: 'Law, whether moral or social, does not provide us with any knowledge; it makes nothing known' (S:PP, 24). Like Nietzsche, Spinoza's frailty ensures that he maintains the capacity to be affected. He is able to give expression to a force which is 'suffused with Life itself' (S:PP, 12). Like Nietzsche, Spinoza emphasises the similarity – and even collusion – between the slave and the tyrant. Both are scared of life, and they consequently combine a boundless desire with superstition and selfishness. Just as much as the tyrant deceives the people by dressing despotism in the finery of religion, so the slave turns guilt and self-hatred inwards.

Deleuze also regards Spinoza as another philosopher who '[...] teaches the philosopher how to become a non-philosopher' (S:PP, 130). There is something in Spinoza's work which cannot be recuperated within philosophy as a system. Likewise, his style means that the very scholastic latin of the *Ethics* is broken up by parentheses, *scholia*. In fact, the *Ethics* contains three books which seem to work in parallel:

> This is the style at work in Spinoza's seemingly calm Latin. He sets three languages resonating in his outwardly dormant language, a triple straining. The *Ethics* is a book of concepts (the second kind of knowledge), but of affects (the first kind) and percepts (the third kind) too. (N, 165)

Similarly, Deleuze argues that a 'double reading' of Spinoza is always possible: a systematic reading, and an affective, intuitive reading (S:PP, 129).[27] The construction of the *Ethics* is itself a plane of immanence, in that neither reading takes precedence. The famous theory of the oneness of substance and the univocity of the attributes cannot be separated from three 'practical theses': consciousness, values and sad passions (S:PP, 28).

We will pause here to consider the 'method' that Deleuze employs when writing about other philosophers. His readings of the work of other philosophers are, of course, highly individual and particular. He is often likely to find something which few others have found, and which brings out previously unexplored aspects of a writer. It is not, therefore, wholly surprising that Pierre Macherey considers Deleuze's concept of 'expressionism' to be somewhat out of tune with, if not completely 'at odds' with Spinoza's own model of 'demonstrative rationality'.[28] What, asks Macherey, can Spinoza's project of a 'scientifically demonstrated ethics' have to do with 'expressionism', a term which is more readily associated with aesthetics, indicating the 'vertical force' of violent gestures and utterances which occur in an atmosphere of 'terror or horror, of sound and fury'?[29] In response to his own question, Macherey shows that Deleuze does in fact find an anti-representational concept of expression in Spinoza. Macherey shows that Deleuze is able to introduce the concept of expression, for which he provides a genealogy which stretches back to Antiquity, by means of the 'double reading' that has already been discussed. Running parallel to the level of demonstrative rationality is another 'differently ordered' level of sudden, expressionistic flashes. Macherey shows that Deleuze works back towards the major thesis of univocity in Spinoza by means of the 'minor' thesis of expressionism. Expressionism in this sense is 'a certain way of thinking' which undermines the notion of representation:

> The logic of expression is basically a logic of power, one might even say a logic of life or a logic of movement, essentially different from the traditional logics of representation that, in their quest for static identity, are constantly threatened by negativity, and therefore dependent on a transcendent principle.[30]

In this way, expressionism can be seen to be at the heart of Deleuze's metaphysical preoccupations which were discussed at the end of the introductory chapter. As Macherey shows, expression means penetrating reality to its 'deepest level'.[31] In this way, Spinoza takes us beyond the conventional limits of philosophy. For this reason, Deleuze considers the 'real Spinozists' to be writers such as Virginia Woolf and Kerouac. Consider the following passage from Woolf's *The Waves*:

> We are only bodies jogging along side by side. I exist only in the soles of my feet and in the tired muscles of my thighs. [...] I am like a log slipping smoothly over some waterfall. I am not a judge. I am not called upon to give my opinion. Houses and trees are all the same in this grey light. Is that a post? Is that a woman walking? Here is the station, and if the train were to cut me in two, I should come together on the further side, being one, being indivisible.[32]

Macherey's essay is a case-study of Deleuze's 'free indirect' style: 'Deleuze's reading of Spinoza powerfully engages us because it distorts without misrepresenting: if he sometimes forces that sense of the text, he does so from within, to bring out the very force that inhabits and empowers it.'[33] Macherey shows that Deleuze may stray from Spinoza's original text, but only to amplify certain relatively undeveloped themes: nothing foreign is imported.

Bergson

> It's what Bergson did in philosophy, what Virginia Woolf or Henry James did with the novel, what Renoir did in cinema (and what experimental cinema, which has gone a long way exploring the states of matter, does). Not becoming unearthly. But becoming all the more earthly by inventing laws of liquids and gases on which the earth depends. (N, 133)

The importance of Bergson for Deleuze cannot be overestimated, and Deleuze indicates this importance with the title of his book on Bergson, first published in 1966 in France: Bergson*ism*. It is as if Deleuze wishes to indicate that Bergson produced a body of thought which deserves to be identified as a coherent system or method in its own right. In *Cinema 1: The Movement-Image* Deleuze remarks upon Bergson's 'profound desire' to produce a philosophy of modern science, which would not be an epistemology but rather an autonomous domain of concepts which would correspond to developments in science (C1, 60). Alain Badiou, for example, sees Bergsonian intuition as being at the heart of Deleuze's project. For Badiou, Bergson is Deleuze's major philosophical reference point,[34] and Constantin V. Boundas argues that, in returning to Bergson, Deleuze has set out a theory of difference which is much more convincing than the versions set out by Heidegger, structuralism and Derrida.[35] We have seen already that Deleuze considers that there is something 'vitalistic' in everything he has written, and any perspective on Deleuze as a vitalist thinker must pass through the lens of his work on Bergson. A recent collection edited by Frederick Burwick and Paul Douglass has located poststructuralism in general, and Deleuze in particular, as a development a of a certain kind of 'critical vitalism':

> [...] a genuine extension of the structuralist urge [...] to find universals, even if those universals involve giving up a certain definition of the 'universal,' as in the *ur*-vitalist thesis that the only thing that does not change is change itself. Seen from this standpoint, the issues of post-structuralism mirror the issues of Bergsonian vitalism: multiplicity, duration, and movement.[36]

This critical vitalism emerged in the nineteenth century with the move from a matter-based physics to an energy-based model.[37] Burwick and Douglass emphasise the importance of the intellectual crisis that this reinterpretation of vitalism precipitated. They suggest that Bergson became the scapegoat of a period of general intellectual confusion at the turn of the century.[38] Deleuze refers to the opposition that Bergson encountered in an interview from 1985, drawing a parallel between the criticism of Bergson and a contemporary attack on any philosophy which rejects eternal values: 'We're back to Benda complaining that Bergson was a traitor to his own class, the clerical class, in trying to think motion' (N, 122).

Bergson believed that 'durée réelle', the real time of 'becoming' could not be apprehended or analysed by conventional scientific methods. We only really grasp reality when we let it 'slip through our fingers'.[39] One of the starting points of Bergson's thought is Zeno's famous paradox: how can we ever say that the arrow which flies is in one place and not another? Accordingly, it is apparently impossible to reconstitute movement from privileged immobile instants. He saw the intellect in general terms as primarily spatial, providing only a sort of snapshot which immobilises the flux of the world in order to permit reflection and subsequent action. He therefore came to think the 'durée réelle' could only be apprehended in memory.[40] As the faculty of understanding has developed along with the evolution of consciousness and action, the human intellect has come to feel at home in the world of inanimate objects.[41] The dominant logic of the intellect is therefore a 'logic of solids'.[42] This immobilising tendency is useful and necessary, but is also potentially limiting and dangerous. In *Creative Evolution* Bergson claims that a real theory of knowledge is inseparable from what he calls a '*theory of life*'.[43] As we saw at the end of Chapter 2, Bergson proposes nothing less than a 'new metaphysics', a world in which things provide their own 'luminosity'. Deleuze finds this same metaphysics at work in art and literature. The paintings of Cézanne and Van Gogh, for example, show a world in which the landscape itself 'sees' (see WP, 169). In this way, Bergson elaborates a thoroughly materialist account of perception. The brain does not create representations of that which is perceived, but rather responds to the movement of matter. What the brain can do is to subtract the actions issuing from an object which do not interest it. Consciousness subtracts something from the world, rather than adding something. The act of perception therefore '[...] puts us at once into matter, is impersonal, and coincides with the perceived object' (B, 25).

Bergson proposes the method of 'intuition' as a way of capturing the 'luminosity' of the world. He defines intuition as a '[...] laborious, and even painful, effort to remount the natural slope of the work of thought'.[44] Deleuze is keen to point out that 'intuition' is, in contrast to the ordinary use of the word, a precise, rigorous method: 'Intuition is neither a feeling, an inspiration, nor a disorderly sympathy, but a fully developed method, one of the most fully developed methods in philosophy' (B, 13). As Paul Douglass points out, Deleuze's pluralism attracts him to Bergson's 'intuitive' method of analysing problems. Intuition is an approach which demonstrates sufficient flexibility to deal with a world of multiplicities which are in flux. According to Douglass, Deleuze treats Bergson '[...] first and foremost as the author of an alternative method of problem-analysis based on a theory of "aggregate images" and irreducible "multiplicities"'.[45] Rather than offering solutions and immobilising perspectives on being, intuition is a 'problematising' method, which corresponds to a pluralist approach to philosophy in that it is 'differentiating' and 'temporalising' (B, 35). In this way, intuition works against the tendency towards artificial closure which exists in the intelligence. Such closure ignores the irreducible pluralism and heterogeneity of being and can lead to the confusion of 'badly analysed composites' (B, 28). According to Deleuze, Bergson considers the clearest example of the badly analysed composite to be the false combination of space and time (B, 86). This can occur either in the conception of time as a series of infinitely small 'snapshots' of the present, or of time as a homogeneous stream. Another example of the badly analysed composite would be the confusion of perception and recollection, since these two faculties tend to overlap and interpenetrate one another in everyday experience (B, 26). Intuition should be a method for inventing a 'liquid' perception, for locating the eye which resides 'within things', a world of flux and mobility. The intuitive method has three basic rules: it is problematising, differentiating and temporalising (B, 35). It is a question of stating and creating problems, of discovering authentic differences in kind, and of apprehending real time. It seems to be not only a tendency of the intellect to come into conflict with these principles – the intellect tends, for example, to spatialise – but a tendency within the world itself: 'Although it is illusion, space is not merely grounded in our nature, but in the nature of things' (B, 34). This leads to an irreducible tension, a doubling of the self, since intellect and intuition each must incorporate the other. Put in abstract terms, a tension is created by the fact that matter finds its home in space, whereas life finds its home in time.[46]

Intuition as a method should take us beyond our own subjective experience towards the 'conditions of experience', experience 'at its source', as Bergson puts it. It is, as Burwick and Douglass point out, a question of becoming free of the self:

> Bergson defines *durée réelle* as that irreversible succession of heterogeneous states melting into one another and flowing in indivisible process which we experience when we return to our

> life below, our Being/Becoming. To be conscious of real duration, however, is to lose a sense of one's individuality in the world (although Bergson later says that *durée* is the ultimate source of true individuality). It is to become aware of the continual novelty generated by the vital impulse.[47]

By using a sort of infinitesimal calculus – reconstituting the curve itself from minute fragments – we can use experience to achieve '[...] an extraordinary broadening out that forces us to think a pure perception identical to the whole of matter, a pure memory identical to the totality of the past' (B, 27).

Intuition necessarily depends upon the concept of duration and seeks to engender a form of thought which acknowledges duration. In going beyond experience to more concrete conditions, intuition is a 'superior empiricism' (B, 30). Bergson acts in this way as the forerunner of a philosophy of difference. According to Bergson, we tend to confuse differences *in degree* with differences *in kind*. Difference in degree is essentially spatial, whereas difference in kind is durational. Deleuze claims that Bergson draws a general distinction, from which all other distinctions derive, which is the distinction between duration and space (B, 31). So, for example, common sense would tell us that there is a difference in kind between the faculty of perception and the matter which is perceived. However, Bergson sees this as a difference in degree:

> We perceive things where they are, perception puts us at once into matter, is impersonal, and coincides with the perceived object. [...] There cannot be a difference in kind, but only a difference in degree between the faculty of the brain and the function of the core, between the perception of matter and matter itself. (B, 25)

It is also possible to misinterpret a difference in kind for a difference in degree. To illustrate this point, Bergson famously uses the example of a lump of sugar. The fact that the lump of sugar has a spatial configuration only enables us to perceive differences in degree between the lump of sugar and other objects. However, the lump of sugar also has a duration. It can dissolve and thus differ in kind from itself. In its temporalising function, intuition reminds us that thought must attempt to achieve mobility and fluidity, accepting no final definition or meaning. In seeking to turn attention away from the spatial in favour of the temporal, Bergson's theory of memory anticipates the poststructuralist concentration on the indeterminacy of meaning. We commonly believe that the past has ceased to exist, and that that which exists is in fact the present moment. This would be, however, to confuse being with being present:

> Nevertheless, the present *is not*; rather, it is pure becoming, always outside itself. It *is* not, but it acts. Its proper element is not being but the active or the useful. The past, on the other hand, has ceased to act or to be useful. But it has not ceased to be. Useless and inactive, impassive, it IS, in the full sense of the word. It is identical with being in itself. (B, 55)

However, it should not be assumed that Deleuze presents Bergson as simply rejecting the spatial. Deleuze notes a twofold evolution which occurs throughout Bergson's work. Firstly, Bergson moves away from the view that duration is a purely psychological experience, and sees it instead as the 'variable essence of things' (B, 34). Secondly, he acknowledges increasingly that, although space can form a homogeneous 'artifice' which separates us from reality, it is also an element of being. One of the consequences of Bergson's understanding of duration is that space itself will have to be analysed in its own terms as a sort of field of durations. This innovative approach to the question of space is present throughout Deleuze's work, particularly in the form of his ongoing dialogue with Michel Foucault (see B, 49).[48]

Bergson's 'intuitive' approach to philosophy is also a 'virtual' form of thinking which attempts to extrapolate from the conditions of ordinary experience. As we have already seen, philosophy might in this way become an 'infinitesimal calculus' which extends the line of experience into a virtual domain (B, 27; see also 42–3). Deleuze presents this philosophical method in terms of a precise geometry, separating composites into diverging lines which will narrow and converge at virtual point:

> When we attain the original point at which the two divergent directions converge again, the precise point at which recollection inserts itself into perception, the virtual point that is like the recollection and the reason of the departure point. (B, 30)

Bergson is of course the starting point for Deleuze's two important volumes on cinema. Bergson provides Deleuze with the inspiration to construct not only a concept of the movement-image, but also the time-image:

> Bergson's position, in *Matter and Memory*, is unique. [...] He no longer puts motion in the realm of duration, but on the one hand posits an absolute identity of motion-matter-image, and on the other hand discovers a Time that's the coexistence of all levels of duration (matter being only the lowest level). (N, 47)

Although Bergson criticises the false combination of space and time, his insistence upon the fact that time actually involves the coexistence and contemporaneity of various levels offers Deleuze a way of working on postwar cinema. This is largely a cinema of time which seeks new ways of representing and analysing the 'sheets of the past'. So, although Bergson opposes the badly analysed composite of space and time, he does leave the way open for a more differentiated and heterogeneous formation of 'space-time'.

The new metaphysics that Bergson explores, and that Deleuze develops, is that of a 'machinic' universe. Deleuze's work on cinema conceives of a 'cinematic' universe without centre, and in a state of constant variation:

> This is not mechanism, it is machinism. The material universe, the plane of immanence, is the *machine assemblage of movement-images*. Here Bergson is startlingly ahead of his time: it is the universe as cinema in itself [...] which is totally different from that which Bergson proposed in his explicit critique. (C1: 59)

Bergson's materialism also points towards the willingness of philosophy to consider the inhuman. A form of philosophy which seeks to incorporate an intuitive approach to duration will be open to permeability of the boundary between that which is human and that which is not human:

> To open us up to the inhuman and the superhuman (*durations* which are inferior or superior to our own), to go beyond the human condition: This is the meaning of philosophy, in so far as our condition condemns us to live among badly analyzed composites. (B, 28)

Intuition is a method by which we can become aware of the existence of these other durations. If we return to the example of the lump of sugar, Bergson points out that we must wait until it dissolves. This simple act '[...] serves to reveal other durations that beat to other rhythms, that differ in kind from mine' (B, 32). As a 'spiritual' materialist, Bergson seeks to come into contact with a level of reality which is in some way prior to human consciousness. For example, Deleuze shows that Bergson does not use the term 'unconscious' in the Freudian 'psychological' sense, but rather '[...] to denote a nonpsychological reality – being as it is in itself' (B, 56). In short, Bergson makes a crucial contribution to the machinic plane of immanence that Deleuze constructs throughout his work.

Kant

> My book on Kant's different; I like it, I did it as a book about an enemy that tries to show how his system works, its various cogs – the tribunal of Reason, the legitimate exercise of the

> faculties (our subjection to these made all the more hypocritical by our being characterized as legislators). (N, 6)

The list of thinkers that Deleuze chooses to write about in his early career is unusual and challenging, but his short work on Kant represents perhaps the most unexpected choice. Is Kant not, along with Hegel, one of Deleuze's philosophical 'enemies'? In *L'Abécédaire de Gilles Deleuze* Claire Parnet asks Deleuze how he came to write about this philosopher who seems furthest from his own thought.[49] He gives two reasons, saying that, in the first place, Kant represents a turning point in the history of philosophy: Kant reverses the subordination of time to movement. Secondly, he is intrigued by the fact that Kant sets up a sort of 'tribunal', a court of reason. Deleuze believes that the idea of the philosopher as a sort of judge of reason is a new persona, possibly derived from the influence of the French Revolution. In contrast, the seventeenth century had tended to think in terms of the philosopher as 'investigator'. Deleuze's reaction to Kant's court of reason is a kind of fascinated horror at this complex architecture which actually founds a 'critical' method that has no need of God, based as it is on reason. There is a way in which Kant can be read which goes 'underneath' his concepts. In one way, he inaugurates a whole critical tradition, inhabited by writers such as Spinoza, Nietzsche, Lawrence and Artaud, which seeks to do away with the judgement of God. Although he constructs a court, he actually sets in motion a tradition which attempts to do without judges.

Kant's Critical Philosophy was published in French in 1963 (*La Philosophie critique de Kant: Doctrine des facultés*), but for the English translation, published in 1984, an important preface was added.[50] Here, Deleuze suggests the use of 'poetic formulae' which would summarise 'Kantian philosophy'. The first is Hamlet's, 'The time is out of joint', a formula which sums up the reversal of the subordination of time to movement that takes place in the *Critique of Pure Reason*. Time is no longer on its hinges, and the straight line itself becomes a 'labyrinth': 'Everything changes, including movement' (KCP, vii). Time can no longer be defined in terms of simple succession. In short, Kant finds himself at the point when philosophy must start to think movement:

> It is not an eternal form, but in fact the form of that which is *not* eternal, the immutable form of change and movement. Such an autonomous form seems to indicate a profound mystery: it demands a new definition of time which Kant must discover or create. (KCP, viii)

The second formula is taken from Rimbaud: 'I is another.' Since the ego is constantly changing in time it is no longer possible to rely on Descartes', 'I think, therefore I am.' In order to speak in the form of the subject *I*, we must synthesise time, and yet the ego is constantly changing through time. The subject becomes an 'infinite modulation' rather than a 'mould'. It is no longer possible to think in terms of a 'unique and active subject'. It is rather a question of a passive ego which represents the activity of thought to itself:

> 'Form of interiority' means not only that time is internal to us, but that our interiority constantly divides us from ourselves, splits us in two: a splitting in two which never runs its course, since time has no end. A giddiness, an oscillation which constitutes time. (KCP, ix)

The third formula is taken from Kafka, and relates to the *Critique of Practical Reason*: 'The Good is what the Law says.' Since time is now unhinged, it is no longer possible to think in terms of a cycle of debt and expiation. Debt is now infinite, and as such becomes guilt: 'Guilt is like the moral thread which duplicates the thread of time' (KCP, xi). In antiquity Law was a sort of 'second resort' in a world abandoned by the Gods. If men knew what Good was, they would not need an imitation in the form of Law. Kant, on the other hand, moves towards a Judeo-Christian conception of Law as a 'pure form of universality'. Kafka places his work within this reversal, but, unlike Kant, invests the themes of Law and guilt with a grim humour (see K, 43).

Kant achieves a 'Copernican revolution' by dismantling the dogmatic rationalism which conceived of a correspondence between the subject and the object. Instead, he thinks in terms of a submission of object to subject:

> The rational being thus discovers that he has new powers. The first thing that the Copernican Revolution teaches us is that it is we who are giving the orders. There is an inversion of the ancient conception of Wisdom: the sage was defined partly by his own submission, partly by his 'final' accord with Nature. Kant sets up the critical image in opposition to wisdom: we are the legislators of Nature. (KCP, 14)

In this way, Kant is undeniably modern, focusing on the complexity of the human subject. However, it is only in the *Critique of Judgement* that Kant takes a late, arguably Romantic turn. The first two *Critiques* outline a relationship between the faculties of the mind whereby one of them is dominant. The various faculties – such as external sense, inner sense, imagination, understanding and reason – enter into relationships, but there is one determining faculty. In the *Critique of Pure Reason* it is the faculty of understanding, whereas in the *Critique of Practical Reason* it is reason which dominates. In the *Critique of Judgement*, on the other hand, Kant speculates upon a 'free and indeterminate accord of the faculties' (KCP, 68). To summarise this late development Deleuze chooses a fourth poetic formula from Rimbaud: 'A disorder of all the senses'. Again, the consequence of this 'discordant accord' is that the subject is problematised: 'It is a tempest in the depths of a chasm opened up in the subject' (KCP, xii).

With the fractured *I* and the notion of a disorder of the senses Kant has the machinery in place to overturn the dominant 'image' of thought. However, he fails to do so, and ultimately he only grants thought a set of 'civil rights' by multiplying the forms of common sense (DR, 137).

Leibniz

> For Leibniz, for Nietzsche, for William and Henry James, and for Whitehead as well, perspectivism amounts to a relativism, but not the relativism we take for granted. It is not a variation of truth according to the subject, but the condition in which the truth of a variation appears to the subject. This is the very idea of Baroque perspective. (LB, 20)

It is undeniable that Leibniz belongs to the rationalist tradition: he is a philosopher of order, preoccupied with the 'policing' of the city. However, Deleuze finds another side, as it were, to Leibniz. This thinker of order also creates some of the most extravagant, 'exuberant', even 'disordered' concepts. Unlike Descartes, who creates several rather sober concepts, Leibniz is one of those 'exasperated' philosophers who engages in a 'crazy' creation of concepts. He never finished creating new concepts: sufficient reason, inherence and inclusion, point of view, incompossibility. Deleuze finds another concept in Leibniz, which tells us much about the others: the fold.

Deleuze's book on Leibniz *The Fold: Leibniz and the Baroque* (*Le Pli: Leibniz et le Baroque*), published in 1988, deals primarily with the concept of the 'fold', ['le pli']. The fold is found everywhere as a feature of matter in the world but, as no two things are ever folded in the same way, it is not 'universal': 'The concept of the fold is always something singular, and you can only get anywhere by varying, branching out, taking new forms' (N, 157). In this way, the fold is a 'differential', a 'differentiator' (N, 156). The fold is in continuous variation. According to Leibniz's philosophy, substance is made up of an infinite number of 'monads'. A monad is not a material element, and consequently it has no parts. Matter is not 'granular', but is made up of ever-smaller folds (N, 158). The monad is completely closed, with no doors or windows. Each monad both contains the entire world within it *and* creates a unique perspective on the world by illuminating a small part of it. Deleuze illustrates this concept of interiority with reference to Baroque art and architecture. He draws attention to the Baroque trait of a contrast between the elaboration of the façade and the 'serene peace' of the inside:

> Baroque architecture can be defined by this severing of the façade from the inside, of the interior from the exterior, and the autonomy of the interior from the independence of the exterior, but in such conditions that each of the two terms thrusts the other forward. (LB, 28)

Since the monad is not a material entity it does not occupy a specific space but is rather a modulation in time. Deleuze uses Leibniz in order to develop his critique of the concept of the One and the Multiple. The idea of the fold expresses a conception of matter which is multiple *and* continuous. In short, it is the triumph of the wave over the particle. Therefore, the fold expresses matter as infinitely complex, such that it is impossible to describe any particular portion or division of matter in terms of a hierarchical organisation of parts or points. Unfolding only serves to open up another fold:

> A fold is always folded within a fold, like a cavern in a cavern. The unit of matter, the smallest element of the labyrinth, is the fold, not the point which is never a part, but a simple extremity of the line. That is why parts of matter are masses or aggregates, as a correlative to elastic compressive force. Unfolding is thus not the contrary of folding, but follows the fold up to the following fold. (LB, 6)

In a recent essay Alain Badiou summarises the concept of the fold as a sort of 'triplet': it is 'an *antiextensional* concept of the multiple', 'an *antidialectic* concept of the event', and 'an *anti-Cartesian* (or anti-Lacanian) concept of the subject'.[51] The fold is the most refined expression of Deleuze's empirical obsession with the multiple. Badiou argues that Deleuze uses Leibniz as a sort of 'spokesman' for the concept of the singular which is so important in Deleuze's work.[52] We will see that Leibniz's concept of the fold provides a point of convergence between Deleuze and Foucault.

Through the concept of the fold Leibniz introduces 'perspectivism' into philosophy. He finds in Nietzsche, Leibniz and the novelist Henry James a subtle perspectivism which is not relativism. Relativism – the idea that everyone has their own point of view ['à chacun son point de vue'] – is an impoverished form of perspectivism.[53] Perspectivism does not mean that truth is relative to a subject, but rather constitutes a 'truth of the relative' (see WP, 130). In the same way that Bergson proposes the possibility of a world without subjects, Deleuze's Leibniz shows that the subject can be substituted for a point of view which is in constant variation. The object has a new status, becoming an *objectile*. The object becomes an 'event'. The 'objectile' corresponds to our current era,

> [...] where fluctuation of the norm replaces the permanence of a law; where the object assumes a place in a continuum by variation; where industrial automation or serial machineries replace stamped forms. The new status of the object no longer refers its condition to a spatial mold – in other words, to a relation of form-matter – but to a temporal modulation that implies as much the beginnings of a continuous variation of matter as a continuous development of form. (LB, 19)

Similarly, the subject becomes a *superject*, a term which Deleuze borrows from Whitehead. Every point of view is now a point of view on variation (LB, 20). Leibniz confronts a world which is in the process of losing its centre, and he replaces this centre with point of view. Great philosophers, Deleuze claims, have an apparently banal concept that they take up in order to have fun ['se marrer'] with it. For Leibniz, this is the concept of point of view. He shows that perspectivism has little to do with everything being relative to the subject. It is rather the case that what makes me is my point of view on the world: point of view is an act. Henry James manages to create innovations in the technique of the novel by exploring such a perspectivism; a 'mobilisation' of points of view. There is no subject in James's novels, only points of view.

CHAPTER 4

Transcendental Empiricism: *Difference and Repetition* and *The Logic of Sense*

> The event does not relate the lived to a transcendent subject = Self but, on the contrary, is related to the immanent survey of a field without subject; the Other Person does not restore transcendence to an other self but returns every other self to the immanence of the field surveyed. Empiricism knows only events and other people and is therefore a great creator of concepts. Its force begins from the moment it defines the subject: a *habitus*, a habit, nothing but a habit in a field of immanence, the habit of saying I. (WP, p. 48)

> Behind the masks, therefore, are further masks, and even the most hidden is still a hiding place, and so on to infinity. (DR, p. 106)

> The task of modern philosophy has been defined: to overturn Platonism. (DR, 59)

> I've never renounced a kind of empiricism, which sets out to present concepts directly. I haven't approached things through structure, or linguistics or psychoanalysis, through science or even through history, because I think philosophy has its own raw material that allows it to enter into more fundamental external relations with these other disciplines. (N, 88–9)

Theatrum philosophicum 1: renverser le platonisme

> To reverse Platonism with Deleuze is to displace oneself insidiously within it, to descend a notch, to descend to its smallest gestures – discrete, but *moral* – which serve to exclude the simulacrum; it is also to deviate slightly from it, to encourage from either side the small talk it excluded; it is to initiate another disconnected and divergent series; it is to construct, by way of this small lateral leap, a dethroned para-Platonism.[1]

In 1969, Deleuze published two major works, *Logique du sens* and *Différence et répétition*, both of which were eventually translated into English in the 1990s. After his series of works on individual philosophers, this was the first time that Deleuze began to elaborate his own concepts, as it were. Taken together, they read like handbooks for the themes that will preoccupy Deleuze throughout his life, offering key insights into later work. In an interview from 1988 he sees the two books as preoccupied with '[...] the nature of the postulates of the image of thought' (N, 149). As far as Deleuze is concerned, philosophy has traditionally been concerned with a 'dominant image' of thought which has depended upon recognition and representation: Hegel and Plato, for example. These two books are an attempt to set out the coordinates of an alternative, non-representational image of thought.

Michel Foucault reviewed both books in 1970, famously declaring that, '[...] perhaps one day, this century will be known as Deleuzian'.[2] Such a claim is hard to ignore, and it is certainly worth looking at Foucault's article in some detail. It should be pointed out that it is more than a straightforward review, reading at times like a lyrical meditation on Deleuze's thought.

Foucault admits that it is difficult even to discuss these books; how can he get to their 'heart', when there is no centre but just a 'problem'? However, he does emphasise a theme which is certainly central to both books; namely Deleuze's desire to 'overturn' Platonism. He recognises that Deleuze has to employ a rather indirect strategy in order to achieve his aim. Deleuze works by noting the oversights, the omissions of philosophy 'as if in passing', working by stealth rather than making grand gestures.[3] We will look briefly at two ways in which Deleuze sets about his task. Firstly, Deleuze seeks to show how Platonism itself contains elements of a certain 'anti-Platonism'. In a useful article on Deleuze's 'anti-Platonism' Paul Patton discusses Deleuze's attempt to outline a non-representational mode of thought which would parallel the question posed by modern art, 'what is art?', by asking 'what is thought'?[4] Patton argues convincingly that Deleuze's critical method – that of emphasising contradictory elements in the works of established 'representational' thinkers, together with the vigorous promotion of a 'minor' non-representational mode of thought – is illustrated by his reading of Plato's own theory of representation. Patton shows how Deleuze's method is similar to the 'double gesture' of deconstruction. Plato himself evinces a certain ambivalence towards the model of representation. Deleuze overturns the dominance established by Plato of identity over difference, and he shows that Plato's figure of the simulacrum, the bad imitation, calls into question the framework of representation itself. In this way, Plato, the founding thinker of representation, is also a thinker of difference:

> To assert the primacy of simulacra is to affirm a world in which difference rather than sameness is the primary relation. In such a world, there are no ultimate foundations or original identities; everything assumes the status of a simulacrum. Things are constituted by virtue of the differential relations that they enter into, both internally and in relation to other things.[5]

Secondly, Foucault shows how, in *The Logic of Sense*, Deleuze demonstrates the importance of one of these omissions: the event. As we have already seen in the introductory chapter, Deleuze's concept of the event is derived from the Stoics. The event belongs to the domain of an 'insolent' metaphysics, in that it is incorporeal, like a sort of fog or mist which rises from the body. It belongs to a discourse which attributes a materiality to incorporeals: 'phantasms, idols and simulacra'.[6] Foucault emphasises the distinction between Platonism as a physics of solid bodies, and the Stoic philosophy of the event as an incorporeal flux which plays upon the surface of the body: 'Physics concerns causes, but events, which arise as its effects, no longer belong to it.'[7] Meaning is not simply a case of the 'knowable object', but rather a question of a flux between words and things. For these reasons, Foucault suggests that *The Logic of Sense* might be subtitled *What is thinking?*; Foucault argues that Deleuze produces a theory of thought that escapes the constraints of the framework of subject and object. It is an approach to thought which allows us to think in terms of problems: 'We must think problematically rather than question and answer dialectically.'[8]

Beyond Common Sense: A New Metaphysics

Foucault shows how Deleuze attacks the image of thought which is based on recognition and assumes the natural goodwill of thought. This image of thought makes the assumption that there are solutions to every problem, and effectively institutes a 'tyranny' of goodwill. Foucault calls this a 'pedagogical' model, which rejects the possibility of 'stupidity'. We must free ourselves from the constraints of 'common sense' which tell us that thought also entails goodwill, and that every problem has a solution. On the contrary, it is necessary to think 'acategorically'; in other words, to think in terms of difference. It is necessary for the philosopher to confront stupidity, to be 'perverse' enough to play the game of truth and error badly in order to escape the limits of 'common sense':

> Common sense extracts the generality of an object while it simultaneously establishes the universality of the knowing subject through a pact of goodwill. But what if it gave free rein to ill will? What if thought freed itself from common sense and decided to function only in its extreme singularity? What if it

> adopted the disreputable bias of the paradox, instead of complacently accepting its citizenship in the *doxa*?[9]

Foucault sees Andy Warhol's 'pop art' as an example of this 'stupidity' which thinks acategorically. Warhol reproduces disparate images – canned foods, film icons, car crashes, the electric chair – and in doing so suggests through repetition 'It's the same either way.'[10] However, at the same time, he manages to think difference. The 'boundless monotony' that Warhol presents us with may give rise to a sudden illumination of singularity amidst the general inertia of equivalences. Foucault claims that drugs can enhance the ability to think acategorically, taking us beyond the 'gloomy dumbshow of stupidity' to an understanding of the acategorical mass as 'variegated, mobile, assymmetrical, decentred, spiraloid'.[11] Foucault is obviously talking here about a plane of immanence, which constitutes the sort of new metaphysics that Deleuze finds in Bergson. We have already seen that Deleuze distinguishes the acentred world of Bergsonism from phenomenology's notion of the 'anchored' subject. Foucault makes the same point when he claims that *The Logic of Sense* is completely alien from Merleau-Ponty's *The Phenomenology of Perception*.[12] Deleuze proposes a new metaphysics of surfaces, which deals with the materiality of the incorporeal.

Difference and Unity: Univocity

> The univocity of being, its singleness of expression, is paradoxically the principal condition which permits difference to escape the domination of identity, which frees it from the law of the Same as a simple opposition within conceptual elements.[13]

In 'Theatrum philosophicum' Foucault also draws attention to Deleuze's concept of 'univocity'. Spinoza and Duns Scotus are rare examples in the history of philosophy who have investigated the radical formulation of the univocity of being. In *The Logic of Sense* univocity is explained as the idea that all events are compatible; they are 'inter-expressive' (LS, 177). Being has one voice but can only express differences:

> It is the eternal return itself, or – as we have seen in the case of the ideal game – the affirmation of all chance in a single moment, the unique cast for all throws, one Being and only for all forms and all times, a single instance for all that exists, a single phantom for all the living, a single voice for every hum of voices and every drop of water in the sea. (LS, 180)

Todd May shows that the concept of univocity is a consequence of the fact that Deleuze's notion of difference must be thought of alongside unity.[14] He argues that the juxtaposition of difference and unity is actually a requirement of Deleuze's particular formulation of difference. After all, it should not be forgotten that Spinoza and Bergson – both unitary, monistic thinkers – are at the heart of this project. Similarly, Deleuze sees philosophy as a process of reterritorialisation as much as a process of deterritorialisation. May is unequivocal: 'Difference, in short, must be thought alongside unity, or not at all.'[15] Spinoza's concept of expression, the plane of immanence that he sets out, precludes the possibility of transcendence. Being may have different expressions, but it remains univocal. We can never look *outside* for a transcendent explanation of the world: 'What univocity implies is not that everything is the same, or that there is a principle of the same underlying everything, but, instead, precisely the opposite. With univocity comes difference, difference for the first time taken seriously in itself.'[16]

Transcendental Empiricism

In 'overturning' Platonism and exploring the paradoxes at the heart of the logic of sense, Deleuze develops further his 'transcendental' empiricism. As we have already seen, the study of Hume constitutes his first discussion of empiricism. This book institutes recurrent references to 'English' thought as a form of empiricism in Deleuze's work. (We must suppose that Deleuze refers to 'British' empiricism.) For example, in a section of *What is Philosophy?*, which displays an appropriately Nietzschean humour, the 'English' are contrasted with their French and German philosophical counterparts (WP, 102–6). All three traditions act as 'reterritorialised' fragments of the Greek philosophical diaspora. French philosophy tends towards the search for a set of shared values which will express themselves through revolutionary aims, a 'republic of the mind'. German philosophy is preoccupied with foundation, with clearing the ground in order to lay these foundations. The 'English', on the other hand, are truly nomadic, habitual, empirical thinkers:

> England, from this point of view, is Germany's obsession, for the English are precisely those nomads who treat the plane of immanence as a movable and moving ground, a field of radical experience, an archipelagian world where they are happy to pitch their tents from island to island and over the sea. The English nomadize over the old Greek earth, broken up, fractalized, and extended to the entire universe. (WP, 105)

It is necessary at this point to pause and consider just what Deleuze means by 'transcendental' empiricism, and the ways in which it generates important concepts such as difference, repetition, becoming, intuition and problematisation.[17] It entails a spirit of experimentation which rejects the distinction between empirical particularities and abstract universals:

> Empiricism is by no means a reaction against concepts, nor a simple appeal to lived experience. On the contrary, it undertakes the most insane creation of concepts ever seen or heard. Empiricism is a mysticism and a mathematicism of concepts, but precisely one which treats the concept as object of an encounter, as a here-and-now, or rather as an *Erewhon* from which emerge inexhaustibly ever new, differently distributed 'heres' and 'nows'. Only an empiricist could say: concepts are indeed things, but things in their free and wild state, beyond 'anthropological predicates'. (DR, xx–xxi)

Bruce Baugh helps to explain this by showing that Deleuze's starting position is the claim that a difference exists between *real* difference and *conceptual* difference.[18] In other words, the 'sensible' differs from the 'conceptual'. In this way, transcendental empiricism is an attempt to overcome the Kantian dualism between real and possible experience.[19] As Baugh shows, Deleuze's transcendental empiricism confronts Hegel directly. Hegel argues that the 'sensible particularity' is empty, since every 'this' is without positive content: 'With respect to its utter indeterminacy and lack of content, being, the here and now existence of something, is identical to nothing.'[20] Deleuze reverses Hegel's epistemological model, claiming that the empirical is the transcendental possibility of the concept and the Idea.[21]

Characteristically, Deleuze does not start from the 'first principle' of empiricism according to which the intelligible comes from the sensible. Instead, he emphasises a neglected principle: the idea that relations are exterior to their terms. In fact, he claims that empiricists really want very little to do with principles. The true empiricist experiments rather than interpreting (D, 55), and is concerned with signs, which are not objects of recognition, and which can only be sensed or felt. The use of the term 'transcendental' here is obviously somewhat confusing, because empiricism quite obviously depends upon a principle of immanence. However, it can be explained in two ways. Firstly, Deleuze refers to a 'transcendental' use of the faculties whereby each faculty discovers its own 'radical difference' (DR, 143). Common sense – the model of recognition – on the other hand, depends upon a harmonious exercise of the faculties. Artaud, in his exchange of letters with Jacques Rivière, reveals himself to be a true transcendental empiricist. Here, Artaud confronts the real difficulty of thought 'without image'; the problem of creating thought which is somehow self-supporting, since it cannot rely on any pre-existing principles:

> He knows that thinking is not innate, but must be engendered in thought. He knows that the problem is not to direct or methodically apply a thought which pre-exists in principle and in nature, but to bring into being that which does not yet exist (there is no other work, all the rest is arbitrary, mere decoration). (DR, 147)

Secondly, Deleuze asserts that the empirical is the 'necessary condition' of any knowledge of actual experience.[22] Deleuze returns to Kant's notion of the radical disjunction of the faculties in order to explain the way in which transcendental empiricism differs from what is normally thought of as empiricism. It is as if each faculty, when freed from the constraints of working with the other faculties, is capable of locating 'things in their free and wild state': 'Each faculty discovers at this point its own unique passion' (DR, 143). Kant also introduces a temporal element, an element of difference, into the tautological certainty of Descartes' 'I think, therefore I am'. I cannot definitively *know* what I think because my being ('I am') is undetermined, unfinished, or, in Deleuzian terms, caught up in a process of becoming:

> Here begins a long and inexhaustible story: *I* is an other, or the paradox of inner sense. The activity of thought applies to a receptive being, to a passive subject which represents that activity to itself rather than enacts it, which experiences its effect rather than initiates it, and which lives it like an Other within itself. [...] It is as though the *I* were fractured from one end to the other: fractured by the pure and empty form of time. (DR, 86)

In this way, Kant opens up the possibility of the self as a fluid, 'larval' subject, and a distinctively modern writer like Beckett has '[...] traced the inventory of peculiarities pursued with fatigue and passion by larval subjects' (DR, 79). In *Difference and Repetition* Deleuze seeks 'a Cogito for a dissolved self' (DR, xxi). The philosopher himself is seen as a 'larval subject of his own system' (DR, 119). As we saw in Deleuze's early work on Hume, the mind is more like a machine than we commonly think, and the construction of the self is nothing more than the habit of drawing difference from repetition: 'The self does not undergo modifications, it is itself a modification' (DR, 79). This possibility as opened up by Kant, almost despite himself, is only a 'furtive and explosive moment', which he does not follow up himself. However, he opens up a 'crack' in the self which continues to haunt philosophy. Kant has, perhaps unwittingly, undermined a traditional notion of consciousness, and has consequently attacked a stable notion of both God *and* Man:

> For when Kant puts rational theology into question, *in the same stroke* he introduces a kind of disequilibrium, a fissure or a crack in the pure Self of the 'I think', an alienation in principle, insurmountable in principle: the subject can henceforth represent its own spontaneity only as that of an Other, and in doing so invoke a mysterious coherence in the last instance which excludes its own – namely, that of the world and God. A Cogito for a dissolved Self [...]. (DR, 58)

Bruce Baugh demonstrates that the model of knowledge that follows from transcendental empiricism is 'intuition' (see Chapter 3 on Bergson).[23] In this way, he claims, Deleuze's empiricism is close to that of Jean Wahl, who draws in turn on the 'metaempirical empiricism' of the later Schelling, Hamann, Whitehead and Marcel. For all these thinkers, the elements of concrete experience are not simply isolated atoms, but rather concrete particulars which also enter into relations to form a plane of immanence.[24]

Difference and Repetition: *Difference and Repetition*

Difference in the specific context of empiricism as defined by Deleuze is first dealt with in Deleuze's first major book-length publication, *Empiricism and Subjectivity*: 'Empiricism begins from the experience of a collection, or from an animated succession of distinct impressions. It begins with them, insofar as they are distinct and independent' (ES, 87). This, claims Deleuze, is the principle of difference itself. In *Difference and Repetition* Deleuze returns to Hume: '*Repetition changes nothing in the object repeated, but does change something in the mind which contemplates it*' (DR, 70). Hume illustrates this thesis with the simple example of a repetition of letters such as AB, AB, AB, A... . The mind experiences a difference, in that it now expects the appearance of B. As one example of this form of habit Deleuze takes Bergson's example of a clock striking four:

> It is not surprising that Bergson rediscovers Hume's analyses once he encounters an analagous problem: four o'clock strikes ... each stroke, each disturbance or excitation, is logically independent of the other, *mens momentanea*. However, quite apart from any memory or distinct calculation, we contract these into an internal qualitative impression within this living present or *passive synthesis* which is duration. (DR, 71–2)

The mind is therefore 'habit', and this habit involves the 'contemplation', or 'contraction' of empirically discrete moments. The mind draws a difference from these empirical elements. In arguing that human beings are really nothing more than habit Deleuze is effectively saying that what we think of as consciousness is in fact 'machinic'. Consciousness and the idea of the self are really only consequences of complexity: 'We speak of our "self" only in virtue of these thousands of little witnesses which contemplate within us: it is always a third party who says "me"' (DR, 75).

Difference and Repetition: *Movement in Philosophy*

Truly 'new' values have the element of difference as a kind of motor. They are always new, and are in this sense untimely. They provide themselves with their own movement:

> What becomes established with the new is precisely not the new. For the new – in other words, difference – calls forth forces in thought which are not the forces of recognition, today or tomorrow, but the powers of a completely other model, from an unrecognised and unrecognisable *terra incognita*. (DR, 136)

The model of recognition, which is ultimately the model of thought favoured by 'philosophical labourers' such as Kant and Hegel, is based upon a particular conception of reason as representation. The four conceptual tools of representation are identity, opposition, analogy and resemblance, and these four principles have traditionally been used by philosophy in order to tame the 'monstrous' potential of difference. Nietzsche, Kierkegaard and Péguy each oppose repetition to all forms of generality. Repetition opposes singularity to the general, a new universality to the particular, a distinctive to the ordinary, and instantaneity to permanence (DR, 1). In all of these thinkers Deleuze considers the problem of movement to be crucial. They reject the 'false movement' of Hegel's philosophy, which 'represents concepts instead of dramatizing Ideas' (DR, 10). Rather than representing movement, they wish to create an unmediated philosophy which is literally *in* motion: thought must dance and leap (DR, 8). In this way they reinvent philosophy as a new kind of 'theatrical' experience. This is not a theatre of representation, which explores the 'inner emptiness' of masks, but rather a theatre which multiplies masks, putting this 'emptiness' into motion so that true movement can be achieved in philosophy. Movement in philosophy and art creates the possibility of a plurality of centres, a 'coexistence of moments which distort representation' (DR, 56). Deleuze considers modern art to be a sort of theatre of flux, where nothing is fixed, 'a labyrinth without a thread' (DR, 56).

As we have already seen, Bergson is one of the thinkers who helps Deleuze to find movement where there had previously been stability or stasis. In fact, Constantin V. Boundas argues that Deleuze models his transcendental empiricism on Bergson's method of intuition.[25] This world of movement is one of problems and questions, rather than representations and solutions: 'There are no ultimate or original responses or solutions, there are only problem-questions, in the guise of a mask behind every mask and a displacement behind every place' (DR, 107). Turning his gaze upon psychoanalysis, which comes under sustained attack in *Anti-Oedipus*, Deleuze sets out a preliminary challenge: 'our loves do not refer back to one mother' (DR, 105).

The Logic of Sense: *A Paradoxical Image of Thought*

> The logic of sense is inspired in its entirety by empiricism. Only empiricism knows how to transcend the experiential dimensions of the visible without falling into Ideas, and how to track down, invoke, and perhaps produce a phantom at the limit of a lengthened or unfolded experience. (LS, 20)

As we have seen in the introduction, *The Logic of Sense* deals with the difficult notion of the event. To understand the relationship between sense and the event it is necessary to recognise that sense is a matter of paradox, '[...] a series of paradoxes which form the theory of sense' (LS, xiii). Paradox is one of the staples of nonsense, a constant theme in *The Logic of Sense*. Nonsense must be distinguished from any philosophy of the absurd, which distinguishes nonsense from sense in terms of a lack. Nonsense is, literally, that which has 'no sense': it goes in both directions at once, and structuralism shows us that there is always an excess of sense (LS, 71). Deleuze draws his main inspiration from two rather ulikely sources: Lewis Carroll and Stoic philosophy. Lewis Carroll was in some ways a collector of such paradoxes, and the Stoics moved away from Socratic philosophy and Platonism to investigate a new image of thought which is 'already closely linked to the paradoxical constitution of the theory of sense' (LS, xiv). Lewis Carroll's *Alice in Wonderland* and *Through the Looking-Glass* are structured around a whole series of paradoxes: the reversal of becoming smaller and becoming larger, the reversal of more and less, and the reversal of cause and effect. Carroll and the Stoics deal with what amounts to a new image of thought, and *The Logic of Sense* is an attempt to give the dimensions of that image. The new image that Deleuze presents is set out as thirty-four 'series' of sense, which form a 'complex place' (LS, xiv).

The idea of sense as a paradox is well illustrated by the first series of 'pure becoming' that Deleuze outlines. In *Alice* and *Through the Looking-Glass* we are introduced to what Deleuze calls 'pure' events. For example, as Alice becomes larger she is also becoming smaller than she will become. Pure becoming in this sense is an affront to common sense, which demands that all things demonstrate one direction, or 'sens' in French. In this way, the paradox of becoming, in eluding the present, undermines the commonsense assumption of fixed identities (LS, 2). Alice's identity, her proper name, is contested: 'Paradox is initially that which destroys good sense [...] but it is also that which destroys common sense as the assignation of fixed identities' (LS, 3). When Alice's identity is contested, the substantive and the adjective are usurped by the importance of the verb. This opposition between, on the one hand, substantives and adjectives and, on the other, verbs is mirrored in the division between Epicureanism and Stoicism, the two great ancient systems of philosophy (LS, 183). For Deleuze, the verb does not express an action, but rather an event: 'That is why, in its most general notion, it envelops the internal temporality of language' (LS, 184).

Deleuze includes some earlier essays as appendices to *The Logic of Sense*. One of these, which deals with the paradox of sense in a literary context, is an essay on Zola's *La Bête humaine*.[26] Zola's novel is part of the Rougon-Macquart series, detailing how the 'flaw' or 'hereditary taint' – what Deleuze calls the 'crack' – of the family plays itself out. Deleuze's reading of Zola's novel is heavily influenced by the ideas that he discusses at length in *The Logic of Sense*. Firstly, Deleuze is at pains to point out that the central character Jacques Lantier is of sound health. He does not embody the crack, which functions according to the Stoic paradox of sense:

> Everything rests on the paradox, that is, the confusion of this heredity with its vehicle or means, or the confusion of what is transmitted with its transmission – the paradox of this transmission which transmits nothing other than itself: the cerebral crack in a vigorous body or the crevice of thought. (LS, 321–2)

Rather than a story of individuals, the Rougon-Macquart series is a history of empirical singularities in what Deleuze calls elsewhere a 'free and wild state'. It is a story of events: 'A terrible encounter between nerves and blood, an encounter between nervous and sanguine temperaments reproduces the Rougon's origin' (LS, 323). Rather than feelings such as love or remorse, it is a question of impersonal physical relations: 'torsions and breakings' or 'lulls and appeasements' (LS, 323).

In summary, then, *The Logic of Sense* shows us that there is a sort of madness at the heart of language, a 'univocity' where the distinctions of first, second and third persons are abolished. This is the fourth person singular; the language of the pure event. Language in this way can express the singularity of the event. The subject of the fourth person singular is 'they'. But this is not the use of 'they' that we encounter in everyday language. It is, as we saw in the introduction, the 'splendour' of an impersonal 'they' (LS, 152):

> The Verb is the univocity of language, in the form of the undetermined infinitive, without person, without present, without any diversity of voice. It is poetry itself. As it expresses in language all events in one, the infinitive expresses the event of language – language being a unique event which merges now with that which renders it possible. (LS, 185)

The Logic of Sense: *A New Image of Thought*

The Logic of Sense constructs an image of thought, based on the thought of he Stoics, which has two temporal dimensions. In Stoic philosophy there are two forms of time: *Aion* and *Chronos*:

> [...] on one hand, the always limited present, which measures the action of bodies as causes and the state of their mixtures in depth (Chronos); on the other, the essentially unlimited past and future, which gather incorporeal events, at the surface, as effects (Aion). (LS, 61)

Aion is a time of pure becoming, a straight line that extends infinitely into the past and future. The Aion also endlessly subdivides the event: 'The event is that no one ever dies, but has always died or is always going to die, in the empty present of the Aion, that is, in eternity' (LS, 63). Since the event is infinitely subdivided on the line of the Aion, running in both directions simultaneously, the Aion is in fact a straight line as a labyrinth; yet another paradox. Chronos is the form of time which contains the present of bodies:

> Chronos is the present which alone exists. It makes of the past and future its two oriented dimensions, so that one goes always from the past to the future – but only to the degree that presents follow one another inside partial worlds or partial systems. (LS, 77)

The third 'Stoic' dimension is that of the surface: 'The empty sky rejects both the highest thoughts of the spirit and the profound cycles of nature' (LS, 137). Stoic surface is opposed to depth and height. Incorporeal events are irreducible to the depth of bodies and 'lofty' Ideas: 'Everything that happens and everything that is said happens or is said at the surface' (LS, 132). The philosopher is no longer a being who dwells in caves, but a creature of the surface such as a tick or a louse, and there is nothing above him but empty sky (LS, 133). The rejection of height and depth is a Stoic adventure of humour. Similarly, Zen wisdom operates on the surface, '[...]

against the Brahman depths and Buddhist heights' (LS, 136). We can see this dismissal of height and depth in the 'marvellous vacuity' of Zen arts such as gardening, flower arranging, archery and fencing (LS, 137).

As Foucault shows, *Difference and Repetition* and *The Logic of Sense* represent a considerable philsophical achievement. These books carefully construct a transcendental empiricism which motivates Deleuze until his very final work.[27]

CHAPTER 5

Capitalism and Schizophrenia: *The Anti-Oedipus* and *A Thousand Plateaus*

Anti-Oedipus

In the early 1970s Deleuze began to write with Félix Guattari, inaugurating a project which would aim at nothing less than a sort of 'universal' history, a genealogy of capitalism.[1] Guattari was a psychoanalyst and political activist who had worked since the 1950s at the experimental La Borde clinic (an activity he continued until his death in 1992). The first volume of this project emerged from the context of the theoretical and social upheavals of France in the late 1960s. French intellectuals took an important part in, and were greatly influenced by the events of May 1968, and *Anti-Oedipus: Capitalism and Schizophrenia*, published in 1972, is often considered to have emerged directly from the intellectual energies set in motion by '68. This book, Deleuze's first collaboration with Guattari, has a more overtly 'political' tone than Deleuze's earlier work. In a similar way, Michel Foucault was also apparently 'politicised' by '68, eventually producing *Discipline and Punish* (*Surveiller et punir: naissance de la prison* 1975) in the mid-1970s. At the risk of oversimplification, *Anti-Oedipus* is an attempt to theorise the new, more permeable relationship between the personal and the political set in motion by 1968.[2]

In *Anti-Oedipus* Deleuze and Guattari react against the Freudian notion of the unconscious as a sort of 'classical theatre' which contains the key to consciousness. Instead they propose an immanent conception of the unconscious as being like a *factory* for producing desire (AO, 24 and 55). Furthermore, *Anti-Oedipus* attempts to expand radically the domain of psychoanalysis, in order to show that '[...] the unconscious isn't playing around all the time with mummy and daddy but with races, tribes, continents, history, and geography, always some social frame' (N, 144). In this way, Deleuze and Guattari attack the theoretical dependence on a certain interpretation of Freud and Marx; a pervasive 'Freudo-Marxism'. That is to say, the view that individuals or societies have essentially innocent energies at their disposal which are blocked or repressed, and which could be released by more benevolent institutions. Against this, they propose a machinic production of desire.

In an interview from 1972 Deleuze and Guattari talk about the background to their collaboration (see N, 13–24). Before meeting Deleuze, Guattari had already begun to develop a notion of the unconscious as a machine, and when he met Deleuze talked of 'desiring machines'. However, as Deleuze points out, his theoretical framework was still heavily influenced by a Lacanian orthodoxy – 'structures, signifiers, the phallus, and so on' – that would be largely dismantled in *Anti-Oedipus*, in order to give Lacan 'some schizophrenic help' (N, 13–14). From the beginning, they experimented with form as well as with content:

> Félix sees writing as a schizoid flow drawing in all sorts of things. I'm interested in the way a page of writing flies off in all directions and at the same time closes right up on itself like an egg. And in the reticences, the resonances, the lurches, and all the larvae you can find in a book. (N, 14)

On one level *Anti-Oedipus* corresponds very closely to a caricatural notion of the ideas in the air in 1968. That is to say, it apparently recommends an anarchic release of desire. It also appears to valorise the experience of the marginal figure of the schizophrenic, since he or she thinks in a manner which escapes the structures imposed upon the 'normal' mind.[3] However, although *Anti-Oedipus* is certainly a product of its time, its importance and relevance cannot be denied.[4] The impact of what happened in France in 1968 remained with Deleuze for the rest of his life. The events had a directness and reality that struck him as having a genuine philsophical significance:

> *Anti-Oedipus* was about the univocity of the real, a sort of Spinozism of the unconscious. And I think '68 was this discovery itself. The people who hate '68, or say it was a mistake, see it as something symbolic or imaginary. But that's precisely what it wasn't, it was pure reality breaking through. (N, 144–5)

It should also be pointed out that Deleuze and Guattari are by no means unaware that their ideas will elicit criticism. In the final pages of the book they acknowledge that readers may have found plenty of reasons to criticise:

> [...] for believing too much in the pure potentialities of art and even of science; for denying or minimizing the role of classes and class struggle; for militating in favor of an irrationalism of desire; for identifying the revolutionary with the schizo; for falling into familiar, all-too-familiar traps. (AO, 378–9)

Yet they feel that they can readily defend themselves against such a 'bad reading'. For one thing, they point out that they at no point equate the schizophrenic with the revolutionary: it is a question of schizophrenia as a process, rather than an entity (AO, 379).

Anti-Oedipus poses extremely important questions which were particularly acute in the early 1970s. Firstly, the problems of fascism and State socialism were historically and geographically close to Western European countries such as France who were enjoying a period of relative economic expansion, whilst at the same time beginning to face the prospect of a genuinely global capitalist economy. So, on one hand the problem of fascism remained unanswered. As Wilhelm Reich had pointed out, fascism cannot be explained as a form of ideology. The masses were not duped; they wanted fascism at a certain time and under certain conditions. An understanding must be sought in terms of desire rather than ideology. Reich poses what is essentially the same question as Spinoza: '[...] why do people still tolerate being humiliated and enslaved, to such a point, indeed, that they *actually want* humiliation and slavery not only for others but for themselves?' (AO, 29). On the other hand, capitalism was moving decisively into a new technological and potentially global era, to a point where the faith that contradictions (irrationalities) would eventually reveal rationalities no longer seemed feasible. Not only were the certainties of dialectical, scientific Marxism under threat, but it was also obvious that living in a society constantly adapting to a developing global capitalism frequently takes a heavy toll on individuals. In short Deleuze and Guattari felt that the twin concept of liberation-repression was, to say the least, an inadequate and restrictive way of thinking about these problems. *Anti-Oedipus*, like the rest of Deleuze's work, is about thinking *differently*.

Oedipus

Anti-Oedipus must be read in the context of the theoretical stakes involved in the discussion of the Oedipus complex. It is almost as if the figure of Oedipus stands as a classically 'overdetermined' signifier for the theoretical debates taking place at the time.[5] The myth of Oedipus and the appropriation of this myth by psychoanalysis represent a sort of 'code' for talking about such apparently diverse subjects as the deficiencies of structuralism and the relationship between French intellectuals and the French communist party. In terms of academic discourse, 1968 can be seen in retrospect as the point at which the dominance of structuralism was finally overturned, making way for what has become known as post-structuralism. Deleuze and Guattari set out to attack a particular sort of 'psychoanalytic' structuralism which posits the Oedipus complex as a transcendental signifier. This has the effect of limiting any meaning which can be generated by an understanding of social and family relations.

Just what Oedipus – this 'overdetermined' term, as I have called it – represented to French intellectuals at this time can be measured by Michel Foucault's own engagement with the tragedy of Oedipus in a lecture course on 'Truth and Juridical Forms' delivered in Brazil in 1973.[6] Foucault reads Sophocles' play as an early example of Greek juridical practices. For Foucault, the play institutes a set of relations between power and knowledge which continue to have an impact in the contemporary world. In a skilful reading he shows that Oedipus has become a superfluous character by the time the truth is revealed at the end of the play. Oedipus *the King* – and it is important that Oedipus is a royal figure – has literally too much knowledge and too much power. Foucault argues that the conclusion that Oedipus Rex reaches, that political power is necessarily 'blind', becomes a dominant myth in Western thought. This myth also feeds into the Platonic belief that power and knowledge are mutually exclusive. It is Nietzsche who shows that, on the contrary, power and knowledge are inextricably linked.[7] Foucault sees a clear link between his reading of Oedipus Rex and *Anti-Oedipus*. Just as Deleuze and Guattari seek to analyse the relations of power that underpin the psychoanalytic process, so Foucault looks at the ways in which the myth of Oedipus helps to establish a dominant conception of political power. There is an Oedipus complex, but it is a collective condition, whereby we are unable to think clearly about the relations between power and knowledge.[8]

Fascism and Ethics: Thinking Beyond Identity

In Foucault's enthusiastic preface to the English translation of *Anti-Oedipus* he emphasises the fact that the book represents a break with 'a certain way of thinking correctly' which dominated the European intellectual scene from 1945–65. One had to be familiar with both Freud and Marx, whilst acknowledging the importance of semiotics. Foucault acknowledges that one possible reading of the book as a consequence of 1968 is as an expression of an anarchic explosion of libidinal energies. As if the force of the unconscious suddenly burned with unprecedented intensity. However, Foucault sees *Anti-Oedipus'* real 'strategic' adversary as nothing less than 'fascism'. That is to say, the fascism which is within us, that 'causes us to love power' (AO, xiii). It is no longer a question of freeing ourselves from repressive institutions and ideologies, but rather of freeing ourselves from our own love of the very things that dominate us. Rather than defending the rights of the individual, who is the product of power, the aim of politics and philosophy should be to 'de-individualise', to find a connection with the collectivity at a level which is underneath that of the individual. Foucault claims that *Anti-Oedipus* is in fact a modern book of ethics, which encourages us to observe the fascism that surrounds us and is part of us.

Anti-Oedipus is driven by a particularly clear attack on conventional notions of identity. The great psychological insights of the century are not necessarily those of Freud, but rather, D.H. Lawrence, Henry Miller, and R.D. Laing: '[...] it is certain that neither men nor women are clearly defined personalities, but rather vibrations, flows, schizzes, and "knots"' (AO, 362). Every individual is actually a little group, a 'groupuscule'. Lawrence attacks the roles – 'fiancée, mistress, wife, mother' – assigned to a woman by the Oedipal model, seeing a man and a woman rather as a 'soft' or 'jarring' 'vibration' (AO, 351). Similarly, Deleuze and Guattari argue that the wild claims of Nietzsche's 'madness' cannot be distinguished from his philosophy in general. If, in his letters, Nietzsche begins to identify with major names in world hsitory, Nietzsche performs a sort of 'schizoanalysis':

> It is not a matter of identifying with various historical personages, but rather identifying the names of history with zones of intensity on the body without organs; [...] No one has ever been as deeply involved in history as the schizo, or dealt with it in this way. He consumes all of universal history in one fell swoop. (AO, 21)

Social Machines

In *Anti-Oedipus* Deleuze and Guattari propose a rapid sketch of human history, locating three main phases to which correspond 'social machines': primitive-territorial, barbarian-despotic, and civilised-capitalist. The primitive-territorial phase is driven by kinship and filiation, which function like a primitive form of capital (AO, 146). Nietzsche's *On the Genealogy of Morals* provides much of the inspiration of this section, since the primitive-territorial phase sets in motion the often cruel process of inscription that constitutes human history: the blood that has dried on the codes of law. Nietzsche reminds us that cruelty is more than a vague, 'ill-defined' drive: '[...] cruelty is the movement of culture that is realized in bodies and inscribed on them, belaboring them' (AO, 145). Nor should we imagine cruelty and culture is a matter of ideology, since the primitive-territorial phase also sets in motion the investment of desire in social production and reproduction. In the barbarian-despotic machine deterritorialised social relations are focused on the despot, and writing is developed as a mode of representation by means of the reterritorialisation of the voice. The civilised-capitalist machine represents something quite different.

Whereas the primitive and barbarian machines 'dread' decoded flows of production and money (AO, 197), the capitalist machine seeks to multiply deterritorialised schizophrenic flows, never reaching a limit: 'If capitalism is the exterior limit of all societies, this is because capitalism for its part has no exterior limit, but only an interior limit that is capital itself and that it does not encounter, but reproduces by always displacing it' (AO, 230–1). The capitalist machine constantly decodes and deterritorialises flows, but it also constantly 'recodes' these flows as axioms. 'Antiproduction' insinuates itself into the process of production, regulating and absorbing dangerous flows. As Philip Goodchild points out, Deleuze and Guattari remind us that capitalism thrives on its contradictions, and it contrives to draw strength from almost any situation.[9] The capitalist axiomatic is never 'saturated'; a new axiom can always be added to the old ones (AO, 250). If this language seems abstract, it is perhaps helpful to consider very similar themes as they are dealt with in Arthur Miller's *Death of a Salesman.* Willy Loman, the salesman, literally loses his mind as a result of being a victim of American postwar capitalism, the American dream. He has a sense of the endless possibilities apparently offered by capitalism – he wants to 'be somebody' – but he loses his job and retreats into his own world. Miller's conclusions may be slightly different from those of Deleuze and Guattari, but they are all concerned with the basic problem:

> On the play's opening night a woman who shall not be named was outraged, calling it 'a time bomb under American capitalism'; I hoped it was, or at least under the bullshit of capitalism, this pseudo life that thought to touch the clouds by standing on top of a refrigerator, waving a paid-up mortgage at the moon, victorious at last.[10]

Schizophrenia and the Schizophrenic

> A schizophrenic out for a walk is a better model than a neurotic lying on the analyst's couch. (AO, 2)

As we have seen already, the concept of schizophrenia and the schizophrenic is one of the most controversial in *Anti-Oedipus.* Even Foucault, who praises the book so highly in his preface, admits elsewhere to being confused over the notion of schizophrenia in the book. Is it, he asks, the way in which society imposes relations of power on individuals at a certain time? Or is schizophrenia the structure of non-Oedipal desire?[11] Deleuze and Guattari seem to be saying that the social world is schizophrenic in that it puts intolerable and contradictory pressures on individuals, but also that schizophrenia is in some ways a valid response to this situation.

The situation is apparently complicated by the fact that Deleuze and Guattari claim, although this was certainly not true, never to have seen a schizophrenic (see N, 12). However, this deliberately provocative statement helps to explain what they mean by schizophrenia. As Brian Massumi points out, the 'schizophrenia' that Deleuze and Guattari seem to promote in *Anti-Oedipus* is not a pathological condition. It is rather a creative process of thinking differently, of 'becoming': 'Schizophrenia is a breakaway into the unstable equlibrium of continuing self-invention.'[12] Even Freud, the discoverer of the unconscious, could not go beyond a limited conception of the ego, constrained as he was by the Oedipal formula for assigning identities: 'daddy-mommy-me' (AO, 23). For this reason, Freud mistakenly attributes a certain autism to schizophrenia: schizophrenics are like narcissistic philosophers, who mistake 'words for things' (AO, 23).[13] For Deleuze and Guattari, on the other hand, it is undeniable that the schizophrenic, or the 'schizo', suffers pain and trauma, but the problems of the schizo are not those of the ego, the habit of saying 'I': 'He is somewhere else, beyond or behind or below these problems, rather than immersed in them' (AO, 23). The clinical schizophrenic does not suffer from narcissism; her/his problem is a 'social' problem. She or he has tried the experiment, but has been blocked, has become a victim of the schizoid process:

> The schizophrenics in hospitals are people who've tried to do something and failed, cracked up. We're not saying revolutionaries are schizophrenics. We're saying there's a schizoid process, of decoding and deterritorializing, which only revolutionary activity can stop turning into the production of schizophrenia. (N, 23–4)

So, Deleuze and Guattari also emphasise the fact that capitalism itself is a 'schizophrenic' process. In the same way that psychoanalysis refuses to acknowledge the desire and schizophrenia which lie at the heart of the unconscious, so capitalism performs the same denial: 'Psychoanalysis is like capitalism: although it tends toward the limit of schizophrenia, it's constantly evading this limit, and trying to get round it' (N, 21). The main tendency of capitalism is the decoding of flows (money-capital and labour) and the deterritorialisation of the socius: 'All that is solid melts into the air.' Jean-François Lyotard argues that Deleuze and Guattari reveal the energy which is potential within Marx's work.[14] Marx was the first to locate the fluidity and deterritorialisation which is axiomatic of capitalism. It constantly draws near to its 'schizophrenic' limit, but also constantly pulls back from that limit:

> What we are really trying to say is that capitalism, through its process of production, produces an awesome schizophrenic accumulation of energy or charge, against which it brings all its vast powers of repression to bear, but which nonetheless continues to act as capitalism's limit. (AO, 34)

As quickly as capitialism deterritorialises, 'ancillary apparatuses', such as the forces of law and order and bureaucratic institutions, carry out a process of reterritorialisation (AO, 35). Just as Marx reminds us that the commodity provides little information on the relations of production that underpin it, so the schizophrenic is a figure isolated from the material process of desire (AO, 25). The 'solution' that Deleuze and Guattari propose is a genuinely schizophrenic production of desire. 'You haven't seen anything yet' is a key slogan of the ethics of 'schizoanalysis'. There is always room for more perversion and more artifice (AO, 321). Capitalism always seems to step back from the brink, as it were, reterritorialising schizophrenic energies into an axiomatic that opposes their revolutionary potential (AO, 246). The solution proposed by Deleuze and Guattari is radical and provocative:

> What we say, in fact, is that there's never anything like enough consumption, never anything like enough contrivance: people's interests will never turn in favor of revolution until lines of desire reach the point where desire and machine become indistinguishable, where desire and contrivance are the same thing, turning against the so-called natural principles of, for example, capitalist society. (N, 19–20)

Machines and Desire

One of the key concepts in *Anti-Oedipus* is the 'desiring machine': 'Desire constantly couples continuous flows and partial objects that are by nature fragmentary and fragmented' (AO, 5). As we have already seen, rather than thinking of the unconscious as a sort of 'theatre', which plays out the archetypes of the Oedipal drama, it should be seen as a machine which is 'constantly whirring, grinding away, churning stuff out [...] (N, 16). Everything is a machine and everywhere there is production. For Deleuze and Guattari the machine is not a metaphor; reality is literally 'machinic'. The concept of the machinic is set against the traditional opposition between vitalism and mechanism. The structural unity of the machine and the discrete unity of the living organism must be fragmented, with the result that, '[...] a direct link is perceived between the machine and desire, the machine passes into the heart of desire, the machine is desiring and desire, machined' (AO, 285).

In short, there is no difference between the categories of the living and the machine. A desiring machine is a fragmented aggregate, whose parts do not constitute a unified whole (AO, 42). The desiring machine depends upon disjunctive synthesis which, as Ronald Bogue points out, would be a contradiction in terms for traditional logic.[15] The concept of the machinic is, therefore, a way of responding to a new way of looking at the world; a new reality. We live in a world of fragments, debris, 'bricks that have been shattered to bits', but we no longer believe that these fragments can be used to reconstruct a whole: we live in a fallen world (AO, 42). Proust's *In Search of Lost Time* is a 'literary machine' which responds to this condition. The novel is constructed from 'non-communicating vessels, watertight compartments', and these fragments are never unified or totalised: 'The whole not only coexists with all the parts; it is contiguous with them, it exists as a product that is produced apart from them and yet at the same time is related to them'(AO, 43–4).

The function of the machine is to produce, and production is one of the key themes of *Anti-Oedipus*: 'everything is production' (AO, 4). The schizophrenic is a figure associated with production: the 'universal producer' (AO, 7). Production escapes idealistic categories such as lack, and constitutes an immanent principle of 'desiring-production' (AO, 5). The traditional logic of desire was flawed from the start, forcing us to make a Platonic choice between 'production' and 'acquisition'. By associating desire with acquisition, it is made to lack a real object, and it becomes an idealistic concept (AO, 25). Desire does not lack an object, and desire is not attached to a fixed subject: 'Desire and its object are one and the same thing: the machine, as a machine of a machine. Desire is a machine, and the object of desire is another machine connected to it (AO, 26). Desire offers us a privileged access to the 'real':

> Lack is a countereffect of desire; it is deposited, distributed, vacuolised within a real that is natural and social. Desire always remains in close touch with the conditions of objective existence; it embraces them and follows them, shifts when they shift, and does not outlive them. (AO, 27)

Desire as a concept is particularly difficult to pin down and, since *Anti-Oedipus* is so obviously inspired by 1968, it is tempting to see Deleuze and Guattari's promotion of 'desire' as the promotion of some sort of anarchy. This would be to caricature their position. It is better to think of desire as a principle of creativity, invention, and possibility. However, it cannot be denied that the notion of 'desire' does have some connotations of a sort of political naturalism.

A Thousand Plateaus

In 1980 Deleuze and Guattari published the second volume of their capitalism and schizophrenia project, *A Thousand Plateaus* (*Capitalisme et schizophrénie tome 2: Mille plateaux*). As we saw in Chapter 2, the concept of the rhizome, an 'acentred' structure, is introduced in this book. A root-radical system is organised around a hierarchy of points and positions, whereas the rhizome is a multiplicity made up of 'lines'. They consciously structure their book as a rhizome, a series of 'plateaus' replacing conventional chapters. The concept of the 'plateau' is borrowed from Gregory Bateson, who uses the term to designate a block of intensity which is not organised around a point of culmination. Bateson uses the term to describe certain elements of Balinese culture, such as mother–child sexual games and quarrels between men. In this way, the idea of the plateau challenges the '[...] regrettable characteristic of the Western mind to relate expressions and actions to exterior or transcendent ends, instead of evaluating them on a plane of consistency on the basis of their intrinsic value' (TP, 22). Deleuze describes the plateaus of the book as being like 'a set of split rings' (N, 25). Any ring will fit into any other ring. 'A plateau is always in the middle, not at the beginning or the end. A rhizome is made of plateaus' (TP, 21).

A Thousand Plateaus also develops and refines several of the themes of the previous volume, such as the notion of the molar and the molecular. In *Anti-Oedipus* desire is positioned within a framework of two poles, the molar and the molecular. In general terms, the molecular is the pure becoming of unmediated desire, whereas the molar represents reterritorialisaion and overcoding. However, it is important to understand that the molar and the molecular do not stand in strict opposition. The distinction between the molar and the molecular is not a distinction of scale; it is qualitative rather than quantitative. Molarity implies organisation and hierarchy, whereas molecularity entails possibility, becoming. The molar is the level at which libidinal energies, that is to say desire, become solidified into transcendental signifiers which tend to restrict the flow and production of meaning. The molecular is the level at which desire moves in 'unstructured' flows. In the second chapter of *A Thousand Plateaus*, '1914: One or Several Wolves?' Freud is accused of reintroducing the molar unities of '*the* father, *the* penis, *the* vagina' at the very moment when he also discovers that the unconscious is composed of molecular multiplicities (TP, 27). Freud himself is engaged in a fetishised relationship with the signifier, which functions as a form of 'lack' in his theory (TP, 28). The molar and the molecular also continue the theme of 'micropolitics' which was introduced in *Anti-Oedipus*. A 'macropolitical' interpretation of May '68 will not provide an adequate understanding. This is why the traditional 'molar' groupings of the Left – unions, parties, politicians – were ultimately confused by the events. They ask themselves how such things could take place when the 'conditions' were not right (TP, 216).

The molecular is rather a potential within the molar. In the chapter entitled '1933: Micropolitics and Segmentarity' the molar and the molecular are linked to the historical development of different forms of 'segmentarity'. Initially, Deleuze and Guattari propose an opposition between the 'supple' segmentarity of so-called primitive societies and the 'rigid' segmentarity of modern societies. Supple segmentarity appears to be rhizomatic, in that there is 'considerable communicability between heterogeneous elements' (TP, 209). Rigid segmentarity, on the other hand, is largely dominated by binary oppositions, such as those between classes and sexes. However, working exclusively in terms of opposition is not enough. Supple and rigid segmentarity are in fact intertwined. The most striking example of this intertwining is the phenomenon of fascism. Fascism does not only exist at the level of the National Socialist State. Fascism is also undeniably 'molecular':

> [...] fascism is inseparable from a proliferation of molecular focuses in interaction, which skip from point to point, *before* beginning to resonate together in the National Socialist State. Rural fascism and city or neighbourhood fascism, youth fascism and war veteran's fascism, fascism of the Left and fascism of the Right, fascism of the couple, family, school, and office [...]. (TP, 214)

The general concept of schizophrenia, however, does not play such an important role in *A Thousand Plateaus*. Schizoanalysis tends to be replaced by the concepts of 'pragmatics' and 'nomadology', together with a general discussion of 'becoming' (see particularly TP, 232–310). If anything, the book is formally and theoretically more adventurous than the earlier volume.[16] However, the experimental structure and provocative ideas are accompanied by an occasionally more sober, cautious tone:

> You have to keep enough of the organism for it to reform each dawn; and you have to keep small supplies of significance and subjectification, if only to turn them against their own systems when the circumstances demand it, when things, persons, even situations, force you to; and you have to keep small rations of subjectivity in sufficient quantity to enable you to respond to the dominant reality. (TP, 160)

A Thousand Plateaus introduces a much more differentiated *geology* and *geography* of capitalism than *Anti-Oedipus*. The book also contains a more differentiated version of the attack upon limited models of meaning that motivated much of *Anti-Oedipus*. Whereas in the earlier volume Deleuze and Guattari promoted a dispersal of libidinal energies away from molar aggregates such as the State and the family, in the later volume they call the opposition between molar and molecular even further into question. By employing the geological vocabulary of strata they convey the idea that meaning is created by the interaction of large, complex blocks of signifying material, rather than by the simplistic tension between signifier and signified:

> Signifier enthusiasts take an oversimplified situation as their implicit model: word and thing. From the word they extract the signifier, and from the thing a signified in conformity with the word, and therefore subjugated to the signifier. They operate in a sphere interior to and homogeneous with language. (TP, 66)

In their attempt to go beyond this relationship between 'words and things' Deleuze and Guattari draw on Foucault's work which seeks to open language to the field of power. The analysis of signification means little without the recognition that power and knowledge are inextricably linked. Deleuze and Guattari take two lessons from Foucault's work on discourse and power: the discursive must always be considered alongside the context of the non-discursive, and social 'meaning' emerges from a network of 'statements'. These statements function rather like a tacit consensus beyond which current thought cannot exist.

Language

The question of language in general is dealt with at length in *A Thousand Plateaus*. Jean-Jacques Lecercle enlists the help of Deleuze and Guattari's work on language in *A Thousand Plateaus* in order to defend his notion of a linguistic 'remainder'.[17] The 'remainder' for Lecercle is basically that which escapes the notion of structure in language. To illustrate this he uses numerous examples of jokes, puns, nonsense, and agrammatical statements, not unlike Bartleby's 'I prefer not to'. In short, he looks at the ways in which language escapes the notion, which has been attributed to Saussure, of *langue* as a structure. In *Anti-Oedipus* Hjelmslev's linguistics is proposed as an alternative to Saussure. Hjelmslev develops an immanent theory of language, which escapes the constraining identity of the signifier, and the 'double game of the voice-graphism domination' (AO, 242). Instead, language is deterritorialised, decoded, subject to the flows of desire.

As Lecercle points out, Deleuze and Guattari reject what they see as the four main postulates of linguistics: the idea that language is essentially communicative; that language operates in isolation from extrinsic factors; that language is a homogeneous system; and that language is defined primarily by the standard version.[18] As Lecercle points out, Deleuze and Guattari propose an approach to language which is derived from the Stoics rather than from Saussure. Rather than seeing language as a system of signs, they see it as a site of contending forces, a system of incorporeal transformations which are social in origin.[19] As Lecercle emphasises, Deleuze and Guattari present language as an institution which is 'non-autonomous and material':

> Language cannot be a simple representation of the world; it is also an intervention within it, to be analysed in terms of positions, advance and retreat, territorial markings, and deterritorialization. We are moving here from the body of the individual to the body politic.[20]

In *What is Philosophy?* logic as the analysis of a discursive series of propositions is dismissed as without interest. In this sense, logic is as banal as a television quiz show. It is only when language is considered as a system which is at once self-referential *and* also traversed by social forces, that something interesting might emerge: 'Instead of a string of linked propositions, it would be better to isolate the flow of interior monologue, or the strange forkings of the most ordinary conversation' (WP, 139–40).

Brian Massumi outlines several ways in which Deleuze and Guattari's treatment of language differs from more familiar linguistic and semiotic themes.[21] For Deleuze and Guattari language is not a transparent medium of communication, and there are no constants in language, marked as it is by dialects, idiolects and jargons. Language is a system which is constantly changing, and which must be seen in a social and political context. They also reject the Saussurian notions of synchrony and diachrony, along with the importance that the latter attaches to the relationship between the signifier and the signified, preferring a pragmatics of language which is developed from Bakhtin and Hjelmslev:

> That's why we turned to Hjelmslev: quite some time ago he worked out a sort of Spinozist theory of language in which the flows of content and expression don't depend on signifiers: language as a system of continuous flows of content and expression, intersected by machinic arrangements of discrete discontinuous figures. (N, 21)

Deleuze and Guattari also admire Foucault's discursive approach to language. Instead of concentrating on the relationship between the signifier and the signified, Foucault looks at the ways in which specific 'discourses' construct their own objects. These discursive formations are networks of knowledge, and consequently networks of power. A particular discursive formation is constructed from linguistic and non-linguistic elements. They take as exemplary Foucault's analysis of the prison. The prison is a form which is related to other forms such as the school, the barracks and the hospital. This 'form-prison' is not reducible to a specific thing – the prison – but to a series of discourses, such as 'delinquency', and to formations of power which may be articulated in non-discursive elements such as architecture:

> Form of content and form of expression, prison and delinquency: each has its own history, microhistory, segments. At most, along with other contents and expressions, they imply a shared state of the abstract Machine acting not at all as a signifier but as a kind of diagram (a single abstract machine for the prison and the school and the barracks and the hospital and the factory ...). (TP, 67)

Language 1: Major-Minor

In *A Thousand Plateaus* and *Kafka: Toward a Minor Literature* (*Kafka: Pour une littérature mineure* 1975) Deleuze and Guattari develop the theme of language as having both a 'major' and a 'minor' inflection. These ideas form part of a wider attack on linguistics as a 'scientific' pursuit. In the fourth chapter of *A Thousand Plateaus*, 'November 20, 1923 – Postulates of Linguistics', the assumptions of Chomskyan linguistics are challenged. In the schema proposed by Deleuze and Guattari language is neither informational nor communicational, it is rather conceived to be 'believed and obeyed' (TP, 76). They also reject the assumption that language is comprised of universals which are part of a homogeneous system. Drawing parallels with language and music, they argue that linguistics functions in a 'major mode' looking for 'dominants, constants and universals', whereas languages themselves are in a state of immanent variation (TP, 97). All languages have a major and a minor mode. Therefore, it is not a question of an opposition between a dominant, major language and a dominated, minor language. For example, even after French effectively lost its position as a world-language it lost nothing of its tendency to be centralised and homogenised. It is rather the case that the more a language assumes a major mode, the more it is inflected by minor potentials. The minor mode of a language is a creative potential within a major mode of language. Rather than being characterised in terms of a creative 'poverty', it is better to think of the minor mode as a potential for *audacity* within a major language. Traditionally, linguists have identified minor languages such as Black English and Québecois with a mixture of poverty and overload.

However, Deleuze and Guattari see these features more positively as a tendency towards continuous variation:

> The poverty is not a lack but a void or ellipsis allowing one to sidestep a constant instead of tackling it head on, or to approach it from above or below instead of positioning oneself within it. And the overload is not a rhetorical figure, a metaphor, or symbolic structure; it is a mobile paraphrase bearing witness to the unlocalized presence of an indirect discourse at the heart of every statement. (TP, 104)

Language 2: Order Words and Free Indirect Discourse

Throughout his career Deleuze is preoccupied with the idea that language is only one element of signification. For example, in his work on cinema he shows that moving images constitute an extremely rich signifying system which is not necessarily structured 'like language'. He is also concerned to demonstrate that language operates on a plane of consistency alongside diverse elements of power and signification. *What is Philosophy?* consistently emphasises the point that philosophy is not a discursive, referential discipline. We have also seen that Deleuze develops a concept of impersonal, indirect discourse, which effectively sidesteps a uniquely discursive approach:

> I always depend on a molecular assemblage of enunciation that is not given in my conscious mind, any more than it depends solely on my apparent social determinations, which combine many heterogeneous regimes of signs. Speaking in tongues. To write is perhaps to bring this assemblage of the unconscious to the light of day, to select the whispering voices, to gather the tribes and secret idioms from which I extract something I call my Self (*Moi*). (TP, 84)

Deleuze shares with Foucault the idea that linguistic formulations only acquire meaning via the non-linguistic. In this way, his conception of language is strongly influenced by Austin's notion of the 'performative'. More often than not, 'meaning' is the same as 'doing'. We can use language to accuse, to blame, to threaten; and we can also use language to effect what Deleuze calls 'incorporeal transformations'. For example, language is used to pronounce people man and wife, and to indicate the passage from non-driver to driver ('I'm pleased to tell you that you've passed, Mr—'). Language can only take on the 'order-word' function because, as Brian Massumi points out: 'If context is immanent to language, language as a whole is nondiscursive.'[22] Meaning is a way of articulating circumstances, as much as it is about what words are saying literally. Massumi shows wittily how this conception of language means that the use of 'I' is ultimately impersonal:

> Language is an endless high school. Every utterance, innocuous as it may seem, takes place in a social or institutional context that inflects it with an imperative, however indirectly. Every utterance is struck, however faintly, with the redundancy of an anonymous murmur. [...] 'I' is not an expressive subject, only a linguistic marker indicating what body is addressed by the whispered imperative immanent to that particular position within that particular state of things.[23]

As Massumi indicates, Deleuze suspects that language often functions as a free indirect discourse, whereby the subject of the utterance is indeterminate. Flaubert developed this conception of language as a literary technique. In *Madame Bovary*, for example, the reader is frequently caught between what might be the thoughts of the author, the narrator, or Emma Bovary herself. *What is Philosophy?* emphasises the literary background to this technique. A novelist such as Dos Passos creates an acentred 'plane of composition', instituting counterpoint between the heterogeneous elements of 'characters, current events, biographies, and camera eyes' (WP, 188).[24] Deleuze and Guattari draw on Bakhtin's theory of the novel to illustrate the idea of free indirect discourse, or 'polyphony'. Bakhtin shows how the novel contains, '[...] from Rabelais to Dostoyevsky, the coexistence of contrapuntal, polyphonic, and plurivocal compounds with an architectonic or symphonic plane of composition' (WP, 188). This element of 'counterpoint' enables the novelist to explore the domain of free indirect discourse, which gives access to the 'madness' which exists within all dialogue, whether it is between characters or internal.[25] Deleuze and Guattari might have extended Bakhtin's analysis to a contemporary 'postmodern' novel such as Don DeLillo's *Libra* (1998). DeLillo explores the polyphonic aspects of narration, and also the free indirect discourse of conspiracy, information and ideology. The fictional character of Lee Harvey Oswald is presented through an indirect commentary on his own thoughts and actions:

> He took Marina boating on Youth Lake. They were the same as anyone, completely ordinary, saying what people say. Every fact about their lives was precious. Marina's weight at birth was a little over two pounds. Alek was in awe of the fact. It was a private charm, something about her to hold dear.[26]

In general terms, Deleuze sees *A Thousand Plateaus* as pointing towards a new linguistics which is a pragmatics, rather than a linguistics which is semantic or syntactic. A similar pragmatics is used in Deleuze's books on cinema. Two insights dominate: all language is always already metaphorical, and all language is indirect. No primary, pre-metaphorical meaning can be atrributed to language since all meaning derives from an unstable system of figures which does not have linguistic constants.

CHAPTER 6

Foucault

> A thought's logic is like a wind blowing us on, a series of gusts and jolts. You think you've got to a port, but then find yourself back out onto the open sea, as Leibniz put it. That's particularly true in Foucault's case. His thought's constantly developing new dimensions that are never contained in what came before. (N, 94)

The mutual influence of Deleuze and Michel Foucault is clear to anybody acquainted with their work. We sense that, particularly in the 1960s and 1970s, each read the other's work closely. We can also see that they were working on very similar problems. Foucault's work on madness, the clinic, prisons and sexuality – which has been widely disseminated and discussed in the English-speaking world – amounts to a sort of history of modern subjectivity, and a shared interest in questioning established notions of the self must be the starting point for a discussion of the links between the two thinkers. In 1972 Pierre Klossowski emphasised the point when he presented the affinity between the work of Deleuze and Foucault in terms of a general attempt to undermine the principle of identity, to dissolve subjectivity.[1] Both are preoccupied with the activity of thinking differently, an activity which Foucault defined in his later work as the struggle 'to get free of the self' ['se déprendre de soi']. Against a politics or a philosophy based on the notion of a stable identity they sought to introduce a principle of constant and inventive creativity. Philosophy, political and social theory, life itself, should never be a question of 'positions' from which one argues, but rather a task of creation, invention and experimentation.[2]

Recent biographies of Michel Foucault also sketch in some of the details of the friendship that developed between the two thinkers. It would appear that they first met through a mutual friend in the 1950s, when Deleuze was teaching at a lycée in Amiens. However, they apparently did not 'click' as friends and colleagues at this point.[3] It was not until the 1960s, when Foucault was working at the university in Clermont-Ferrand and Deleuze was working in Lyons that their friendship began to develop.[4] Deleuze remembers 1962 as the time when he first got to know Foucault (N, 83). It seems that Deleuze and Foucault initially recognised each other as fellow

Nietzscheans. Foucault was greatly impressed by *Nietzsche and Philosophy*, and the 1965 Royaumont conference on Nietzsche that they both atttended was an important point in their friendship.[5] At this point, they had started work on the production of a new French edition of Nietzsche's work.[6] This editorial work led to a joint publication, the introduction to Klossowski's French translation of *Die Fröhliche Wissenschaft*.[7] In the late 1960s Deleuze joined Foucault and Daniel Defert in their Prison Information Group (GIP).[8] This inaugurated a period of militant activity during which Foucault and Deleuze signed numerous petitions, and were involved in many demonstrations together. They set out a new ethics, as it were, for the intellectual. It would no longer be appropriate for intellectuals to 'totalise' their political engagement. Rather than acting as 'universal' intellectuals, it was now necessary to become involved in specific struggles over specific points.[9] So, for example, the rationale for the GIP was inspired not by some higher goal of universal justice, but by the more specific aim of disseminating information about prisons (see also N, 87–8). In an obituary of Deleuze, David Macey offers a snapshot of the two young philosophers from this period. Macey believes that it was this shared political activity which brought them together as much as the intellectual interests that they had in common:

> In June 1971, the novelist and journalist Claude Mauriac met two philosophers: one young, tanned and with a shaven head; the other with 'long grey hair and a worn, tired face'. Foucault and Deleuze were organizing a 'commission of enquiry' into the case of a journalist who had been badly beaten by the police. Although they obviously admired one another's work [...] it was really the micro-politics of a turbulent period that brought them together as philosophers militant.[10]

However, this period of militancy and friendship was broken fairly abruptly in in the late 1970s when, amongst other things, Deleuze and Foucault disagreed over a particular set of events. All three of Foucault's biographers describe the situation in some detail. Along with Deleuze, Foucault had become involved in supporting the West German lawyer Klaus Croissant, who had defended the members of the *Rote Armee Faktion* (often known as the 'Baader-Meinhof gang') in 1975. Croissant sought asylum in France since he risked imprisonment in West Germany for allegedly seeking to provide material assistance for the members of the gang, who eventually committed suicide in Stammheim prison in 1977. As he applied for asylum the West German government began extradition proceedings, and he was imprisoned by the French authorities.[11] Both opposed the extradition, but Foucault would not sign the petition that Deleuze had signed, which referred to West Germany as a fascist state and appeared to support the activities of the members of the RAF. Foucault argued rather in terms of the inalienable right of the 'governed' to be represented and defended in the courts.[12] It seems that Foucault and Deleuze ceased to see each other as friends at this point. Didier Eribon refers to the memoirs of Claude Mauriac, who recalls talking to Foucault in 1984, when Foucault confirmed that he had not seen Deleuze since the Klaus Croissant affair.[13] It should be pointed out that it was not only this affair which marked the increasingly divergent political analyses of the two men. Foucault was briefly associated with the so-called 'nouveaux philosophes' (although he distanced himself from them fairly rapidly), against whom Deleuze launched a stinging attack.[14] In general terms, Foucault was moving away from some of the political preoccupations of the 1960s and 1970s, spending more time outside France, particularly in the United States. Deleuze acknowledges this in his own generous assessment of the 'split': 'I got the impression that he wanted to be left alone, to go where none but his closest friends could follow him. I needed him much more than he needed me' (N, 83). Deleuze suggests that the fact that their paths diverged was regrettable, but that it may have been a necessary stage in a philosophical friendship.

Deleuze-Foucault: Influence as Variation

After Foucault's death in 1984 Deleuze talked of their friendship as a part of the work that they both accomplished. Their personal relations fed into, and also helped to illuminate the ideas that they produced. Deleuze's *Foucault* is, in this way, an attempt to 'draw a picture' of a friend who has died. *Foucault* is a philosophical 'portrait' of someone whom Deleuze regards as 'the greatest thinker of our time' (N, 102). It is striking that on several occasions Deleuze refers to Foucault in terms of violence, rupture and upheaval. According to Deleuze, Foucault's work did not so much evolve, as move from one crisis to another: thought as variation. Deleuze also recalls a sense of violence which clung to Foucault's personality. This violence was present in Foucault's everyday life, trembling with rage at demonstrations, and also in his books: 'An intense violence, mastered, controlled, and turned into courage' (N, 103). In terms of the subject matter of Foucault's work we might consider, for example, the awful description of the torture and execution of Damiens which opens *Discipline and Punish.* But there is also a violence in the style of Foucault's writing; a sort of rhythmical, musical violence. In seeking to think differently from what has gone before, thinking becomes '[...] a violence whose first victim is oneself' (N, 103). In musical terms, Deleuze considers Foucault to be something like Varèse, 'metallic and strident' in his critique of our actuality (N, 118). However, this style changed in Foucault's later work, which was '[...] no longer scintillating, with sudden flashes of brilliance, but taking on an ever more austere, ever purer linearity, almost calm' (N, 105).

Foucault and Deleuze describe individual trajectories which, nonetheless, share points of influence and connection. Deleuze remarked after Foucault's death: 'It's not a question of points I thought we had in common, or on which we differed. What we shared was bound to be rather indefinite, a sort of background that allowed me to talk with him' (N, 102). Deleuze also remarks that, for anybody who uses Foucault's thought: 'It's not just a question of intellectual understanding or agreement, but of intensity, resonance, musical harmony' (N, 86). What is certain is that Deleuze is frequently present, discreetly, often silently, in some of Foucault's most important and celebrated work. Deleuze himself admits, although with characteristic modesty, that he may have provided Foucault with 'raw material' for his historical work.[15] When asked to comment on Foucault's claim that the century would one day be 'Deleuzian', he says the following:

> He may perhaps have meant that I was the most naive philosopher of our generation. In all of us you find themes like multiplicity, difference, repetition. But I put forward almost raw concepts of these, while others work with more mediations. [...] Maybe that's what Foucault meant: I wasn't better than the others, but more naive, producing a kind of *art bru*, so to speak [...]. (N, 88–9)

However, despite the complexity of the links between Deleuze and Foucault, it is possible to discern four general segments, which we will look at in turn, in their joint trajectory. It is necessary to talk of 'segments', since each segment corresponds roughly to a period of time and also goes beyond that period, linking the two projects in a complex and multiple way. The first segment is inaugurated in the 1960s, when they shared a developing interest, as we have seen, in Nietzsche. In the late 1960s and early 1970s a second segment was set in motion when Foucault was particularly struck by *Difference and Repetition* and *The Logic of Sense*, singling them out for extravagant public praise. In the late 1970s there was, as already discussed, a cooling of relations which related to political choices and, to a certain extent, theoretical divergences. Then, as Foucault completed his final work on sexuality in the Greek and Roman eras, Deleuze perceived a link with his own work on Leibniz: we might talk of a Leibniz-segment.

Nietzsche-Foucault-Deleuze

The first contact between Foucault and Deleuze emerged out of the former's admiration for *Nietzsche and Philosophy*. Just as Deleuze had done, Foucault experienced a feeling of exhilaration and liberation when he first read Nietzsche. For Foucault, Nietzsche is both within and outside the tradition of Western philosophy. Traces of Nietzsche can be found in thinkers as disparate as Spinoza, Plato and Hegel, but he also '[...] has all the roughness, the rusticity, of the outsider, of the peasant from the mountains [...]'.[16] Nietzsche remained an important influence throughout Foucault's career, to the extent that, in his very last interview, he acknowledged a 'fundamental Nietzscheanism'.[17] Foucault felt that his Nietzschean preoccupation with the neglected subject of power was a project that he shared with Deleuze and Guattari.[18]

In an interview from 1986 Deleuze sets out three themes in Foucault's work which were influenced by Nietzsche: a conception of power enables us to think in wider terms than violence, including the power to be affected; the relation of forces to form, which leads Foucault to question the stability of the 'Man-form'; and finally the process of 'subjectification', of inventing new possibilities of life (N, 117–18). In this way, Deleuze reads Foucault and Nietzsche through his own lens: they are both philosophers of force, expanding the notion of power to include notions such as seduction and the capacity to be affected, investigating the links between force and the forms which must contain it, and looking at the way in which force works upon itself. Through Nietzsche, Foucault worked for much of his career on what amounts to a critique of three of the main moral and political assumptions of modernity: the sovereignty of the State; the sovereignty of the individual; and the stability of the contract which has supposedly developed between them.[19] In assuming that the individual is sovereign and therefore 'free', apart from the freedom that is given up to the State in return for the protection afforded by the rule of law, we misjudge the workings of power. Rather than being the property of a dominant class or the State, power is a matter of strategy and politics. Foucault argues that power is essentially productive, which, as Ansell-Pearson points out, closely follows Nietzsche's argument in *The Genealogy of Morals*.[20] Foucault is unequivocal; behind the discourse of 'right', or legitimacy, that has traditionally preoccupied modern political theory there lies a network of power.[21] As far as political theory is concerned, we must finally cut off the king's head and understand that what we think of as our individuality is frequently just another ruse of power:

> As in *The Genealogy of Morals*, Foucault understands the exercise of power not in terms of 'right' but in terms of technique, not in terms of law but in terms of normalization, not in terms of

> abuse but in terms of punishment and control. Our modern political rationality, according to Foucault, has developed alongside a new political technology of power which has produced the 'individual' as a subject of the state with rights and obligations: a subject not in the sense of sovereignty but in the sense of discipline.[22]

Deleuze concurs with this reading of Foucault's Nietzsche, showing how Foucault's critique of law is also a critique of the notions of ideology and repression: 'Power "produces reality" before it represses. Equally it produces truth before it ideologizes, abstracts or masks' (F, 29). It is wrong to think of ideology and repression as the conscious projects of a dominant class or of the State. That is not to say that ideology and repression do not exist, but rather that, '[...] as Nietzsche had already seen, they do not constitute the struggle between forces but are only the dust thrown up by such a contest' (F, 29). To illustrate this point Deleuze turns to Foucault's *The History of Sexuality* (*Histoire de la sexualité*, vol. 2 1984), which seeks to move the discussion of sexuality away from the notion of repression. The problem is not that we are repressed, but that we are rather constantly incited, seduced even, into searching for the truth that sexual behaviour constitutes. The words and phrases that our societies produce would seem to indicate a degree of repression, but the network of power is only revealed if '[...] we isolate the dominant statements, and especially the verbal procedures in use in churches, schools and hospitals, which simultaneously search for the reality of sex and the truth in sex' (F, 29). Deleuze sums up the link between Foucault and Nietzsche as a criticism of truth, whereby truth cannot be considered separately from the will it conceals. So, just as Nietzsche analyses the psychology of priests as a method of control by means of guilty conscience and *ressentiment*, so Foucault looks at the increase in social control which accompanies the construction of the modern 'individual' (N, 116–17). For Deleuze, Foucault-Nietzsche is the expression of a 'certain vitalism':

> When power becomes bio-power resistance becomes the power of life, a vital power that cannot be confined within species, environment or the paths of a particular diagram. Is not the force that comes outside a certain idea of Life, a certain vitalism, in which Foucault's thought culminates? Is not life this capacity to resist force? [...] for Foucault as much as for Nietzsche, it is in man himself that we must look for the set of forces and functions which resist the death of man. (F, 92–3)

Theatrum philosophicum 2: difference/problematisations

'Theatrum philosophicum', Foucault's review of *Difference and Repetition* and *The Logic of Sense*, has already been discussed earlier in terms of its reading of Deleuze's themes of the event, difference and repetition, and the univocity of being.[23] However, the article also yields useful information on the ways in which Deleuze influenced Foucault's own work. In a recent issue of the same journal, looking back at some of the most influential articles it has published, Judith Revel assesses the importance of this influence.[24] She is quite clear that Foucault's reading of these two books by Deleuze was a turning point in his work, opening up for him the question of *difference*. Revel argues that Foucault's article shows him in the process of problematising his earlier work. She suggests that Foucault realised that the analysis that he had formulated throughout the 1960s in terms of exclusion and binary oppositions might lead on to a subtler examination of the difference which lies at the heart of philosophy and rationality itself.[25]

As an example of this 'differentiated' approach, it is clear that Foucault is inspired by the theme of problematisation which he finds in Deleuze's work. He admires Deleuze's rejection of the pedagogical model of thought, which assumes the goodwill of the thinker and treats thought as taking place in a 'classroom'. To think problematically is to think more maturely, and with more integrity; to think *differently*.

> Far from being the still incomplete and blurred image of an Idea that eternally retains our answers in some upper region, the problem lies in the idea itself, the Idea exists only in the form of a problem: a distinctive plurality whose obscurity is nevertheless insistent and in which the question ceaselessly stirs. What is the answer to the question? The problem. How is the problem solved? By displacing the question.[26]

Although, as Judith Revel suggests, Foucault is influenced by Deleuze to think in terms of problematisations as opposed to binary oppositions from the late 1960s onwards, it is in the very final phase of his career that Foucault begins to look explicitly at what he calls the concept of 'problematisation'.[27] For him, the notion of problematisation is an adequate description for the way in which a new object, such as sexuality, appears in discourse. For example, Foucault looks at the way in which sexual behaviour is problematised in the transition from the elitist aesthetics of the Greeks to the confessional Christian mode. In short, desire is no longer a matter of appetite and moderation, but an index for the movements of the soul. The choice of the term 'problematisation' has a dual purpose. Firstly, to move away from the idea of an ideological shift imposed from above, towards a concept of care or concern which develops around a particular subject. Secondly, Foucault also indicates by the use of this term that particular problematisations are open-ended sets of statements which leave us, politically, without the comfort of positions which can be chosen from a range of possibilities. Foucault views the history of thought precisely as a history of problematisations; of the way in which objects – such as madness or crime – become areas for concern. A history of problematisations is a history of thought for Foucault, in that it represents a history of the relationship of, as he puts it, the self to the self. Deleuze emphasises that the notion of problematisation in Foucault's late work is the development of the concept of heterogeneity in previous work. In his late work, Foucault shows that truth can only become an object of knowledge by means of problematisations.

In *Foucault*, Deleuze draws attention to the question of problematisation. He argues that *The Use of Pleasure* draws out explicitly what was already present implicitly in previous books. For Deleuze, these problematisations frequently consist of disjunctions between seeing and saying:

> These practices, the process and the method, constitute the procedures for truth, 'a history of truth'. But these two halves of truth must enter into a relation, problematically, at the very moment when the problem of truth denies any possible correspondence or conformity between them. (F, 64)

As an example Deleuze proposes psychiatry, where there is often a discrepancy between what we can *see* and what we can *articulate* as madness. Psychiatry in the nineteenth century recognises this dilemma and so actively problematises the notion of madness. Both Foucault and Deleuze show us that critical thought must not suppose that its objects are unreflective. It is always a case of problematising what has already been problematised.

Difference, Desire and Pleasure

Although the theme of problematisation only appears explicitly at the end of Foucault's career, it can be clearly seen that, by the late 1960s, he was conscious of the need to explain what he calls a 'pluralist' method in his own historical work. In a reply to questions put to him by the readers of the journal *Esprit*, he points out that his method is 'pluraliste'. Rather than looking for an overall *Weltanschauung* or system, Foucault claims that he wishes to add to the plurality of existing systems, by means of locating the individuality of discourses.[28] For example, according to Foucault, we are faced with two conventional historical explanations of the new medical practices linked to the birth of the clinic. Firstly, one might look at the development of the clinic and the acceptance of the *post mortem* in the late eighteenth century as evidence of a more enlightened form of medical practice. Secondly, this new attitude might be seen as the medical correlate of a new political practice which treats society as an organic body. Foucault claims that his own method is different, in that he prefers to maintain that a new political practice does not produce a new medical object, but rather that the growing political interest in the welfare of the population changes the system of formation of a specific scientific discourse. The creation of teaching hospitals only provides the conditions for the emergence of new discourses. In this way, he attempts to show that an apparently seamless discourse or practice may in fact be constructed from plural sources: a discourse is a composite form.

Foucault aims in this way to show that his project cannot be that of uncovering historical repressions or ideological errors. Instead, he seeks to analyse the dynamic relationship between subject and object whereby both must in some way be 'problematised' in order for new effects of truth to be produced.

Deleuze sees Foucault as one of the major contemporary practitioners of a pluralist concept of 'heterogeneity': the science of 'mixed forms'. Abstractions conceal difference:

> We had no taste for abstractions, Unity, Totality, Reason, Subject. We set ourselves the task of analyzing mixed forms, arrangements, what Foucault called apparatuses. We set out to follow and disentangle lines rather than work back to points: a cartography, involving microanalysis [...]. (N, 86)

In *Foucault* (1986) Deleuze builds his analysis on the observation that Foucault's work is organised around a preoccupation with light and language, visibilities and statements, as heterogeneous 'arrangements'. The two forms are heterogeneous, 'anisomorphic' as Deleuze puts it, but may engage in a communication through a 'mutual grappling'. In short, the two can never come together to form a totality; they are separated by a sort of fissure or cleft. For example, in *Discipline and Punish* the prison system is shown to be a mechanism formed from disparate elements; the *visible* element is the disciplinary mechanism of the panopticon, and the *articulable* element is a discourse of humanitarian reform in the field of punishment.[29] In *The History of Sexuality: An Introduction* he considers the growth of a State interest in reproduction and health, but emphasises that the family and the State are not reflections of the same power. They are rather separate series which call upon each other for tactical support.[30]

In the 1970s then, Foucault develops the concept of 'le dispositif', which might be described as a social mechanism or rationality. ('Le dispositif' is often translated as an 'apparatus'.) A 'dispositif' – the prison system, for example – is an effect derived from a series of separate constituent parts; discourses on punishment and reform, economic interests, and the architecture of the prison: it is a heterogeneous series. This 'series' interacts in turn with the general series of training and discipline in the form of hospitals, asylums, schools, prisons and factories. Foucault's own analysis of the prison is the analysis of a 'mixed' category. He uses genealogy as a method of separation and division in order to undermine the notion that the prison is a discrete object. In fact, Foucault's project of genealogy as a 'history of the present' is very close to Deleuze's definition of Bergsonian intuition. This historical approach to the concept of structure introduces the possibility of instability, of difference, into that which characterises the present moment. Taking the example of the prison again, Foucault looks at the transformations which take place around the body of the criminal. He claims that the development of a generalised prison regime is not solely the result of humanitarian reformist discourse, since this discourse itself intersects with a new concern for education and training, which is in turn linked to the idea of a social contract. Controversially, Foucault implies that the spectacular cruelty of the *ancien régime* has been replaced by a more subtle and pervasive form of physical and mental cruelty. This might be seen as Foucault's own 'intuitive' method. It is only by separating the discourses on reform and the new social contract that he is able to look at the body of the criminal in the context of a history of the present.

So, it seems that Foucault may well have been influenced by Deleuze in the development of a method of analysis which acknowledges the complexity and difference at the heart of social reality. However, as mentioned above, in the late 1970s the paths of Deleuze and Foucault diverged. We have seen that one reason for this divergence was to do with the political choices that they both made at this time. However, it is also clear that certain theoretical differences had begun to emerge. Shortly before his death in 1995 Deleuze allowed a series of notes to be published which he had written in 1977. The notes, which refer primarily to Foucault's *The History of Sexuality: An Introduction*, were passed on to Foucault via a third party, François Ewald.[31] As Ewald points out in his introduction to the notes, Foucault's *The History of Sexuality*, which amongst other things challenged a current orthodoxy concerning sexual repression, had been generally poorly received. Foucault was entering a period of theoretical, political and personal crisis, and Deleuze was seeking to help his friend in this period of upheaval. Deleuze's notes are invaluable in showing the proximity of their projects in the 1970s, whilst also pinpointing definite areas of tension. Deleuze begins by outlining his general agreement with the ideas advanced in *Discipline and Punish*, which immediately preceded *The History of Sexuality*. The book is important in three respects: Foucault moves away from theories of power which refer ultimately to the State; he goes beyond his own earlier opposition between the discursive and the non-discursive; and he looks at normalisation and discipline rather than repression and ideology. For Deleuze, Foucault has developed a form of analysis which goes in two directions, but which is not at all contradictory. That is to say, Foucault looks on the one hand at 'micro-apparatuses' ['micro-dispositifs'] which constitute a diffuse, heterogeneous multiplicity. He also shows how these micro-apparatuses refer to a 'diagram' – *Discipline and Punish* outlines the rise of 'panopticism' – which constitutes an 'abstract machine' which is immanent to the social field.[32] As we have seen above, the encounter with difference in the early 1970s enables Foucault to construct a subtle analysis which begins to confront the ways in which power works in a differentiated, variable mode.

Deleuze then moves on to the publication which was to precipitate a sort of 'crisis' for Foucault, *The History of Sexuality: An Introduction.* He argues that Foucault has taken the rejection of repression and ideology a step further: power is not only seen as normalising, but also as *productive*. Previously, Foucault had shown how power produced knowledge; now he shows how power produces *truth*. Deleuze thinks that the new concept is important, but that Foucault tends, as a consequence, to make the category of power too diffuse, and too abstract. Deleuze's main disagreement with Foucault hinges on the categories of power and desire. Whereas Foucault emphasises 'apparatuses of power' ['dispositifs du pouvoir'], Deleuze prefers to concentrate of 'arrangements of desire' ['agencements du désir'].[33] In short, Deleuze prefers to think in terms of desire rather than power. He cannot go as far as Foucault in dispensing completely with the repressive hypothesis. It is not the case that a 'natural' category of desire is consciously repressed by power, but power does seem to block 'arrangements of desire'.[34]

Deleuze also shows how his concept of desire differs from Foucault's preoccupation with pleasure ['le plaisir']. He recounts the last discussion he had with Foucault, when Foucault told him that he could not go along with Deleuze's notion of 'desire', since this implied the category of 'lack'. Perhaps, Foucault suggested, his own category of 'pleasure' ['le plaisir'] was closer to Deleuze's use of desire. However, Deleuze insists in his notes that it is not simply a question of their choice of words, since he cannot accept the notion of pleasure. Deleuze points out that desire does not entail lack; it is rather an arrangement of heterogeneous elements, a 'haecceity'.[35] As far as Deleuze is concerned, pleasure simply interrupts the immanent process of desire, and in this way seems to be on the side of 'organisation', the molar. Pleasure is a way in which the individual 'reterritorialises' during the process of desire, and is therefore linked with lack and normalisation. It is not surprising, Deleuze suggests in passing, that Foucault 'attaches a certain importance' to Sade, and he to Masoch. What interests

Deleuze in Masoch is precisely the idea that pleasure is postponed in order to prolong the positive, immanent process of desire.[36]

In general, Deleuze is unsure whether Foucault has in fact made any advances in the project that they had, at one stage, worked on fairly closely: a 'micro-analysis' of power as a differentiated, heterogeneous, variable field. Deleuze parts company with the Foucault of *The History of Sexuality*, where power is posited as productive and new concepts of truth and pleasure appear. It is undeniable that these theoretical differences in some ways run parallel to political differences, as Deleuze himself acknowledges.[37] Foucault was becoming disenchanted with what he saw as the need to be politically 'on the right side', and the rejection of the repressive hypothesis was a way of attacking a certain version of 'Freudo-Marxism'.[38] Although Deleuze and Guattari had also attacked a similar target in *Anti-Oedipus*, Deleuze seems to have retained more sympathy with the radical Left than Foucault. As Deleuze suggests, the integrity of Foucault's project inevitably led to such 'violent' ruptures. It was necessary for Foucault to pursue his own path which would, for the time being, diverge from that followed by Deleuze.

The Life of Infamous Men: Deleuze-Leibniz-Foucault

At first sight, Foucault's article 'The Life of Infamous Men' might appear to be a minor text in his œuvre.[39] It is a short and enigmatic preface for a projected publication based on archival research on the registers of internment and the system of 'lettres de cachet' maintained by the *ancien régime*. However, Deleuze holds it in high regard: 'I often turn to that text, because although it's one of Foucault's minor pieces, it's inexhaustible, potent [...]' (N, 90). The piece emerges from an unrealised project, which was to have been published in Gallimard's 'Le Chemin' series, and was conceived of as an anthology of these memoirs, biographies and accounts. Foucault treats these texts as 'fragments' of the real, rather than representations of the real, arguing that the accounts are part of the process whereby the 'ordinary' became a fit and interesting subject to be described. They are in some ways the crude prototype of a modern literature of the 'everyday'.

For Deleuze, these 'infamous men' help Foucault to confront the problem with which he is faced after the publication of the first volume of *The History of Sexuality*, where he had become trapped by his own conception of power. In crude terms, he had described the web of power in modern societies so well that there now appeared to be no way out, no possibility of liberty or free-will for the individual:

> What Foucault felt more and more, after the first volume of *The History of Sexuality*, was that he was getting locked into power relations. And it was all very well to invoke points of resistance as 'counterparts' of foci of power, but where was such resistance to come from? Foucault wonders how he can cross the line, go beyond the play of forces in its turn. (N, 98)

Foucault thinks of the texts he reads as providing a sudden illumination of these 'vies infimes' – lowly, wretched lives – caught as they are in a brief shaft of light. Similarly, Deleuze sees the 'infamous man' as being like a 'particle' caught in a pencil of light and a sound wave: an individual summoned to 'appear and speak' by power (N, 108). In this sense, Foucault creates a literary effect worthy of Chekhov, who writes of the peasant who is taken to court for using bolts from railway lines to weight his fishing line.

Deleuze reads 'The Life of Infamous Men' as a sort of anticipation of the concept of *le pli*, the 'fold'. The infamous man, caught in the spotlight of power, poses the question of how we might learn to resist, not to allow power to crush us. The answer that Foucault comes up with in his final work on Antiquity is to find 'folds' in power: 'Crossing the line of force, going beyond power, involves as it were bending force, making it impinge on itself rather than other forces: a "fold", in Foucault's terms, force playing on itself' (N, 98). According to Deleuze, in discovering this new dimension of the 'fold', Foucault presents the possibility of an axis which is different from those of power and knowledge. This axis represents a final, optimistic turn in Foucault's work, by proposing ways in which life might be affirmed as a set of vital forces. This dimension of the 'fold' depends on a pluralist conception of the individual.

Postscript on Control Societies: from Moles to Snakes

In 1990 Deleuze published a short article which effectively acts as a gloss on Foucault's concept of the disciplinary society. In this short piece Deleuze emphasises an aspect of Foucault's work which is often neglected by commentators. Foucault is not only a theorist of the disciplinary society, he also shows that this type of society is part of the history of our present. The disciplinary society is part of what we are, but also a part of what we are ceasing to be. As Deleuze points out, Foucault saw these disciplinary societies in Europe as being essentially a product of the eighteenth and nineteenth centuries, succeeding earlier 'sovereign' societies where power was concentrated very much at the apex. Individuals move from one closed space to another in disciplinary societies: factory, barracks, hospital, school, prison.

As far as Deleuze is concerned, Foucault pointed forward to a new form; societies of control. In these new forms of society, the ones in which we live at the end of the twentieth century, the old disciplinary sites of confinement are breaking down. The hospital is increasingly replaced with community psychiatry and day hospitals: 'It's not a question of asking whether the old or new system is harsher or more bearable, because there's a conflict in each between the ways they free and enslave us' (N, 178). The American novelist William Burroughs has written about the 'new monster' of control, and the French theorist Paul Virilio has analysed the question of control in terms of variable speeds.

At this point, Deleuze goes on to incorporate Foucault's work into his own theoretical framework. Deleuze outlines a series of differences between disciplinary and control societies, and emphasises that these differences are generated by a transformation in capitalism. Nineteenth-century capitalism was essentially 'concentrative', based largely on production. Contemporary capitalism, on the other hand, tends towards 'metaproduction': it is directed towards the buying and selling of finished products. It will be recalled from earlier discussions of *What is Philosophy?* that Deleuze deplores what he sees as a contemporary obsession with 'marketing':

> We're told businesses have souls, which is surely the most terrifying news in the world. Marketing is now the instrument of social control and produces the arrogant breed who are our masters. Control is short-term and rapidly shifting, but at the same time continuous and unbounded, whereas discipline was long-term, infinite, and discontinuous. (N, 181)

Societies of control function according to a familiar image in Deleuze's reconstruction of thought. Control is based on forms which are 'inseparable variations', whereas disciplinary forms are 'independent variables'. In other words, in disciplinary societies individuals move from one site of confinement to another, each time starting the process over again. In control societies, forms of control function according to a continuously varying geometry (N, 178). The stakes have changed: 'Confinements are *molds*, different moldings, while controls are a *modulation*, like a self-transmuting molding continually changing from one moment to the next, or like a sieve whose mesh varies from one point to another' (N, 178–179). To illustrate this point Deleuze uses the example of the factory as opposed to the business. In the factory it is a fairly simple question of achieving an equation between the highest possible level of production and the lowest possible wages. In the business it is a question of a 'deeper level of modulation' as far as wages are concerned. In terms of labour, disciplinary societies function according to the model of the factory, with management confronting organised mass resistance in the form of trade unions. Control societies function according to the more individualised model of the business. Life becomes a question of an endless seminar, organised along the lines of the 'stupidest TV game shows' (N, 179). School is replaced by continuing vocational education and schools and universities are encouraged to compete for the 'best' results.

Disciplinary societies both amass *and* individuate, and Foucault saw the origin of the dual attitude in the 'pastoral' power of priest over his flock. Individuals in disciplinary societies consequently have a signature, a 'precept' or 'order-word', whereas control societies demand codes, or passwords. Money also illustrates the differences between the two types of society. Money in disciplinary societies is based on a gold standard, whereas control societies employ a floating exchange rate: 'If money's old moles are the animals you get in places of confinement, then control societies have their snakes' (N, 180). Similarly, disciplinary societies worked with thermodynamic machines, and control societies use information technology and computers.

It is a mark of Deleuze's respect and admiration for Foucault that he wanted to take Foucault's own ideas a step further after his death in 1984. Deleuze also took over Foucault's lecture course at the Collège de France for a short time, and it was Deleuze who read a passage from *The Use of Pleasure* at Foucault's funeral which captures the notion of thinking differently:

> There are times in life when the question of knowing if one can think differently than one thinks, and perceive differently than one sees, is absolutely necessary if one is to go on looking and reflecting at all. [...] what is philosophy today – philosophical activity, I mean – if it is not the critical work that thought brings to bear on itself? In what does it consist, if not the endeavor to know how and to what extent it might be possible to think differently, instead of legitimating what is already known.[40]

CHAPTER 7

The Literary Machine

The Critical and the Clinical

> As Nietzsche said, artists and philosophers are civilisation's doctors. (N, 143)

In an interview from 1988 Deleuze is asked why literature, which is a constant presence in his work, is not treated as a distinct art form which needs to be rationalised and ordered, as he has done with cinema. Is it, the interviewers ask, because literature is too close to philosophy to be treated separately? He responds by saying that he does not recognise this difference (N, 142). Deleuze does not make a hard and fast distinction between literature and 'l'écriture' in general, as demonstrated by the authors he writes about in his collection of 'literary' criticism *Critique et clinique*. Melville and Kafka rub shoulders with Kant and Spinoza: all are writers. However, it is undeniable that literature – a diverse collection of authors which includes Proust, Kerouac, Kafka, Melville, Sacher-Masoch and D.H. Lawrence – has an important part to play in Deleuze's work. This chapter looks at some of the reasons why these authors are accorded importance in Deleuze's work.

Deleuze published a series of essays which concentrate, for the main part, on literature in 1993. He had spoken of this project, *Critique et clinique* ['The Critical and the Clinical'] in earlier interviews (see N, 142–3). The title is not meant to imply that writers are frequently frail individuals, but rather that they are great 'symptomatologists': they are adept at reading and creating signs. 'Signs imply ways of living, possibilities of existence, they're the symptoms of life gushing forth or draining away' (N, 143). In *Critique et clinique* Deleuze presents what at times looks like the outline of a literary manifesto. This 'manifesto' proposes a way of both writing and commenting upon literature which is resolutely opposed to metaphor. In fact, the starting point of Deleuze's approach to literature is a sceptical stance with regard to language itself. Writers worthy of attention, as Proust says, will tend to write in a 'new language', they will create what is almost a 'foreign language' (see WP, 176). They will push language towards its 'asyntaxic' and 'aggrammatical' limits (CC, 9). Deleuze alludes to Beckett's comments in his 'German Letter of 1937' in which he says that, in order to spare no effort in undermining language, it is necessary to '[...] bore one hole after another in it, until what lurks behind it – be it something or nothing – begins to seep through; I cannot imagine a higher role for a writer today.'[1] The writer must find a 'minor' mode within an already existing major language. This must be the effect of literature upon language:

> [...] as Proust says, it opens up a kind of foreign language within language, which is neither another language nor a rediscovered patois but a becoming-other of language, a 'minorization' of this major language, a delirium that carries it off, a witch's line that escapes the dominant system.[2]

Deleuze goes so far as to say that literature and linguistics stand in strict opposition to each other.[3] Linguistics conceives of language ['la langue'] as a system which is always in balance: all variation is attributed to speech ['la parole']. Literature, on the other hand, confronts the fact that language is a heterogeneous system which is in perpetual disequilibrium. In this way, important writers are 'stylists' who create their own syntax. A great stylist, such as Charles Péguy, will embrace this disequilibrium and make language 'stutter'. Rather than sentences which follow one another in a linear narrative sequence, Péguy repeats the same sentence with an addition in the middle. The stuttering effect is created by sentences which proliferate from the middle. In short, Péguy constructs his own 'crazy' syntax. Another way of achieving a style would be the sobriety and simplicity – like a Japanese line drawing – that Deleuze finds in the writing of Jack Kerouac at the end of his life. Consider, for example, the closing lines of *Big Sur*:

> I'll get my ticket and say goodbye on a flower day and leave all San Francisco behind and go back home across autumn America and it'll all be like it was in the beginning — Simple golden eternity blessing all — Nothing ever happened — Not even this — St Carolyn by the Sea will go on being golden one way or the other — The little boy will grow up and be a great man — There'll be farewells and smiles — My mother'll be waiting for me glad — The corner of the yard where Tyke is buried will be a new and fragrant shrine making my home more homelike somehow — On soft Spring nights I'll stand in the yard under the stars — Something good will come out of all things yet — And it will be golden and eternal just like that — There's no need to say another word.[4]

Literature is also a matter of becoming, of instigating a zone of indiscernibilty rather than creating identification or imitation, and literature is capable of putting into practice the principle that runs throughout Deleuze's work: becoming:

> Writing is a question of becoming, always incomplete, always in the midst of being formed, and goes beyond the matter of any livable or lived experience. It is a process, that is, a passage of Life that traverses both the livable and the lived. Writing is inseparable from becoming: in writing, one becomes-woman, becomes-animal, or -vegetable, becomes-molecule, to the point of becoming-imperceptible.[5]

It is a way of entering into a 'zone-which-neighbours-on' rather than a process of transformation. Since writing is an act of becoming it is not a question of recounting memories and experiences, nor is it a way of explaining the Oedipal drama. Literature is characterised by 'the force of the impersonal', freeing us from the first and second person. The effect is that of an impersonal mode of enunciation which is not a generality but a singularity: *a* man, *a* woman, *a* child.[6]

As mentioned already, great writers are the physicians of society, symptomatologists, who read and invent signs in an innovative way. They may themselves be physically frail, may even have a 'shaky hold on things' (N, 143), but this only increases their affective potential. Their work is vital rather than communicative, liberating the '[...] power of non-organic life that can be found in a line that's drawn' (N, 143). They invent ways of living, of surviving, resisting, and freeing life.[7] The signs that Deleuze finds in literature are always signs of life: 'Signs imply ways of living, possibilities of existence, they're the symptoms of life gushing forth or draining away' (N, 143). The writer has in some way 'heard and seen' things – events which are collective – which overpower him/her, and it is through this capacity to be affected that the writer can liberate life where it is imprisoned:

> [...] he possesses irresistible and delicate health that stems from what he has seen and heard of things too big for him, too strong for him, suffocating things whose passage exhausts him while nonetheless giving him the becomings that dominant and substantial health would render impossible. The writer returns from what he has seen and heard with red eyes and pierced eardrums.[8]

Deleuze emphasises that literature does not spring from personal experience. The writer goes beyond the personal, and in this way engages in a free indirect discourse with the world. Writing is not a question of recounting our *personal* experiences, feelings, dreams, and memories: 'It is the same thing to sin through an excess of reality as through an excess of imagination.'[9] Memory can only ever play a small role in art, since the artist is 'a seer, a becomer' (WP, 171). Literature is always collective, often attempting to 'invent a people', a 'minor' people. This is the case for Kafka and central Europe and Melville and America: they are writing for a people who do not yet exist. 'Perhaps it only exists in the atoms of the writer, a bastard people, inferior, dominated, always in becoming, always incomplete.'[10]

Wolfson: A Book in a Foreign Language

In 1971 Deleuze wrote the preface to Louis Wolfson's *Le Schizo et les langues.*[11] Wolfson, a schizophrenic born in 1931, wrote this 'autobiographical' work in the late 1960s when he lived in a small apartment with his mother and stepfather, spending much of his time studying foreign languages. He produces a work which is literally a book written in a foreign language: Wolfson lived in New York, but chose to write his book in French. However, this is only the first element of disequilibrium that Wolfson introduces into the system of language. He describes in detail the elaborate word-games that he employs to blot out his 'maternal' language, English. These linguistic 'procedures', which frequently involve substituting foreign words – or fragments of foreign words – for the original English that he finds so painful, are described in exhaustive detail. So, for example, the sentence, 'Don't trip over the wire', becomes – via German, French and Hebrew – 'Tu'nicht tréb über èth hé zwirn' (CC, 19). Wolson sets about a systematic dismantling of his 'mother' tongue, and this obsessive activity is obviously linked to his problematic relationship with his mother. However, Deleuze argues that it would be wrong to explain Wolfson's 'condition' uniquely in terms of psychoanalytic categories, the 'eternal mummy-daddy' (CC, 29). The explanation of the schizophrenic individual should not be sought in the family, but rather 'global', even 'cosmic' categories. What Wolfson calls 'mother' is a particular way of organising words that he rejects. The student is sick of the world, not just his stepfather and mother (CC, 30). Wolfson attempts to locate that which is most 'impossible' in language: the 'outside' of language. In other words, Wolfson explores the madness which lies at the heart of language (CC, 32). Ultimately, Deleuze suspects that Wolfson may not have succeeded in crossing triumphantly the frontier of 'unreason'. Perhaps he remains a prisoner of madness, but he carries out a unique experiment with language.

American Literature: Lines of Flight

> What we find in great English and American novelists is a gift, rare amongst the French, for intensities, flows, machine-books,

> tool-books, schizo-books. All we've got in France is Artaud and half of Beckett. (N, 23)

In his own work, and that which is co-authored with Félix Guattari, Deleuze returns several times to the question of American, or sometimes 'Anglo-American' literature.[12] In *Dialogues* Deleuze argues that Anglo-American literature is somehow 'superior' to French literature, which is weighed down with 'manifestos' and 'ideologies', since it is a literature of flight, rupture, deterritorialisation. French literature is critical of life rather than creative (D, 49-50), since it is obsessed with what Lawrence called a 'dirty little secret' which lies at the heart of a writer's life, work and neurosis, whereby Kafka is childish and Lawrence himself impotent (N, 143). The pursuit of the secret represents in general terms the disease of interpretation as opposed to the relative health of experimentation. In the case of Thomas Wolfe or Henry Miller, American literature can aspire to be a genuinely popular literature, in which the most personal, 'autobiographical' material is also necessarily collective. In this way, the 'Anglo-Saxon' self is fragmented, dispersed, relative, compared to the 'solipsistic' European self (CC, 76). American literature seems to incorporate an instinctive understanding of the fragmentary nature of experience and selfhood, along with a 'democratic' celebration of the ordinary 'man without qualities'. In short, the experience of the American writer is never very far from the experience of America itself. In this sense American literature is, unexpectedly, a 'minor' literature. Paul Auster concurs with Deleuze's belief that the American novelist experiences a becoming-minor:

> In his *American Notebook*, Hawthorne wrote an extraordinary and luminous sentence about Thoreau that has never left me. 'I think he means to live like an Indian among us.' That sums up the project better than anything else I've read.[13]

Even the most autobiographical of narratives, a common American form epitomised by Whitman, seeks to convey a collective message, or to make some connection with collective experience: 'American literature has an exceptional power to produce writers who can recount their own memories, but as those of a universal people composed of immigrants from all countries.'[14] Consider as an example this central passage in Kerouac's *On the Road*:

> I was far away from home, haunted and tired with travel, in a cheap hotel room I'd never seen, hearing the hiss of steam outside, and the creak of the old wood of the hotel, and footsteps upstairs, and all the sad sounds, and I looked at the cracked high ceiling and really didn't know who I was for about fifteen seconds. I wasn't scared; I was just somebody else, some

> stranger, and my whole life was a haunted life, the life of a ghost. I was halfway across America, at the dividing line between the East of my youth and the West of my future, and maybe that's why it happened right there and then, that strange red afternoon.[15]

Literature should abandon interpretation in favour of 'fluxes' or flows (D, 47), and American literature in particular is able to articulate these flows and intensities. Flight in American literature is distinguished from the voyage, which always offers the possibility of reterritorialisation, of interpreting the voyage and of discovering an identity. As well as physical, geography is 'no less mental and corporeal' (D, 38). Deleuze develops this geographical reading of American literature from the notion of the 'West' proposed in Leslie Fiedler's *The Return of the Vanishing American.*[16] A note in the introduction to *A Thousand Plateaus* provides a brief summary of Fielder's geographical topology of American literature, which proposes Northern, Southern, Eastern and Western books.[17] As a locus of deterritorialisation, the West creates the possibility of a literature where 'becoming is geographical' (D, 37). Anglo-American literature therefore expresses a unique relationship with the earth:

> Thomas Hardy, Melville, Stevenson, Virginia Woolf, Thomas Wolfe, Lawrence, Fitzgerald, Miller, Kerouac. In them everything is departure, becoming, passage, leap, daemon, relationship with the outside. They create a new Earth; but perhaps the movement of the earth is deterritorialization itself. American literature operates according to geographical lines: the flight towards the West, the discovery that the true East is in the West, the sense of the frontiers as something to cross, to push back, to go beyond. (D, 36–7)

Deleuze argues that the potential for experimentation in the American novel cannot be extinguished by what he calls the failure of the American revolution. Melville imagines American literature as a minor literature in the same way that Kafka talks of 'minor' nations (CC, 114). American literature creates something schizophrenic from the neurosis of the Old World (CC, 100). Trees and roots are not absent in this literature, but there is also a constant minor inflection which constitutes '[...] the route of the American rhizome: the beatniks, the underground, bands and gangs, successive lateral offshoots in immediate connection with an outside' (TP, 19).

In this short essay on Walt Whitman, Deleuze presents what might be called a 'geophilosophical' sketch of the differences between European and American literature (CC, 75–80). In keeping with the concept of America as a federation of states, American writers tend to express a democratic ideal which is fragmentary rather than organic, as is the case with European literature. In this way, American literature also reflects the 'empiricist' preoccupations of Anglo-Saxon thought; a totality which does does not preclude the continued existence of discrete elements. In a rather longer essay in *Critique et Clinique*, 'Bartleby, ou la formule', Deleuze explores further this geophilosophical approach to American literature. Here, he considers links between literature and the American pragmatist tradition. Whereas the European novel (including the English novel) is frequently motivated by the desire to rationalise the world, the American novel expresses a pragmatism which is anti-rational in that it conceives of the world as an open-ended whole (CC, 110).

Proust: Signs

> The notions of the Search are: sign, meaning, and essence; the continuity of apprenticeship and the abruptness of revelation. (PS, 90)

Deleuze's first work to deal with literature at length is – perhaps surprisingly given his admiration for literature written in the English language – a reading of one of the major texts of French literature, *Proust and Signs,* which was originally published in French as *Marcel Proust et les signes in* 1964.[18] Deleuze uses a reading of Proust's *A la recherche du temps perdu* to consider a particular notion of the sign. The *Recherche* is shown to be a general semiology, a 'symptomatology' (see N, 142). In this book Deleuze continues his method of developing and multiplying the philosophical concepts with which he works. He continues the Nietzschean theme of truth as a matter of interpretation and creation, and also anticipates his later work on Leibniz and the 'fold', together with the question of philosophy and communication in *What is Philosophy?* We can also perceive the presence of Bergson and Kant: the theme of the 'errors' of natural perception recalls Bergson, and the notion of a disjunctive, 'transcendent' use of the faculties is the main theme of *Kant's Critical Philosophy*. Deleuze shows how Proust constructs a literary 'machine'; a fragmented world which generates signs.

It should not be surprising that Deleuze's reading of Proust is provocative, since he is so adept at inhabiting other authors and finding something new and vital in them. For example, it is frequently assumed that the act of 'involuntary memory' which the narrator experiences upon eating the madeleine is the definitive moment of Proust's masterpiece. However, according to Deleuze, the main theme of *A la recherche du temps perdu* is not that of memory. Similarly, he argues that the madeleine and the cobblestones have less importance as signs than 'the steeples of Martinville and Vinteuil's little phrase' (PS, 3). It is, rather, the 'narrative of apprenticeship' which is important; the way in which the narrator learns to read signs (PS, 4). Deleuze feels he has plenty of textual evidence to back up this claim. 'Sign' ['le signe'] is frequently mentioned in *La recherche*, particularly in 'Le Temps retrouvé'.

According to Deleuze, then, the novel is an exploration of different worlds of signs, forming circles which intersect at various points (PS, 5). There are basically four types of signs in Proust's novel: worldly signs, signs of love, sensuous signs, and signs of art. Worldly signs are essentially stereotyped and vacuous (which also gives them an extreme formalism and a 'ritual perfection'). They stand as a replacement for action or thought: 'One does not think and one does not act, but one makes signs' (PS, 6). To fall in love with someone is to become sensitive to the signs that they emit, to 'explicate' or 'develop' the possible and unknown world that the beloved represents. Friendship may well be a matter of conversation and interpretation, but love is a matter of jealousy and 'silent interpretation' (PS, 7–9). Sensuous signs, including the madeleine, are perhaps the most famous in *La recherche*. All of these signs, whether it is the madeleine, cobblestones or the noise of a spoon, entail a similar procedure. An initial joy is proceeded by a feeling of obligation to locate the meaning of the sign, which is in turn followed by the revelation of that meaning. Sensuous signs are certainly more joyous and affirmative than empty worldly signs, or the deceptive signs of love. However, unlike the signs of art they are still *material* (PS, 11–12). The signs of art, such as the steeples of Martinville, are 'dematerialised', and therefore reveal an essence (PS, 12–13). These signs are immaterial, appealing only to desire and imagination, rather than to memory: 'As long as we discover a sign's meaning in something else, matter still subsists, refractory to spirit. On the contrary, art gives us the true unity: unity of an immaterial sign and of an entirely spiritual meaning' (PS, 40). Essence, as revealed in the work of art, is 'the absolute and ultimate Difference', insofar as difference is what enables us to conceive of being (PS, 41). This is not an 'empirical difference' between two objects, but rather an 'internal' difference: 'Each subject expresses the world from a certain viewpoint. But the viewpoint is the difference itself, the absolute internal difference. Each subject therefore expresses an absolutely different world' (PS, 42). This internal difference which is essence goes beyond the framework of subject and object (PS, 36). Essence is also a matter of repetition: 'What can one do with essence, which is ultimate difference, except to repeat it, since it is irreplaceable and since nothing can be substituted for it?' (PS, 48)

Proust is, for Deleuze, 'Leibnizian', since the essences are like monads (PS, 41). Things, that is to say beings, are not points of view on a whole; they are themselves irreducible points of view. Essence is the complication of envelopment and development:

> The sensitive man liberates the souls implicated in things: somewhat as we see the pieces of Japanese paper flower in the water, expanding or extending, forming blossoms, houses, and characters. Meaning itself is identified with this development of the sign, as the sign was identified with the involution of meaning. So that Essence is finally the third term which dominates the other two, which presides over their movement: essence complicates the sign and the meaning, it holds them *in complication*, it puts the one in the other. (PS, 89)

The world that Proust explores in *La recherche* is a fragmentary world of plural viewpoints which do not refer back to a unifying whole. It is as if we move from one irreducible viewpoint to another. Proust shares this aesthetic of the viewpoint with Henry James, and in this way confronts the definitive problem of modernism (PS, 98). The notion of order has collapsed: 'The world has become crumbs and chaos' (PS, 98). Proust rejects the idea of organic totality in favour of

> [...] the new conception of unity he was in the process of creating. For it is surely from here that we must begin: the disparity, the incommensurability, the disintegration of the parts of the Search, with the breaks, lacunae, intermittences which guarantee its ultimate diversity. (PS, 103)

Proust allows us to be present as meaning is explicated, but he shows that this process of unfolding only produces truths which are heterogeneous and fragmented.

The theme of heterogeneity is crucial. In the case of the famous example of the madeleine in Proust, Deleuze emphasises the point that there is no identity or resemblance between the madeleine and Combray. It is rather the fact that two 'heterogeneous' presents coexist to create Combray in a totally new form. The essence of Combray therefore depends upon the immanent difference between the two presents (PS, 59). The way in which the past and the present moments are brought together is closer to a struggle than an agreement (PS, 109). But even such a 'sensuous memory' depends, in the last instance, upon an association which compromises the principle of difference and means that 'reminiscences are inferior metaphors' (PS, 63). Involuntary memory – the sudden reminiscence that overtakes the narrator when he eats the madeleine – is not the most important form of memory in the novel. Sensuous signs are superior to worldly signs and signs of love, but they remain inferior to the dematerialised signs of art.

For Deleuze, Proust creates a plural world of signs as a project which sets itself against the generally accepted models of truth proposed by philosophy and science. Proust does not subscribe to the idea that there is a natural 'will-to-truth' (PS, 15). We go in search of truth only when incited to do so by the shock, or violence, of a sign. Truth is not a matter of 'affinity' or 'good will', but rather of shock, contingency, constraint, chance. Philosophy is mistaken when it assumes that we are imbued with a natural love of truth:

> Truth depends upon an encounter with something which forces us to think, and to seek the truth. The accident of encounters, the pressure of constraints are Proust's two fundamental themes. Precisely, it is the sign which constitutes the object of an encounter, and which works this violence upon us. It is the accident of the encounter which guarantees the necessity of what is thought. (PS, 16)

An example of such a shock might be the jealousy which is stimulated in a love affair. The jealous lover goes in search of the truth stimulated by the lies and betrayal of the partner. For this reason, a mediocre love affair is of more interest than a serious and profound friendship, since the former lends itself to the proliferation of signs. Similarly, a work of art is frequently more rich in signs than a work of philosophy (PS, 21).

In insisting upon the idea that it is one of the errors of philosophy to believe that we have a natural love of truth, *Proust and Signs* initiates a theme which continues throughout Deleuze's work, and which is discussed at length in *What is Philosophy?* When it works by good will, and refuses to waste time, the faculty of intelligence tends towards conversation, friendship and philosophy, which in turn implies a voluntary impulse towards community, communication and an objective perspective. In art and literature intelligence operates in a different way, and 'comes after' rather than before (PS 22). Proust opposes art and love to philosophy and friendship, since both circumvent the dull clarity of conventional, communicated wisdom, and tend towards a creative proliferation of signs (PS, 29). According to Deleuze, the Proustian vision of the world excludes the disciplines of physics and philosophy in favour of the vocation of the 'Egyptologist'. Philosophy presupposes minds which engage in intersubjective communication and which share an unequivocal desire for truth: physics presupposes objective access to an unproblematic mechanical reality. Egyptology, on the other hand, takes us into the labyrinth of implication and complication (PS, 90–1).

In *Proust and Signs* Deleuze presents another generally 'deconstructive' reading. This time he sees Proust's 'Platonism' as an attempt to 'overthrow' ['renverser'] one sort of Platonism. One strand of Plato's thought is concerned with that which is the same, which is an 'object of recognition'. In Deleuze's reading of Proust, the act of recognition precludes thought by lapsing into a sort of banal objectivity:

> We recognize things, but we never know them. What the sign signifies we identify with the person or object it designates. We miss our finest encounters, we avoid the imperatives which emanate from them: to the exploration of encounters we have preferred the facility of recognitions. (PS, 26)

In his preoccupation with recognition, Plato denigrates the concept of pure difference which is exemplified by the figure of the simulacrum, the copy of which there is no original. However, Deleuze claims that Proust concentrates on another, rather different, aspect of Plato's philosophy. That is to say, the Plato who makes a distinction between 'objects of recognition' and things which are no longer recognisable, objects which have a violent effect on intelligence and perception. It is the latter which appear in Proust's work as 'essences'. When we are forced to think by the signs of art, a sort of 'pure thought' is released. In this way, thought is able to conceive of essences (PS, 164). To conceive of essences, then, entails a disjunctive use of the faculties of intelligence, memory and imagination (PS, 94). Involuntary thought is the thought that forces us to think and conceive of essences: 'Involuntary exercise is the transcendent limit or the vocation of each faculty' (PS, 165).

Proust presents us with a new image of thought, which opposes sensibility to observation, thought to philosophy, and translation to reflection (PS, 94). This new image of thought leads us to essences, which inhabit 'dark regions', where we must be forced to go (PS, 165). The novel that Proust creates to convey this image of thought is a sort of 'literary machine' which opposes pathos to logos: 'antilogos'. Proust is a literary modernist, and he is consequently less concerned with meaning than with the use of the literary machine: 'No one has insisted more than Proust on the following point: that the truth is produced, that it is produced by orders of machines which function within us [...]' (PS, 129). The machine is not a whole, a logos, to which the parts refer back, it is a *fragmentary* whole. The parts of the novel are fragmented, but nothing is lacking in the machine (PS, 142–3).

Sacher-Masoch: Desire and Immanence

> With Sade and Masoch the function of literature is not to describe the world, since this has already been done, but to define

> a counterpart of the world capable of containing its violence and excesses. (M, 37)

In *Masochism*, published in 1967 in France as *Présentation de Sacher-Masoch*, Deleuze makes an attack on received wisdom.[19] The aspect of masochism that is normally emphasised is pain ['la douleur'], whilst the importance of the idea of the contract is neglected. Also, it is commonly believed that Sade and Masoch stand in a dialectical relationship and that, consequently, sadism and masochism are complementary components of a single illness called sado-masochism. In Bergsonian terms, however, sado-masochism is a badly analysed composite, and the new concept that Deleuze proposes is a dissociation of sadism and masochism. Rather than a single entity it is, in medical terms, a *syndrome*. Sado-masochism is a syndrome that should be split into irreducible causal chains (M, 14). Since symptomatology is an art, Deleuze takes this opportunity to stake a claim for the specificity and cultural importance of literature: '[...] sadism and masochism are not separable from the literary values peculiar to Sade and Masoch' (M, 14). More than being important literary figures they are also 'great anthropologists'. In considering the questions of 'man, culture and nature' they are artists who have introduced something genuinely new into thought. Masoch, in particular, invents a new set of signs which seek to liberate life where it is imprisoned:

> Why has Masoch given his name to a perversion as old as the world? Not because he 'suffered' from it, but because he transformed the symptoms, he set out a novel picture of it by making the contract its primary sign and also by linking masochistic practices to the place of ethnic minorities in society and the role of women in those minorities: masochism becomes an act of resistance, inseparable from a minority sense of humor. Masoch's a great symptomatologist. (N, 142)

According to Deleuze, neither Sade nor Masoch are pornographers, since pornography depends upon a series of imperatives; 'do this', 'do that'. They are rather 'pornologers', since they create a world where language confronts its own limits. In different ways, both attempt to construct a plane of thought across which sexuality breaks away fom the limits of expression conventionally attributed to it. Sade does this by pushing language towards the description of a reason which ultimately becomes unreasonable. Ultimately, Sade wishes to mock the law by demonstrating that reasoning is itself a form of violence. Reason can simply be a way for the powerful and 'unreasonable' to enforce their institutional domination. Masoch's intent is perhaps more 'humorous', in that he shows how contracts can be used to allow desire to proliferate in a way that the law would apparently prohibit. Behind this common project to undermine the Kantian notion of law through the humour and irony they use strikingly different methods. Sade demonstrates a '[...] surprising affinity with Spinoza – a naturalistic and mechanistic approach imbued with the mathematical spirit' (M, 20). Masoch demonstrates a similar drive to go beyond the imperative and descriptive functions of language. In contrast to Sade's concentration on reasoning as violence, Masoch is preoccupied with persuasion and education. Pointing out that *Venus in Furs* begins with a dream that occurs during an interrupted reading of Hegel, Deleuze claims that Masoch's project has a dialectical spirit: 'While Sade is spinozistic and employs demonstrative reason, Masoch is platonic and proceeds by dialectical imagination' (M, 22). The literary figure of the masochist constructs a plane of immanence from desire. The ideal is suspension, the postponement of pleasure. For this reason, Masoch's descriptions often have an 'oppressive atmosphere', a sort of 'sickly perfume' of 'suspended gestures and suspended suffering' (M, 31).

As we have seen already, Masoch has a political significance: his is a 'minor' body of work, as Deleuze and Guattari show to be the case with Kafka several years later. Of Slav, Spanish and Bohemian descent, Masoch's work is pervaded by the problems of nationalities and minority groups in the Austro-Hungarian Empire. The minorities of the Austrian Empire provide a source of stories and folklore for the folktales that form the basis of much of his work. In this way, he manages to sexualise language and narration in general. He goes some way towards the scandalous aim of eroticising the problems of politics.

Ronald Bogue has argued convincingly that, in the case of Sade, Masoch and Proust, Deleuze chooses to write about three literary 'idealists'. Although Proust's idealism is 'aesthetic' as compared to the 'carnal, perverse' idealism of Sade and Masoch, all three show that the ideal world contests the sensible world from inside. The ideal and the sensible function as a plane of immanence: 'Proust, Sade, and Masoch all explore a curious interworld, in which bodies and words, things and ideas interpenetrate and the traditional demarcations between the physical and the metaphysical become blurred.'[20] This plane of immanence generates signs of life.

Kafka: Minor Literature and Machinic Assemblages

> If we try to sum up the nature of the artistic machine for Kafka, we must say that it is a bachelor machine, the only bachelor machine, and, as such, plugged all the more into a social field

> with multiple connections. Machinic definition, and not an aesthetic one. (K, 70)

In *Kafka: Toward a Minor Literature* Deleuze and Guattari seek to overturn just about every piece of received critical knowledge concerning Kafka. Rather than being a lonely and tortured artist, Kafka is actually able to conceive of a collective, political literature. It is, they claim, 'grotesque' to oppose life to writing in the case of Kafka, to claim that he only wrote out of a sense of weakness, as a form of retreat from life. His bachelor existence, far from cutting him off from social life, allows him a fluid, even 'dangerous' social nature. Kafka's 'solitude', and that of his narrator/character K, allows Kafka to construct a literary 'machine':

> Kafka's solitude opens him up to everything going on in history today. The letter K no longer designates a narrator or a character but an assemblage that becomes all the more machine-like, an agent that becomes all the more collective because an individual is locked into it in his or her solitude (it is only in connection to a subject that something individual would be separable from the collective and would lead its own life). (K, 18)

There is no psychoanalytic significance in his work, and the use of animals in the short stories is in no way metaphoric. Instead, Kafka aims for a sober hyperrealism, a realism that deals with metamorphosis rather than metaphor. His work is driven by the principles of anti-lyricism and anti-aestheticism. The world must be grasped as it is – 'objects, characters, events' – rather than as a series of impressions: 'Kill metaphor' (K, 70). The machinic assemblage constitutes a field of immanence. Such an assemblage is constructed from contiguous segments, and as such does not correspond to a transcendent principle which would explain the way that it functions. *The Castle* and *The Trial* function as machinic assemblages: 'Writing has a double function: to translate everything into assemblages and to dismantle the assemblages' (K, 47). Rather than illustrating the transcendence of law, as some critics would have it, they set out abstract machines which function as immanent fields for the workings of desire: 'The contiguity of the offices, the segmentalization of power, replaces the hierarchy of instances and the eminence of the sovereign [...]' (K, 50). In this way, justice becomes a question of desire and chance. Rather than finding its reference in the transcendent principle of the Law, justice is the product of desire, of judges who are like children, of gossip, maliciousness and caprice.

The 'collective' literature that he produces in this way is prophetic, in that it anticipates the arrival of the 'diabolical' powers of the future; 'capitalism, Stalinism, fascism' (K, 83). In fact, Deleuze claims that

Kafka writes at the juncture between disciplinary and control societies. (See Chapter 6 for a fuller discussion of this distinction).

> Kafka, already standing at the point of transition between the two kinds of society, described in *The Trial* their most ominous judicial expressions: *apparent acquittal* (between two confinements) in disciplinary societies, and *endless postponement* in (constantly changing) control societies [...]. (N, 179)

It is the machinic nature of Kafka's writing that allows him to analyse the segments of the social world as he sees it: (K, 70). As a 'bachelor machine' he dismantles the bureaucratic world that he sees around him into segments. From these segments he builds strange and prophetic machines such as the Castle (K, 50). Deleuze and Guattari also reject the idea that Kafka's work has a straightforward psychoanalytic, Oedipal drive. Drawing on Kafka's 'Letter to the Father', they show how he deterritorialises the Oedipal image of the father until the figure covers the entire globe. If there is an Oedipal element in Kafka it is global, unlimited and impersonal. In this way, apart from producing a machinic literature, Kafka's work also constitutes a 'minor' literature. Minor literature is the literature that a minor group – in this case Prague Jews – constructs within a major language – in this case German. Deleuze and Guattari see a minor literature as having three defining characteristics. Firstly, it has a 'high coefficient of deterritorialization'. Secondly, everything in a minor literature ultimately has a political inflection. Thirdly, everything in a minor literature has a collective inflection. It is as if the more that Kafka succeeds in his aim of becoming a stranger in his own language, the more he can make that language resonate with the forces that traverse and surround it.

Tournier: a 'Posthuman' Novel

> The self is the development and the explication of what is possible, the process of its realization in the actual. (LS, 307)

For Deleuze, the literary machine also acts as a site for the exploration of subjectivity. The act of writing itself, particularly fictional writing, involves a dispersal of subjectivity: writing is an enactment of multiplicity. In *A Thousand Plateaus* Deleuze and Guattari choose as an example Virginia Woolf's *The Waves*. The wave is a figure which suggests 'shifting borderlines' between all the elements of the narrative; characters, ages, sexes. The book is constructed around a wave-like motion of becoming (TP, 252). In a similar way, the literary 'genius' is an artist who can create an effect of 'becoming' for everybody, rather than being an extraordinary individual

(TP, 200). The writer is someone who '[...] is traversed by strange becomings that are not becomings-writer, but becomings-rat, becomings-insect, becomings-wolf, etc.' (TP, 240). Literary texts can also be read as experiments with subjectivity. An example of this would be his essay on Michel Tournier's *Friday, or the Other Island*.[21] Tournier's novel, published in French in 1967, is an interpretation of the Robinson Crusoe myth. Deleuze reads Tournier's version as an investigation of an experimental 'world without others'. Defoe's original work is, Deleuze considers, 'well-intentioned', but the problem of what becomes of a man without others is badly posed in terms of 'origins' rather than 'ends' (LS, 302–3). By 'origin' Deleuze means that Defoe tries to show how a man alone, without others, will refound the economic order, the 'reality', that we know. Tournier's reading of the Robinson myth, on the other hand, is a question of genuine experimentation, of becoming: 'The effects of the absence of Others are the real adventures of the spirit: this is an experimental, inductive novel' (LS, 305).

Tournier's Robinson initially tries to remake the island on which he is stranded in the image of the society he has come from. He attempts to order the island and his life on it by means of agriculture, a clock, and even a penal code. However, Robinson's 'humanity' breaks down as he becomes 'elemental':

> The end, that is, Robinson's final goal, is 'dehumanization,' the coming together of the libido and of the free elements, the discovery of a cosmic energy or of a great elemental Health which can surge only on the isle – and only to the extent that the isle has become aerial or solar. (LS, 303)

The main effect of the absence of others is to eradicate the field of virtualities and potentialities which surround objects when we are in a world with others. We suppose that the part of the object that we cannot see is visible to others, and so experience a *possible* world. In short, the presence of others gives depth and meaning to the world. The world without others is a 'posthuman' world in which there is no longer this 'softening' force of contiguity and resemblance. All that is left for Robinson is the harsh opposition of light and darkness. Tournier's Robinson now lives in a world which resembles the pure consciousness of which Bergson dreams:

> Consciousness ceases to be a light cast upon objects in order to become a pure phosphorescence of things in themselves. Robinson is but the consciousness of the island, but the consciousness of the island is the consciousness the island has of itself – it is the island in itself. (LS, 311)

In the absence of an 'other' Robinson's self is gradually dismantled, decomposed. As Moira Gatens argues, Deleuze shows how

Robinson's 'humanity' is contingent upon the framework of a human society around him. Consequently the novel calls into question the notion of an essential human ontology.[22] Literature, like philosophy, can explore the world without subject.

CHAPTER 8

Cinema: New Art, New Thought

> We can consider the brain as a relatively undifferentiated mass and ask what circuits, what kinds of circuit, the movement-image or time-image trace out, or invent, because the circuits aren't there to begin with. (N, 60)

In many ways, the reasons that Deleuze has chosen to devote two relatively lengthy volumes – *Cinema 1: The Movement-Image* and *Cinema 2: The Time-Image* – to the study of cinema are simple. Firstly, cinema depends upon movement, and, as we have seen already, movement, becoming – that which challenges conventional notions of perception – is central to Deleuze's philosophy. There are certainly indications in earlier work that Deleuze finds cinema philosophically intriguing. For example, in *Anti-Oedipus* Deleuze and Guattari suggest that cinema may in fact be able to capture the 'movement of madness', since it explores a general 'field of coexistence' (AO, 274). In *A Thousand Plateaus* they point out that movement is 'by nature imperceptible' (TP, 280–1). It is only if perception somehow functions in the middle, on the plane of immanence, that it can perceive the imperceptible:

> Perception will no longer reside in the relation between a subject and an object, but rather in the movement serving as the limit of that relation, in the period associated with the subject and object. Perception will confront its own limit; it will be in the midst of things, throughout its own proximity, as the presence of one haecceity in another, the prehension of one by the other or the passage from one to the other: Look only at the movements. (TP, 282)

For Deleuze and Guattari, Kierkegaard is therefore acting as a precursor of the cinema and of cinematic thought when he adopts the motto, 'I look only at the movements' (TP, 281). Secondly, cinema in the widest sense is the youngest of the major art-forms. It has now existed for a century, and has inevitably reflected and participated in the political, intellectual and social world around it. Deleuze's work on cinema emphasises the 'newness' of cinema, and he concentrates in particular on the idea that cinema is a form of thought in its own right. For Deleuze, cinema and philosophy are in a situation of 'aparallel evolution'. Both started to investigate the problem of movement at the same time: cinema came on the scene at the same time that philosophy was trying to 'think motion' (N, 57). Deleuze claims that there can exist 'points of indiscernibility' whereby the same idea could be expressed by a painted image, a scientific model, a cinematographic image or a philosophical concept.[1] It is a matter of bringing cinema and philosophy into contact, rather than philosophy being used to write 'about' cinema. Richard Dienst considers this method, whereby Deleuze provides a 'conceptual illustration' of films, to be a sort of poststructural 'pragmatism'.[2] In placing his work on cinema within the wider philosophical question of a 'new image of thought' Deleuze implies that cinema might be able, under certain circumstances, to function as just such a new image. Cinema can function in this way because it can escape the constraints of representation. At their most innovative and powerful, the images created by the cinema cease to 'represent' reality and constitute their own reality.[3]

The overall theoretical framework for the analysis of cinema is provided by a combination of Henri Bergson and Charles Sanders Peirce. According to Deleuze, cinema has undertaken an extremely condensed version of the transformation that it has taken philosophy centuries to achieve. In looking at the question of movement philosophy and cinema have moved towards an appreciation of time as mobility, flux, difference and provisionality. In both spheres, time is no longer subordinated to movement. Deleuze draws on Bergson to show that an image, and particularly the cinematic image, is not a representation, but the result of movement between the world of matter and the memory:

> There are images, things are themselves images, because images aren't in our head, in our brain. The brain's just one image among others. Images are constantly acting and reacting on each other, producing and consuming. There's no difference at all between *images*, *things*, and *motion*. (N, 42)

We find ourselves once again confronted with Bergson's new metaphysics: a world without a subject. In this way, Bergson inspires Deleuze's concept of cinema as a concrete example of 'universal variation', an acentred system which is constantly in flux. Cinema can transcend the sluggish and stereotyped tendencies of what Bergson called natural perception. For Deleuze, Bergson's distinction between perception, action and affection as an analysis of motion can be applied directly to cinema. In the same way that cinema – which was born as Bergson was developing his thought – finds a way of giving motion to images, so Bergson finds a way of giving movement to thought:

> Bergson presents one of the first cases of self-moving thought. Because it's not enough simply to say concepts possess movement; you also have to construct intellectually mobile concepts. Just as it's not enough to make moving shadows on the wall, you have to construct images that can move by themselves. (N, 122)

As Paul Patton points out, in his review of *Cinema 1* and *Cinema 2* for *Screen*, the decision to base his approach to cinema on a reading of Bergson is in keeping with the move away from theories of representation: '[...] the world as assemblage of movement-images, not images *of* something, but images *in* the flow of time'.[4]

Peirce provides a generalised, non-linguistic semiotics which inspires Deleuze to look at cinema in terms of thought and the superior empiricism of relations.[5] Deleuze attempts to develop a semiotics which is no longer based on language and metaphor. In this way, Deleuze draws a fine distinction between 'semiology' and 'semiotics'. Semiology identifies non-verbal language systems, and Deleuze expresses a preference for semiotics which he defines as '[...] the system of of images and signs independent of language in general' (C2, 29). Just as philosophy must constantly come into contact with 'non-philosophy', so language comes into contact with 'non-language material'. In effect, Deleuze challenges the notion that cinema is an essentially 'narrative' form: 'Narration is grounded in the image itself, but it is not given' (C2, 29). Narrative is an 'indirect product' of motion and time (N, 59).

Critical reaction to the books on cinema has in general been enthusiastic, with particular attention being paid to the innovation of an approach to reading film which is not based on a linguistic model. However, two important critical reservations should be noted, both of which have been levelled at Deleuze's work in general. Firstly, Deleuze concentrates rather too much, for someone who is apparently bringing something new to the study of of cinema, on the great *auteur* figures: Welles, Resnais, Hitchcock, Renoir, Godard, etc. Secondly, Deleuze's perspective has been seen as Eurocentric.[6] As for the first objection, Deleuze attempts to pre-empt such criticisms by presenting the proper name of the author as nothing more than a useful label for that which is new, unexpected ('inattendu'), and innovative.[7] He also argues that signs always have a 'signature'; they must be created and re-created by individuals. For this reason, an analysis of signs must deal with the great *auteurs* (N, 49). As for the second criticism, it is true that Deleuze concentrates on European authors, although he does refer frequently to American cinema, and the later part of *Cinema 2* includes a short discussion of Third World cinema.

Summary: Time, Motion and Thought

> Cinema sets out to produce self-movement in images, autotemporalization even: that's the key thing, and it's these two aspects I've tried to study. (N, 58)

Before looking in some detail at the ideas developed in both books on cinema, it is worth summarising briefly the main lines of argument. In the first volume Deleuze looks at cinema mainly from the first half of the century, arguing that it is organised around the 'movement-image'. Deleuze starts from the premiss that cinema does not add movement to the image, but rather that it creates something new which is called the movement-image: '[...] that is, pure movement extracted from bodies or moving things' (C1, 23). In general terms, the movement-image indicates a philosophy of action, which corresponds roughly to the twin ideologies of Soviet dialectical materialism and American liberalism. This early cinema is a cinema of action, in which characters react according to their perceptions of a given situation.

In *Cinema 2: The Time-Image* Deleuze looks mainly at postwar cinema, in which the perception-action link of prewar cinema has largely broken down:

> Now, suppose a character finds himself in a situation, however ordinary or extraordinary, that's beyond any possible action, or to which he can't react. It's too powerful, or too painful, too beautiful. The sensory-motor link's broken. He's no longer in a sensory-motor situation, but in a purely optical and aural situation. There's a new type of image. (N, 51)

In this way, Deleuze points to what he considers to be a 'Kantian' revolution in cinema. The subordination of time to movement is reversed, and cinema is able to produce complex 'time-images' (C2, xi and 22). The time-image corresponds to a new kind of thought, calling into question the philosophies which underpinned the movement-image. A new kind of character also appears, who is a seer rather than an actor (C2, 3). Although Deleuze does argue that postwar cinema is dominated by time, he avoids positing an absolute historical break between the movement-image and the time-image. It is as if, between them, they articulate the two aspects of movement that Bergson elucidates. The first aspect involves the way in which bodies physically change either position or state. This corresponds roughly to the movement-image. The second aspect involves what Deleuze sometimes calls an 'incorporeal transformation'. This is movement as time – time being no longer subordinated to movement – and corresponds to the time-image.

However, it is not just by means of the time-image that postwar cinema goes beyond the movement image. The new complexity of aural and optical elements in cinema means that the image becomes more 'legible'. Directors like Godard begin to experiment with a 'pedagogy' of the image. Cinema also also tends to produce images which capture and influence directly the mechanisms of thought. So, the time-image, the 'chronosign', is accompanied by 'lectosigns' and 'noosigns'. The idea that cinema can come into contact with thought itself is extremely important, telling us much about Deleuze's materialist approach.

With the movement-image and the time-image cinema offers the possibility of exploring a 'cinematographic' world which has no centre, and which is in constant flux. As a form of thought, cinema offers us the possibility of discovering the 'inner becoming of things': a world of constant modulation.

The Movement-Image

In *The Movement-Image* Deleuze offers a reading of Bergson which quite consciously 'starts in the middle'. In general, Bergson would appear to be a rather unhelpful thinker to choose for work on cinema, since in *Creative Evolution*, published in 1907, he is unimpressed by the very earliest forms of cinema. Here, Bergson refers to a 'cinematographic illusion' of false movement based upon the reconstitution of movement with immobile sections or instants:

> Such is the contrivance of the cinematograph. And such is that of our knowledge. Instead of attaching ourselves to the inner becoming of things, we place ourselves outside them in order to recompose their becoming artificially. We take snapshots, as it were, of the passing reality [...]. Whether we would think becoming, or express it, or even perceive it, we hardly do anything else than set up a kind of cinematograph inside us. We may therefore sum up what we have been saying in the conclusion that the *mechanism of our ordinary knowledge is of a cinematographic kind.*[8]

Deleuze points out that here Bergson was only aware of the fixed camera of cinema's infancy, and that cinema developed relatively quickly a more mobile form of perception. Deleuze labels this first 'mature' stage of cinema as a genuinely new form, the movement-image. The movement-image is the first real form of genuinely cinematic perception, and responds to the development of various forms of transport, which represent a new attitude towards time and movement. The modern world of the car and aeroplane helps to move the conception of movement away from the arrangement of a series of fixed poses. In this way the cinema of the movement-image actually strives towards the expression of the mobility of which Bergson is so acutely aware:

> One might conceive of a series of means of translation (train, car, aeroplane ...) and, in parallel, a series of means of expression (diagram, photo, cinema). The camera would then appear as an exchanger or, rather, as a generalised equivalent of the movements of translation. (C1, 4–5)

However, Deleuze does not allow himself to be deterred by Bergson's apparent dismissal of cinema. He turns instead to *Matter and Memory*, published before *Creative Evolution* in 1896, where Bergson sets out a unique consideration of movement and time which, Deleuze argues, anticipates both the movement-image and the time-image of cinema (see N, 48). Here, Bergson advances the dual thesis of mobile sections – the ability of an image to convey movement – and temporal planes; the coexistence of several levels of *durée* (C1, 1–7). Bergson shows how the movement-image breaks down the distinction between the object and the image:

> This is what Bergson showed from the first chapter of *Matter and Memory*: if movement is taken from the moving body, there is no longer any distinction between image and object [...] The movement-image is the object; the thing itself caught in movement as continuous function. The movement-image is the modulation of the object itself. (C2, 27)

Deleuze picks up Bergson's theoretical framework and continues the project that Bergson might have completed. In *Creative Evolution* Bergson concentrated on what happened in the apparatus of the camera – a 'procession' of individual images – and consequently believed that cinema was incapable of producing pure movement. However, Deleuze claims that cinema is in fact 'eminently capable' of extracting this sort of movement. He refers to the example of Renoir's *The Crime of Monsieur Lange*, when the camera leaves a character and continues its own movement, only to rejoin the character at the end of this movement (C1, 23).

Peirce: Firstness, Secondness, Thirdness

Deleuze's deployment of Peirce is occasionally difficult to follow, but it is worth pursuing, since it is central to the non-linguistic approach of the cinema books. Peirce bases his complex system of semiotics on a simple triadic structure: sign, referent and interpretant. This triadic structure can also be expressed in terms of firstness, secondness and thirdness. In *Cinema 1* firstness, secondness and thirdness are shown to correspond to the affection-image, the action-image and the relation-image respectively.[9] As an example of cinematic 'firstness', the affection image, Deleuze proposes the close-up of the face of Joan of Arc in Dreyer's *The Passion of Joan of Arc* (C1, 70). Firstness is difficult to define, since it concerns the 'quality of a possible sensation' and is 'felt, rather than conceived' (C1, 98). It is a question of that which is new and fleeting in experience. In short, it is cinema's way of expressing instantaneous consciousness. Firstness is another version of the concept of *haecceity* which recurs throughout Deleuze's work. That is to say, an effect which is impersonal and unindividuated, and yet which has a distinctive singularity (C1, 98–9). An example of cinematic 'secondness', the action-image, is provided by Fritz Lang in *Dr. Mabuse the Gambler*: '[...] an organised action, segmented in space and time, with the synchronised watches whose ticking punctuates the murder in the train, the car which carries off the stolen document, the telephone which warns Mabuse' (C1, 69). Secondness in this case involves the individuation of the unindividuated singularity of cinematic firstness. The action-image is concerned with milieux and modes of behaviour, and the relationship between the two. It is central to the triumph of the American 'Realist' model of cinema, adopted by film-makers of all nationalities who have aspired to this model. The milieu conspires to set the character a challenge, and in responding to the challenge, the character attempts to modify the situation (C1, 141). Deleuze associates secondness with a peculiarly American expression of dialectical thinking:

> Everything which only exists by being opposed, by and in a duel, therefore belongs to secondness: exertion-resistance, action reaction, excitation-response, situation-behaviour, individual-milieu ... It is the category of the Real, of the actual, of the existing, of the individuated. And the first figure of secondness is that in which power-qualities become 'forces', that is to say are actualised in particular stages of things, determinate space-times, geographical and historical milieux, collective agents or individual people. (C1, 98)

Finally, as an example of cinematic 'thirdness', the relation-image (or the mental image), Deleuze makes reference to the films of Hitchcock, drawing on the analysis of Rohmer and Chabrol.[10] Hitchcock uses the figure of the 'murder' from the detective film, but rather than an exploration of secondness, that is to say the crime and the criminal, he examines the way in which the crime has been done for somebody else. Rather than the question of who did the action, Hitchcock is preoccupied with the relations which surround the action. As Rohmer and Chabrol point out, the criminal has always done the crime *for* another. Beyond the acting and the action, there is always a 'third' situation or person (C1, 201). Hitchcock is one of the first directors to experiment with a 'camera-consciousness' which stands apart from individual characters. For these reasons, Hitchcock does not necessarily require 'method acting':

> The characters can act, perceive, experience, but they cannot testify to the relations which determine them. These are merely the movements of the camera, and their movements towards the camera. Hence, the opposition between Hitchcock and the Actors Studio, his requirement that the actor acts in the most simple, even neutral, way, the camera attending to what remains. (C1, 201)

Even in the way that Hitchcock conceives of cinema as a function of three terms – film, director, public – we can see an element of 'thirdness'. Hitchcock is, therefore, primarily a director of 'relations', rather than a psychologist or a 'Platonic and Catholic metaphysician', as some would have it. In Hitchock's cinema, the shot has two 'faces', one of which is turned to the characters, and the other towards the relations which constitute an evolving whole (C1, 203).

The Time-Image

Cinema 2: The Time-Image locates a shift away from the action-image and the movement-image in postwar cinema. In the cinema of action which characterises the movement-image, characters find themselves in 'sensory-motor situations'. As a consequence, they react dynamically, and reactions become intertwined with perceptions. However, in postwar cinema, characters find themselves in situations which do not appear to allow for action. This new cinema finds initial expression in the Italian neo-realist movement. Here, characters become 'seers' who find themselves in purely optical situations. The definitive neo-realist character goes on a journey and becomes the viewer of that journey. In the cinema of the movement-image the viewer identified to a greater or lesser extent with the characters' options for action in a given sensory-motor situation. However, in the cinema of the time-image the characters themselves become viewers. Hitchcock makes a step towards this new paradigm by including the viewer in the relations which evolve throughout the film. Hitchcock also introduces one of the first 'seers' in the history of cinema in *Rear Window*:

> [...] the hero of *Rear Window* has access to the mental image, not simply because he is a photographer, but because he is in a state of immobility: he is reduced as it were to a pure optical situation. If one of Hitchcock's innovations was to implicate the spectator in the fim, did not the characters themselves have to be capable – in a more or less obvious manner – of being assimilated to spectators? (C1, 205)

Following on from this, neo-realism creates a cinema in which the possibilities for action are consistently thwarted:

> He shifts, runs and becomes animated in vain, the situation he is in outstrips his motor capacities on all sides, and makes him see and hear what is no longer subject to the rules of a response or an action. He records rather than reacts. He is prey to a vision, pursued by it or pursuing it, rather than engaged in an action. (C2, 3)

The 'sensory-motor connections' of the action-image are loosened, and a 'dispersive reality' – as Bazin calls it – is presented (C2, 2). Hitchcock had taken a step towards the new cinema by including the viewer in the film, but neo-realism goes even further by making the character a viewer (C2, 3). Deleuze argues that the form of space used and illustrated in these films is 'disconnected' or 'empty', corresponding to the process of change and rebuilding in Europe after the Second World War. Instead of being organised around the axis of movement, postwar cinema is structured around the question of time: 'And thanks to this loosening of the sensory-motor linkage, it is time, "a little time in the pure state", which rises up to the surface of the screen' (C2, xi). In the films of Antonioni the body itself 'reveals' the time of tiredness and waiting. By means of further commentary on Bergson, Deleuze considers this preoccupation with time as manifesting itself in the form of the 'crystal-image'. That is to say, the coalescence of the actual and the virtual image:

> Instead of a linear development, we get a circuit in which the two images are constantly chasing one another around a point where real and imaginary become indistinguishable. The actual and its virtual image crystallize, so to speak. (N, 52)

The crystal-image is based on Bergson's fundamental thesis that the past is constituted at the same time as the present. A director such as Fellini understands this intuitively: 'Fellini recently said we're in infancy, old age, and middle age all at once: that's thoroughly Bergsonian' (N, 47–8). Images crystallise and layers of time can be seen. These 'layers', or 'slivers', of time coexist according to a principle of indiscernibility within the crystal-image. Cinema frequently uses the mirror in order to construct such a circuit of indiscernibility, and Orson Welles provides a celebrated example of the crystal-image in *The Lady of Shanghai*:

> [...] where the principle of indiscernibility reaches its peak: a perfect crystal-image where the multiple mirrors have assumed the actuality of the two characters who will only be able to win

> it back by smashing them all, finding themselves side by side and each killing the other. (C2, 70)

In *Sculpting in Time* Andrey Tarkovsky argues that cinema as an aesthetic activity is preoccupied with time.[11] Like Deleuze, he regards cinema as a major aesthetic innovation, since the technical means becomes available, for the first time in the history of the arts, '*to take an impression of time*'.[12] Rather than the rhythm of montage, Tarkovsky is concerned with time within the shot, and he shows that film is a matter of sculpting with individual shots, which are like 'blocks' of time. This entails a concern with the 'pressure of time' within each shot.[13] In his analysis of *Citizen Kane* Deleuze acknowledges that the time-image is, in part at least, conveyed by means of an innovative use of montage. The most famous example is the rapid succession of 'shot-reaction shots' – a series of 'former presents' – which outline in an extremely condensed form the breakdown of communication between Kane and his first wife. However, another form of the time-image is closer to Tarkovsky's notion of the pressure of time within the shot. Deleuze gives as an example the scene in which Kane goes to Chicago to confront his friend Jedediah. Here, Welles uses the technical innovation of depth-of-field to show Kane entering the office which is at the back of the shot. Kane literally emerges from the past:

> The images in depth express regions of past as such, each with its own accents or potentials, and mark critical moments in Kane's will to power. The hero acts, walks and moves; but it is the past that he plunges himself into and moves in: time is no longer subordinated to movement, but movement to time. Hence in the great scene where Kane catches up in depth with the friend he will break with, it is in the past that he himself moves; this movement *was* the break with the friend. (C2, 106)

Like Deleuze, Tarkovsky considers cinema to be in its infancy, since commercial cinema in particular has not capitalised upon this technical and aesthetic innovation of capturing time. Cinema can have a 'colossal' future if it learns to use these untapped resources and refine its capacity to 'sculpt' time. The image in cinema enables the viewer to observe a phenomenon as it passes through time. In this way, both Deleuze and Tarkovsky find links between cinema and Proust's work. Deleuze points out that idea that bodies can occupy places in time which are not commensurate with their positions in space is dealt with in Proust's *Time Regained*, the sixth volume of *A la recherche du temps perdu*. At the Guermantes' reception, the narrator sees the guests as puppets expressing the complexity of time:

> These were puppets bathed in the immaterial colours of the years, puppets which exteriorised Time, Time which by habit is made invisible and to become visible seeks bodies, which, wherever it finds them, it seizes upon, to display its magic lantern upon them.[14]

As far as Tarkovsky is concerned, the experience of going to the cinema can, at best, have a spiritual dimension. It is possible that the spectator is reacting against the alienating conditions of modern existence and seeking to the fill the gaps in experience, literally searching for 'lost time'.[15] Just as Deleuze feels that a linguistic framework for film analysis is an insufficiently flexible tool for the potential richness of cinema's system of signs, so Tarkovsky claims that a 'real picture' has a plural sense of time which flows beyond the frame.[16] In this assessment of the role of the past and the future in the constitution of the present Tarkovsky seems to be close to Deleuze's Bergsonian reading of cinema. The time-image itself deals not with things occurring in time, but with 'new forms of coexistence, ordering, transformation' (N, 123).

In the same way that Deleuze takes Bergson's theses on movement as his starting point for the analysis of the movement-image, so he develops the time-image from Bergson's theses on time:

> [...] the past coexists with the present that it has been; the past is preserved in itself, as past in general (non-chronological); at each moment time splits itself into present and past, present that passes and past which is preserved. (C2, 82)

In Deleuze's hands these theses on time actually offer us something which is very different to a conventional reading of Bergsonism as the idea of duration as constituting a subjective, 'internal' life. Deleuze argues that Bergson increasingly shows us how time is not internal to us, but how we are interior to time: our subjectivity is fractured in the labyrinth of time. In this way, Bergson is close to the Kant of *Kant's Critical Philosophy*. One of the films which explores the way in which time 'inhabits' us is Hitchcock's *Vertigo*, in which the hero cannot escape the past: 'Subjectivity is never ours, it is time, that is, the soul or the spirit, the virtual' (C2, 82–3).

New Art, New Thought

Cinema converts the possibility of intimate contact with the mechanisms of thought into a powerful potential: 'It is only when movement becomes automatic that the artistic essence of the image is realized: producing a shock to thought, communicating vibrations to the cortex, touching the nervous and cerebral system directly' (C2, 156). In prewar cinema montage is the general technique employed to explore thought, and in *Cinema 1* four types of montage are outlined: the empiricist montage of American cinema, the dialectical montage of Soviet cinema, the 'quantitative-psychic' montage of French cinema, and the 'intensive-spiritual' montage of German cinema. Eisenstein considers the cinematic technique of montage to be a dialectical form (C2, 158). The hope exists that cinema will constitute a sort of intellectual 'punch':

> If Eisenstein is a dialectician, it is because he conceives of the violence of the shock in the form of opposition and the thought of the whole in the form of opposition overcome, or of the transformation of opposites: 'From the shock of two factors a concept is born'. This is the cinema of the *punch* – 'Soviet cinema must break heads.' (C2, 158)

In general terms the cinema of the movement-image forms three relationships with thought: a movement towards 'higher awareness', an exploration of the subconscious unfolding of images, and the sensory-motor relationship (C1, 163). As well as montage as a dialectical form, Eisenstein referred to his own ideal of cinematic thought as an 'internal monologue': 'This is a primitive language or thought, or rather an *internal monologue*, a drunken monologue, working through figures, metonymies, synecdoches, metaphors, inversions, attractions ...' (C1, 159). One of the aims of this cinematic form of thought is to create a genuinely collective, 'mass' thought:

> It is as if the cinema were telling us: with me, with the movement-image, you can't escape the shock which arouses the thinker in you. A subjective and collective automaton for an automatic movement: the art of the 'masses'. (C2, 156–7)

Montage provides Eisenstein with a framework which means that cinema does not have the individual as its subject, or history as its object: '[...] its object is nature, and its subject the masses, the individuation of mass and not that of a person' (C1, 162).

In the first half of the twentieth century, then, the hope had existed that cinema would be a genuine art of the masses. It would be capable of communicating the 'shock' of thought to the people, and would therefore be a revolutionary form of art. New art would produce a new thought. Soviet cinema would be an 'intellectual' cinema, and, by means of a dialectical spiral, it would also enhance the emotional aspect of the image. But these great hopes for 'new art, new thought' have been called into question, both by contemporary commercialism, and the genuine success of a fascist art of the masses as produced by a film-maker such as Leni Riefenstahl. Deleuze has to turn to Artaud to find some hope for cinema as a form of thinking. Artaud, like Eisenstein, thinks that cinema might be able to produce a shock or a vibration which will have an effect on thought. However, unlike Eisenstein, instead of basing this hope upon the power of thought, he is more concerned with its 'impower':

> It is precisely this which is more important than the dream: this difficulty of being, this powerlessness at the heart of thought. What the enemies of cinema criticized it for (like Georges Duhamel, 'I can no longer think what I want, the moving images are substituted for my own thoughts'), is just what Artaud makes into the dark glory and profundity of cinema. (C2, 166)

The putative subject of thought in Artaud's cinema – Deleuze refers to the handful of film scripts – is a subject whose thoughts have been 'stolen', and who can no longer keep hold of thoughts. This is in contrast to the revolutionary mass subject of thought in Eisenstein's Soviet cinema. For Artaud, the most creative possibility open to cinema is to come into contact with the 'innermost reality of the brain', a dislocated form of thought (C2, 167). Artaud wishes to bring into cinema an awareness of the fragmentation of the process of thought. The dream of early cinema was that of the *spiritual automaton* within us which would react to the 'shock' of automatic movement in cinema. It was hoped that cinema would touch the nervous system directly, producing a revolutionary shock to the masses (C2, 156–7). However, Artaud takes things one step further, whereby the internal monologue becomes multivocal: it is always a question of a voice within another voice. In its most intense relationship with thought cinema can attempt to come into contact with what Artaud calls the 'innermost reality' of the brain (C2, 167). Like literature, cinema can approach the problem of '[...] the presence to infinity of another thinker in the thinker, who shatters every monologue of a thinking self' (C2, 168). Some cinema can provide us with access to the 'pure' materiality of thought. The spiritual automaton is no longer the mass-subject of Eisenstein, but the '[...] Cartesian diver in us, unknown body which we have only at the back of our heads whose age is neither ours nor that of our childhood, but a little time in the pure state' (C2, 169).

Free Indirect Discourse

The notion of an internal monologue for Eisenstein also entailed a sort of internal coherence in the film, whereby there was '[...] a whole of the film which encompassed the author, the world and the characters, whatever the differences or contrasts' (C2, 182). However, in postwar cinema this monologue is dispersed, losing its unity, whether personal or collective: '[...] stereotypes, clichés, ready-made visions and formulas took away the outside world and the interiority of the characters in the same decomposition' (C2, 182). So, in Godard's *A Married Woman*, the woman merges with the pages of the magazine or catalogue that she is reading. Consequently, internal monologue is replaced by a sequence of images characterised by 'dissonant tunings' or 'irrational cuts'. The potential that Eisenstein saw for harmony and metaphor disappear. As the image is 'unlinked', free indirect discourse replaces the internal monologue:

> In short, Pasolini had a profound insight about modern cinema when he characterized it by a sliding of ground, breaking the uniformity of the internal monologue to replace it by the diversity, the deformity, the otherness of a free indirect discourse (C2, 183–4)

Deleuze refers here to Pasolini's paper 'The Cinema of Poetry', delivered at the Pesaro New Film festival in 1965.[17] Pasolini acknowledges that cinema must now be talked of in terms of semiotics, but rejects a uniquely linguistic conception of sign systems. In fact, the language of cinema cannot be compared with the language of words, since the film-maker has no existing dictionary of cinematic 'words' to draw from. Whereas the writer must engage in aesthetic invention, the film-maker has the double task of linguistic, and only then, aesthetic invention. It is through the use of the 'free indirect subjective' that film can achieve a technical language of poetry. In this way, film shows itself to be stylistically differentiated from literature, although it takes its cue from formal experiments in literature. 'Free indirect discourse' in literature involves the insertion of a linguistic difference between the author and the character, whereas the technique of 'free indirect subjective' – the film-maker seeing through a character's eyes – creates a zone of indiscernibility between author and character which is genuinely poetic. Film can therefore be considered as a poetic 'language of reality'. Deleuze alludes to the idea of free indirect discourse in *The Movement-Image*. He suggests that the technique is inherent in cinema from the beginning, but that it reaches a more mature stage in the cinema of the time-image. It is no longer simply a question of a mobile and indiscernible point of view: the images themselves enter into a situation of continuous modulation. The internal monologue is replaced by a sequence of images: 'There are no longer any perfect and "resolved" harmonies, but only dissonant tunings or irrational cuts, because there are no more harmonics of the image, but only "unlinked" tones forming the series' (C2, 182).

Cinema takes up the train of thought set in motion by Bergson, in showing itself to be eminently suited to undermining the prejudices of 'natural' perception:

> The cinema can, with impunity, bring us close to things or take us away from them and revolve around them, it suppresses both the anchoring of the subject and the horizon of the world. Hence it substitutes an implicit knowledge and a second intentionality for the conditions of natural perception. (C1, 57)

As Richard Dienst points out, Deleuze considers film and the viewer to be part of an 'open plane of images' in which physical and psychic realities are seen to be in a constant process of combination: 'Cinema catches Deleuze's eye because it begins without prejudice to the subjective point of view.'[18] Cinema can institute an 'acentred' perception of the world, suggesting a Bergsonian perspective whereby '[...] images are luminous by themselves without anything illuminating them' (C1, 57). This Bergsonian principle provides Deleuze with what Dienst calls the 'scandalous premise' that viewers must be considered on the same plane as filmic images.[19] In this way, Dienst claims that Deleuze turns to Bergson in order to reverse the presuppositions of phenomenology, encouraging a view of cinema as '[...] spewing the inward out, forcing consciousness to become a wandering orphan among the things called images'.[20]

In general terms, Deleuze does not deny that the cinema of the first half of the century is to a large extent dominated by a relatively stable notion of human perception. However, this cinema already demonstrates the potential for more 'acentred' modes of perception, which Deleuze terms 'fluid', 'liquid' or 'gaseous'. According to Deleuze, prewar French cinema often demonsrates such a 'liquid' perception. This is shown in the predilection of various authors – particularly Jean Renoir – for images of running water. For these early French film-makers water offered the '[...] promise or implication of another state of perception: a more than human perception' (C1, 80). In discussing these new forms of cinematic perception Deleuze draws heavily on literary modernism. For example, Dos Passos talks of the 'eye of the camera' when attempting to convey an anonymous viewpoint which cannot be attributed to a single character (C1, 72). Likewise, Pasolini talks of a use of the camera which is ' free indirect subjective' (C1, 74). In this way, the camera enacts in a particularly vivid way the doubling of the subject which takes place in all art: (C1, 73). As we have seen, a character acts and constructs a certain perspective upon the world, and yet at the same time the camera conveys another viewpoint. Cinema can therefore aspire to go beyond images which are purely objective or subjective. As shown in the introduction, the use of *discours indirect libre* is crucial in Deleuze's work. Zourabichvili, for example, sees it as a general principle which runs across many of the themes which Deleuze sets in motion.[21] In *Cinema 1* free indirect discourse is discussed as an essential component of the perception image.[22] Deleuze starts from the problem of distinguishing between objective and subjective perception-images in cinema. In fact, Deleuze goes so far as to suggest that free indirect discourse, entailing as it does a 'dividing-in-two' of the subject, is characteristic not only of cinema, but of thought and art in general:

> It is the *Cogito*: an empirical subject cannot be born into the world without simultaneously being reflected in a transcendental subject which thinks it and in which it thinks itself. And the *Cogito* of art: there is no subject which acts without another which watches it act, and which grasps it as acted, itself assuming the freedom of which it deprives the former. (C1, 73)

In cinema, the subjective character of the image derives from the fact that it is compared with '[...] the modified, restored image, which is supposed to be objective' (C1, 71). So, in Gance's *La Roue*, for example, a character sees his pipe in soft focus because his eyes are damaged. In this way, cinema can convey a subjective perception which is indexed against a notional real. However, how can an image be defined as 'objective'? Some film sequences initially appear to be external, 'objective' perspectives, but are in fact themselves subjective perceptions. A sequence seen through a character's eyes, as it were, may not reveal itself initially as such. Deleuze uses the opening long shot of Lewin's *Pandora and the Flying Dutchman* to illustrate this point. The characters seen through the telescope on the beach are actually characters who also inhabit the house in which the telescope is placed. Deleuze concludes that it is '[...] cinema's perpetual destiny to make us move from one of its poles to the other, from an objective perception to a subjective perception' (C1, 71–2). The very nature of cinema is to produce and experiment with what Jean Mitry calls a 'semi-subjective' perception. The camera does not give us direct access to the character's perceptions, nor is it completely 'outside' the character: it rather expresses a 'being-with' the character.

> Very early on, the mobile camera anticipated characters, recaptured them, let them go or picked them up again. Very early too, in Expressionism, it filmed or followed a character from behind (Murnau's *Tartuffe*, Dupont's *Vaudeville*). Finally, the liberated camera performed 'tracking shots in a closed circuit' (Murnau's *The Last Laugh*) in which it no longer confines itself to following characters, but moves amongst them. [...] It is a kind of truly cinematographic *Mitsein* – or what Dos Passos aptly called the 'eye of the camera', the anonymous viewpoint of someone unidentified amongst the characters. (C1, 72)

Deleuze turns to Pasolini and Bakhtin to show how free indirect discourse is an 'assemblage of enunciation' which involves a differentiation of two heterogeneous subjects: 'It is no longer metaphor which is the fundamental act of language, inasmuch as it "homogenises" the system; it is free indirect discourse, inasmuch as it testifies to a system which is always heterogeneous, far from equilibrium' (C1, 73). Cinema, and particularly the 'cinema of poetry' produced by auteurs such as Antonioni, Godard and Pasolini, achieves this use of free indirect discourse by developing the self-consciousness of the camera. It is no longer a question of subjective or objective images, but of a heterogeneous '[...] correlation between a perception-image and a camera-consciousness which transforms it' (C1, 74). The films of Antonioni characterise this 'cinema of poetry' as defined by Pasolini. The camera makes its presence felt by an 'insistent' framing. A character enters the frame and subsequently exits, and the camera continues to frame the space which is now empty, with the result that the scene is left to 'its pure and absolute signification as scene' (C1, 74). It would be wrong to conclude from these empty, disconnected spaces, however, that Antonioni is preoccupied with alienation and the 'impossibility' of communication. It is rather a case of an 'any-space-whatever', which does express fear and detachment, but also freshness and speed, as elements of the new postwar European experience. These new spaces of postwar Europe, the docks, warehouses and urban deserts, are not metaphors for alienation, but rather components of an enunciative assemblage which is articulated through free indirect discourse.

Cinema and Belief in the World

> The link between man and the world is broken. Henceforth, this link must be an object of belief: it is the impossible which can only be restored within a faith. Belief is no longer addressed to a different or transformed world. [...] The cinema must film, not the world, but belief in this world, our only link. (C2, 171–2)

In *Cinema 2* Deleuze develops the notion that cinema has, from the beginning, been concerned with the general question of belief: it has been preoccupied with the two 'faiths' of Christianity and revolution. In short, cinema investigates the link between man and the world. Early cinema, the films of Eisenstein, for example, expresses a revolutionary faith. On the other hand, certain postwar directors, such as Rossellini, Bresson and Ford, express a sort of 'Catholicism' (C2, 171). The revolutionary, sensory-motor link has broken down, and any link between man and the world must be an object of faith (C2, 172). The fact that we can no longer believe in revolution, the possibility of a transformed world, means that we must believe in the body: cinema must become vitalist:

> We must believe in the body, but as in the germ of life, the seed which splits open the paving stones, which has been preserved and lives on in the holy shroud or the mummy's bandages, and which bears witness to life, in this world as it is. (C2, 173)

As far as politics is concerned, cinema now faces the problem of finding a 'people'. For the 'classical' cinema of Eisenstein the people exist, but they are oppressed or tricked. Similarly, American cinema up to and during the war, although it does not deal with class struggle and ideology, is built around a certain unanimity. Soviet and American cinema of this period hold out the hope of a mass, democratic art. However, as discussed above, this dream is compromised by the tyranny of Hitler and Stalin, and the failure of the American 'melting-pot': 'In short, if there were a modern political cinema, it would be on this basis: the people no longer exist, or not yet ... *the people are missing*' (C2, 216).

Modern cinema can also be a cinema of the *brain*. In the films of Stanley Kubrick, for example, a journey undertaken in the world is also a journey in the brain (C2, 206). Similarly, Alain Resnais has quite consciously developed an 'intellectual' cinema which investigates the '[...] cerebral process as object and motor of cinema' (C2, 210). Michelangelo Antonioni strives for a 'double composition' in which brain and body coexist in the world but are out of step with each other. The brain adapts to new beliefs and knowledge, whereas the tired, 'neurotic' body clings to old values and myths: 'The world awaits its inhabitants, who are still lost in neurosis' (C2, 205). This new cinema of the brain corresponds to a change in the way we conceive of the brain itself. Eisenstein, like a 'cinematographic Hegel', worked according to a cerebral model of internal monologue according to which the principles of montage correspond to the process of thought. This was a 'classic cerebral model', organised on a vertical axis of integration-differentiation and a horizontal axis of association (C2, 211). However, we now have a different relationship with the brain:

> Our lived relationship with the brain becomes increasingly fragile, less and less 'Euclidean' and goes through little cerebral deaths. The brain becomes our problem or our illness, our passion, rather than our mastery, our solution or decision. (C2, 212)

What is Cinema? What is Philosophy?

In the closing sentences of *Cinema 2* Deleuze defends a theoretical approach to cinema. In doing so, he returns once again to the debate on representation which is so important as far as the search for a new image of thought is concerned. Paul Patton defines this as the question of 'aboutness'. As Patton notes, Deleuze is opposed to the 'traditional' view of philosophy as being about external objects, just as representational painting is 'about' objects which '[...] are given outside the artist's work'.[23] Cinema itself is an intervention in reality, rather than a representation of reality. Similarly, Deleuze claims that he is not writing *about* cinema, but an interference *with* cinema. This allows him to conceive of cinema and theory as an eclectic plane of activity:

> A theory of cinema is not 'about' cinema, but about the concepts that cinema gives rise to and which are themselves related to other concepts corresponding to other practices, the practice of concepts in general having no privilege over others, any more than one object has over others. (C2, 280)

Ultimately, we must conclude that film is philosophically important for Deleuze because it sets out a plane of immanence and indiscernibility. Cinema is, quite simply, a moving image of thought; and an image of thought which undermines any conventional notion of subject and object. Instead cinema's plane of immanence, particularly in the postwar era, institutes a complex zone of indiscernibility: 'We run in fact into a principle of indeterminability, of indiscernibility: we no longer know what is imaginary or real, physical or mental' (C2, 7). Just as other forms of art, such as the paintings of Francis Bacon, aspire to act directly upon the nervous system,[24] so cinema will attempt to arouse the thinker in us, or remind us of the 'impower' of the thinker within the thinker.

Conclusion

How are we to assess Deleuze's work, with and without Félix Guattari? We might initially turn to Deleuze's own reflections on the subject. Two years before his death Deleuze talked to Didier Eribon about his career, and extracts from this interview are published posthumously.[1] Here, Deleuze reinforces the idea of philosophy as the creation of concepts, referring to the 1960s and early 1970s as a period during which there was a 'new functionalism' in the domain of ideas. Rather than having recourse to the notion of transcendence or of philosophy as 'reflection on' something, this 'functionalism' entailed the creation of concepts which would 'function' within a given social field. It is a question of thought as an 'event'; thought as something immanent rather than transcendent; ethics rather than morals.[2]

This, then, must be regarded as one of Deleuze's major contributions to contemporary philosophy: thought as an event.[3] Nick Millett assesses Deleuze's work in a similar way when he draws attention to the fact that, as far as Deleuze is concerned, philosophy should have a 'horror' of abstraction.[4] As Millett points out, Deleuze's philosophy of immanence, the event and empiriscism – a 'wild' creation of concepts – depends upon a systematic dismantling of identity; a 'disenfranchisement' of the subject.[5] Millett also goes on to discuss Deleuze's style, and in doing so touches upon the theme of 'free indirect discourse'. Millett quite rightly shows how this practice of free indirect discourse is a consequence of Deleuze's general critique of representation and ideology.[6] Deleuze has little time for the 'clarity' of abstractions, communicative rationality and the model of false consciousness that ideology entails. It is only in that space where the 'I' is disenfranchised, where enunciation is indirect that something interesting takes place.[7] As we saw in the introduction, Alain Badiou considers Deleuze's use of free indirect discourse to be an expression of perspectivism. For these reasons, Badiou shows that Deleuze's style of thought is necessarily one of description and narration, as opposed to argument or 'dialectic development':

> Deleuze lets thought roam through the labyrinth of the world; he lays down marks and lays out threads, sets mental traps for

> beasts and shadows. [...] He likes the question to be indirect and local, the mirror to be tinted. He likes there to be a tight-woven screen that forces us to squint to perceive the outline of being. The aim is to sharpen perception, to make hypothetical assurances move about and stray.[8]

Of course, it is not really possible to discuss the overall impact of Deleuze's thought without considering Foucault's much-cited comment to the effect that the century will one day be Deleuzian. Kenneth Surin takes on the task of considering the ways in which Deleuze's work is 'epochal'.[9] Whilst acknowledging that the search for a given philosopher's 'epochality' runs the risk of reducing a body of thought to a set of slogans, he argues that the exercise is worthwhile if it entails the attempt to locate the 'reciprocity and congruence' between Deleuze's thought and the imaginary 'episteme' of *le siècle*. Approaching the question in this way, Surin claims that the concept of the rhizome is associated with a sort of 'new' Baroque. The 'cyberspaces' that are dealt with in fictional form by William Gibson and Bruce Sterling represent a congruence of previously diverse elements such as computer technology, the human nervous system and commodity production. Surin argues that Deleuze's concept of the fold has strong affinities with these new cyberspaces.[10] Similarly, Surin points out that the *Capitalism and Schizophrenia* project is epochal, in that it attempts to introduce 'homeopathically' into thought the mutations that took place in capitalism in the 1970s: 'The rhizome is explicitly invoked in *A Thousand Plateaus* as the image of thought "for" this capitalist world order.'[11] The rhizome is an image of thought which sets out a 'univocity of strata' responding to a similar univocity in contemporary capitalism. Surin concludes by arguing that ultimately, as we have already seen, Deleuze offers a practical philosophy as event. In such a philosophy politics precedes being (see TP, 203), and we can no longer rely on transcendental forms.

However, it should not be thought that all of the commentary on Deleuze's work is unreservedly positive in its assessment. Jonathan Ree, for example, claims that Deleuze and Guattari's final work only confirms that their project has lost the freshness of *Anti-Oedipus*, *Kafka* and *A Thousand Plateaus* and has become an exercise in 'philosophy for philosophy's sake'.[12] He considers *What is Philosophy?* to be a 'good book', but ultimately a 'cry for help', revealing its authors to be a 'terrible pair of snobs'. Deleuze and Guattari are portrayed as a sort of philosophical 'odd couple', unable to come to terms with a changing world:

> In this last book, the improbable collaboration between a university philosopher [...] and a rascally anti-psychiatrist (Guattari could never forgive Laing and Cooper for selling out

> to the capitalist-therapeutic system), has changed its tune: this is not a call to arms by a post-Marxist revolutionary, but the melancholy memoir of a philsophical connoisseur.[13]

Ree savours the irony of two 'poststructuralists' writing a book which often seems to convey the love which its authors have for the Western canon of philosophy. He is willing to go along with what he sees as the discussion of philosophical taste that Deleuze and Guattari oppose to historicism in the first part of the book. However, he cannot go along with the 'haughty assertiveness' of the second half of the book which describes the relationship between science, art and philosophy.[14]

There are also challenges to Deleuze's concepts of univocity, immanence, and empiricism. Some commentators accuse Deleuze of somehow reintroducing a transcendent, almost mystical, category of the 'Real'. Peter Hallward, for example, challenges the notion that Deleuze is a thinker of radical pluralism, or a thinker of difference at all.[15] For Hallward, Deleuze's spinozism, rather than expressing a continuous form of difference, a line of 'variation', is rather a quasi-religious notion whereby Deleuze '[...] writes an attack on specific, worldly knowledges and worldly differences, in favour of an other-worldly redemptive force'.[16] Deleuze's 'redemptive paradigm' is not really any different from a Christian model, whereby he seeks to return to an 'original harmony or Reason'.[17] Hallward argues that Deleuze's project is ultimately incoherent, since his philosophy of immanence ultimately depends upon a more primary transcendence:

> If Deleuze's radical philosophy of immanence of course entails the critique of transcendence just as it implies the refusal of negation, this very critique obtains only through a preliminary transcendence of what might be called the 'Given' (relative, worldly, specific, human, significant) as opposed to the 'Real' (absolute, other-worldly, singular, inhuman or impersonal, asignificant).[18]

There is, Hallward claims, an ontological univocity which is central to Deleuze's essentially redemptive philosophical enterprise. Like Spinoza, Saint Paul, or the Muslim thinker Suhrawardî, Deleuze wants to redeem us from the 'Given'. Hallward sees three accounts of the Given in Deleuze: the Bergsonian critique of the human; the critique of capitalism and psychoanalysis; and Foucault's critique of the constitution of the modern subject.[19] The philosopher or the artist, as a clinician, attempts to recover the 'Real' on our behalf: the given must be exploded or paralysed.[20] In this way, Hallward seeks to undermine one of the established starting points of Deleuze's work, his avowed opposition to Hegel. For Hallward,

'Deleuze's redemptive philosophy always works from, within and toward the assumption of ontological univocity, the redemptive identity of the One and the multiple.'[21] He also criticises Deleuze for underestimating the important position that his philosophy ultimately reserves for the 'agent of redemption', which is usually the thinker, artist or philosopher: 'through the finite power of the philosopher, the infinite expression of the Real'.[22] The writer/artist has a privileged position which allows him or her to operate 'alone, outside history'.[23] Deleuze's project, rather than undermining theoretical imperialism, is itself a form of 'State-thought'. Deleuze erects his own philosophy as a form of unlimited judgement, a judgement which '[...] is no longer relative to a judge, a faculty, a place, a constitution or a set of criteria of judgement, but coincides with itself alone – as redemptive of all'.[24] Ultimately, and although Hallward does acknowledge that there are virtues in Deleuze's work, he claims that Deleuze is not what he claims to be: 'His multiple is not the plural, but the internal consequence of univocity.'[25] This blunts the political efficacy of Deleuze's philosophy, since he has no convincing way of dealing with that which is equivocal in human affairs. Focusing on Deleuze's analysis of Spinoza's ethical vision in *Expressionism in Philosophy*, Hallward suggests that Deleuze's political philosophy is authoritarian, in that Spinoza's sovereign City is built upon the renunciation of plural interests.

Alain Badiou proposes a similar reading, in a short book on Deleuze published after the latter's death which emerges from an exchange of correspondence with Deleuze in the 1990s.[26] Badiou highlights three elements in Deleuze's work as a whole: it is a philosophy which, as Hallward argues, is based upon the model of univocity; it is a philosophy which demands an ascetic approach to the self, an ethic of 'getting free' of the self; finally it is a systematic and abstract philosophy.[27] Badiou considers the second and third of these dimensions to be positive aspects of Deleuze's thought. It is the first aspect which Badiou finds more problematic, and which led to an exchange of letters between the two. Badiou bases his reading on carefully selected quotations, such as the following from *Difference and Repetition*: 'There has only ever been one ontological proposition: Being is univocal. There has only ever been one ontology, that of Duns Scotus, which gave being a single voice' (DR, 35). In this way, Badiou argues that Deleuze seeks to 'reconstruct' Platonism, rather than overturning it. At heart, he claims, Deleuze's work is a 'reaccentuated' Platonism.[28]

It cannot be denied that Deleuze's work leaves us with a set of paradoxes which undoubtedly add to the interest of his work, but also leave us with difficulties in reading this work. These contradictions are summarised concisely by Paul Patton shortly after Deleuze's death:

> In his pursuit of this project, Deleuze became an increasingly paradoxical figure: a philosopher who defended the autonomy of philosophical thought in relation to art and science but denied any hierarchy between them; a proponent of nomad thought who believed in philosophy as a system; a Nietzschean political thinker who never ceased becoming Marxist.[29]

I would add one further 'contradiction', which is not really a contradiction but rather an unexplored path. Deleuze developed a notion of the machinic which embraced a certain vitalism. This in itself does not entail a contradiction: machinic vitalism is quite simply a philosophy of transcendental empiricism, a philosophy of multiplicity. As Deleuze shows in his books on cinema, the machinic nature of the brain has little to do with information technology: we need to look more and more to the brain, not to computers. However, he also acknowledges that we are increasingly coming into contact with new forces from the outside: 'Nineteenth-century man, for example, confronts life and combines with it as the force of carbon. But what happens when human forces combine with those of silicon, and what new forms begin to appear?' (N, 100). Perhaps Deleuze would have written more about this problem in the 'philosophy of Nature' that he planned to write with Félix Guattari (see N, 155), and perhaps the twenty-first century will reveal itself to be at least a little 'Deleuzian'.

Notes and References

Preface

1. See Pascal Engel, 'La philosophie analytique peut-elle être française?', *Magazine littéraire*, no. 339 (janvier 1996), pp. 47–51. This distinction between 'Continental' and 'analytic' traditions is borrowed largely from Engel's provoking article. As an example of the analytic approach as academic practice Engel refers to the numerous objections and responses found in journals such as *Mind* and *Journal of Philosophy*.

Chapter 1

1. See Félix Guattari, *Chaosmose* (Paris: Galilée, 1992). Translated as *Chaosmosis: an Ethico-Aesthetic Paradigm*, translated by Paul Bains and Julian Pefanis (Bloomington and Indianapolis: Indiana University Press, 1995). Deleuze's friend and collaborator Guattari discusses just what is meant by such a 'collective' subjectivity:

   > We know that in certain social and semiological contexts, subjectivity becomes individualised; persons, taken as responsible for themselves, situate themselves within relations of alterity governed by familial habits, local customs, juridical laws, etc. In other conditions, subjectivity is collective – which does not, however, mean that it becomes exclusively social. The term 'collective' should be understood in the sense of a multiplicity that deploys itself as much beyond the individual, on the side of the socius, as before the person, on the side of preverbal intensities, indicating a logic of affects rather than a logic of delimited sets. (p. 9)

2. See 'Gilles Deleuze, un penseur pluriel et pourtant très singulier', *Le Monde* (7 novembre 1995), pp. 1 and 28.

   'Le plus philosophe des philosophes Gilles Deleuze s'est suicidé à 70 ans', *Libération* (6 novembre 1995), pp. 8–11.

Jean-François Lyotard, et al., 'À Gilles Deleuze, l'inventeur, l'innocent, le fugueur: l'adieu des philosophes', *Libération* (7 novembre 1995), pp. 36–8.

Paul Patton, et al., 'Symposium: Gilles Deleuze, 1925–1995', *Radical Philosophy* (March/April 1996), pp. 2–6.

Christian Deschamps, et al., 'Dossier: Gilles Deleuze', *La Quinzaine littéraire*, no. 686 (1–15 février 1996), pp. 16–24.

3. See note 2, Jean-François Lyotard, 'Il était la bibliothèque de Babel'.
4. See James Miller, *The Passion of Michel Foucault* (London: Simon & Schuster, 1993), p. 196.
5. See Philip Goodchild, *Deleuze and Guattari: An Introduction to the Politics of Desire* (London: Sage Publications, 1996). Goodchild makes a similar point when he argues that Deleuze and Guattari's 'opinions' cannot be abstracted from their 'concepts' (p. 45).
6 See Michel Foucault, 'Theatrum philosophicum', *Critique*, no. 282 (1970), p. 885. Translated as 'Intellectuals and Power', in *Michel Foucault: Language, Counter-Memory, Practice*, edited by Donald F. Bouchard, translated by Donald F. Bouchard and Sherry Simon (Ithaca: Cornell University Press, 1977), pp. 165–96.
7. Michel Tournier, 'Gilles Deleuze', *Critique*, nos 591–2 (août–septembre 1996), pp. 725–6. See also Gilles Deleuze, 'Le "je me souviens" de Gilles Deleuze', *Le Nouvel Observatur*, no. 1619 (16–22 novembre 1995), pp. 50–1. Here, Deleuze speaks of his great admiration for Sartre, seeing 'Les Mouches' as an act of resistance during the Occupation. See also Tournier's autobiographical work *Le Vent paraclet* (Paris: Gallimard, 1977). Deleuze also speaks of his admiration for Sartre in *Dialogues*:

> Fortunately there was Sartre. Sartre was our Outside, he was really the breath of fresh air from the backyard [...]. Among all the Sorbonne's probabilities, it was his unique combination which gave us the strength to tolerate the new restoration of order. And Sartre has never stopped being that, not a model, a method or an example, but a little fresh air – a gust of air even when he had just been to the Café Flore – an intellectual who singularly changed the situation of the intellectual. (D, 12)

8 Gilles Deleuze and Claire Parnet, *L'Abécédaire de Gilles Deleuze*. This consisted of a series of interviews with Claire Parnet filmed in 1988. The programmes were shown fortnightly from 15 January 1995 on the Franco-German channel *Arte*. The

interviews are published in the form of three video cassettes by Editions Montparnasse, 1997.

9. See James Miller, *The Passion of Michel Foucault*; Didier Eribon, *Michel Foucault*, translated by Betsy Wing (London: Faber & Faber, 1992); David Macey, *The Lives of Michel Foucault* (London: Hutchinson, 1993).
10. In *What is Philosophy?* Deleuze and Guattari suggest that the philosopher 'plunges into' chaos to bring back infinite variations (p. 202).
11. Paul Patton, 'Gilles Deleuze, 1925–1995: One of the Saints', *Radical Philosophy* (March/April 1996), p. 2. See note 2.
12. All translations from *Nietzsche* are my own.
13. Friedrich Nietzsche, *Beyond Good and Evil*, trans. R.J. Hollingdale (Harmondsworth: Penguin, 1973), p. 19 (6).
14. Michel Cressole, *Deleuze* (Paris: Editions Universitaires, 1973).
15. See 'Dossier: Gilles Deleuze, un philosophe nomade', *Le Magazine littéraire*, no. 257 (septembre 1988), pp. 14–59. In this dossier of articles on the work of Deleuze the editors produce a series of 'biographical reference points'. Under 'distinguishing marks' they list, 'travels little, was never a member of the Communist party, was never a phenomenologist nor a Heideggerian, has never renounced Marx, has never given up on May '68 (p. 19). In fact, Deleuze was very occasionally persuaded to travel to conferences in the USA, Canada, and once in Lebanon.
16. See note 8.
17. Gilles Deleuze, 'Literature and Life', translated by Daniel W. Smith and Michael A. Greco, *Critical Enquiry*, vol. 23 (Winter 1997), p. 227.
18. See *L'Abécédaire de Gilles Deleuze*, 'P comme professeur'.
19. See note 2.
20. See Gilles Deleuze, 'La Méthode de dramatisation', *Bulletin de la société française de philosophie*, no. 61, vol. 3 (juillet–septembre 1967), pp. 89–118. The central question for Platonic philosophy is 'what' (e.g. 'what is justice'). This question should, however, be 'dramatised' (e.g. 'who is just?').
21. Ibid., p. 92. Deleuze claims that Hegel is perhaps the only philosopher to have concentrated on the question 'what?' as opposed to 'who?' (He is challenged strongly on this point by Ferdinand Alquié in the questions that follow.)
22. Alexandre Kojève, *Introduction à la lecture de Hegel: Leçons sur 'La Phénoménologie de l'Esprit'* (Paris: Gallimard, 1947).
23. See Vincent Descombes, *Le Même et l'autre: quarante cinq ans de philosophie française* (Paris: Minuit, 1979). Translated as *Modern French Philosophy*, translated by L. Scott-Fox and J.M. Harding (Cambridge: Cambridge University Press, 1980).

24. See Ronald Bogue, *Deleuze and Guattari* (London: Routledge, 1989), pp. 2–3. Bogue points out that Kojève's reading of Hegel appealed to the postwar intellectual movements of phenomenology, existentialism, and humanistic Marxism, but that the theory of negation was unsatisfactory for Deleuze:

> To Deleuze and many of his generation, however, the Hegelian dialectic only *seemed* to engage the non-rational; its logic of negation and contradiction was based ultimately on a logic of identity, within which the non-rational 'other' could only be conceived of as the shadow of the rational 'same'. What was needed, according to Deleuze and others, was a philosophy of difference *as* difference, irreducible to the concepts of identity and representation. (pp. 2–3)

25. Michael Hardt, *Gilles Deleuze: An Apprenticeship in Philosophy* (London: UCL Press, 1993), p. x.
26. See Jacques Derrida, *Spectres de Marx* (Paris: Éditions Galilée, 1993). Translated as *Specters of Marx: The State of Debt, the Work of Mourning, & the New International*, translated by Peggy Kamuf (London: Routledge, 1994). Here, Derrida returns to the question of Hegel and the 'end' of history.
27. Hardt, *Gilles Deleuze: An Apprenticeship in Philosophy*, p. xi.
28. Ibid., p. 115.
29. See Michael George, 'Marx's Hegelianism', in David Lamb, ed., *Hegel and Modern Philosophy* (Beckenham: Croom Helm, 1987), pp. 119–42. George points out that the 'conventional' reading of the dialectic as the triadic relation of thesis, antithesis and synthesis should be attributed to Fichte rather than Hegel or Marx. Fichte's triadic form of the dialectic presupposes an opposition between two discrete concepts which are subsequently synthesised as a third concept, the synthesis. George argues that Hegel rejects the process of synthesis as the guiding principle of the dialectic in *Science of Logic.* Instead of emphasising the distinct and discrete nature of opposing concepts, Hegel considers the act of perceiving opposition to be itself a form of 'abstraction'. In perceiving opposition between concepts we ignore the fact that opposition is pre-existed by a greater Whole. In the Hegelian form of the dialectic, ideas which are initially seen as distinct are ultimately understood, by means of the use of Reason, to be interdependent. George prefers the German term *Gegenstaz*, which he translates as 'against positing', to *synthesis* as the guiding principle of the Hegelian dialectic (p. 126). In this way, George reaches a similar conclusion to that reached by Foucault. The concept must always be supplemented and expanded by means of a careful consideration of the Whole within which it stands.

Reason must push thought beyond the limits of an identity between concepts. Similarly, Deleuze's logic of relations, whilst being anti-Hegelian, takes the Hegelian form of *Gegensatz.*

30. Michel Foucault, *L'Ordre du discours* (Paris: Gallimard, 1971), p. 8. Translated by Ian McLeod as 'The Order of Discourse', in R. Young, ed., *Untying the Text: A Poststructuralist Reader* (London: Routledge, 1981), pp. 48–78. I have used the translation of this passage by David Macey in *The Lives of Michel Foucault*, p. 243.
31. Hardt, *Gilles Deleuze: An Apprenticeship in Philosophy*, p. xi. Hardt acknowledges Judith Butler, *Subjects of Desire* (New York: Columbia University Press, 1987).
32. Catherine Malabou, 'Who's Afraid of Hegelian Wolves?', in Paul Patton, ed., *Deleuze: A Critical Reader* (Oxford: Blackwell, 1996), pp. 114–38.
33. Ibid., p. 116.
34. Ibid., p. 115.
35. Ibid., p. 121.

Chapter 2

1. See Jean-Jacques Lecercle, 'The Pedagogy of Philosophy', *Radical Philosophy*, no. 75 (January–February 1996), pp. 44–6. Lecercle portrays the following scene:

   > The underground is taking you, rather fast (this is Paris, not London), towards the skyscrapers of La Défense and, a little further west, the University of Nanterre. On the seat facing you, a bespectacled yuppie, complete with tailored suit and regulation tie, is reading Deleuze and Guattari's latest book, *What is Philosophy?* The incongruity of the scene induces a smile – after all, this is a book explicitly written against yuppies, who, with their culture of advertising and marketing, have kidnapped the very term 'concept' to denote the sales promotion of their marketable 'ideas'. Your smile turns into a grin as you imagine that this enlightenment-seeking yuppie bought the book because of its title, because he wanted a textbook, a primer in philosophy. And what he got is a book that reads like the third volume of *Capitalism and Schizophrenia*. Already you see the puzzled look on the yuppie's face, as he reads page after page of vintage Deleuze ... (p. 44).

2 See *Negotiations*, 'The key thing, as Nietzsche said, is that thinkers are always, so to speak, shooting arrows into the air, and other thinkers pick them up and shoot them in another direction' (p. 118).

3. See Gilles Deleuze and Michel Foucault, 'Les intellectuels et le pouvoir', *L'Arc* 49: *Deleuze* (1972), pp. 3–10. Translated as 'Intellectuals and Power', in *Michel Foucault: Language, Counter-Memory, Practice*, edited by Donald F. Bouchard, translated by Donald F. Bouchard and Sherry Simon (Ithaca: Cornell University Press, 1977), pp. 205–17. Also published in *Telos*, no. 16 (Summer 1973), pp. 103–9.
4. Lecercle, 'The Pedagogy of Philosophy', p. 46.
5. See N, 152:

> If you're talking about establishing new forms of transcendendence, new universals, restoring a reflective subject as the bearer of rights, or setting up a communicative intersubjectivity, then it's not much of a philosophical advance. People want to produce 'consensus', but consensus is an ideal that guides opinion, and has nothing to do with philosophy.

6. Friedrich Nietzsche, *Untimely Meditations*, translated by R.J. Hollingdale (Cambridge: Cambridge University Press, 1983).
7. Ibid., p. 133.
8. See Richard Rorty, *Contingency, irony, and solidarity* (Cambridge: Cambridge University Press, 1989).
9. See Arnaud Villani, 'Méthode et théorie dans l'œuvre de Gilles Deleuze', *Les Temps modernes*, no. 586 (janvier–février 1996), pp. 142–53.
10. Michel Foucault, 'Theatrum philosophicum', *Critique*, no. 282 (1970), pp. 885–908. Translated as 'Intellectuals and Power', in *Michel Foucault: Language, Counter-Memory, Practice*, edited by Donald F. Bouchard, translated by Donald F. Bouchard and Sherry Simon (Ithaca: Cornell University Press, 1977), p. 181.
11. See Philip Goodchild, *Deleuze and Guattari: An Introduction to the Politics of Desire* (London: Sage, 1996): Goodchild argues that Deleuze and Guattari's thought developed 'in parallel' with that of Jacques Derrida, the author most often associated with deconstruction:

> Deconstruction [...] is a political activity which involves the dissolution of fixed boundaries that shape hierarchical structures. In addition to declaring that the search for truth or presence is impossible, deconstruction subverts the desire to pursue such a search. (p. 115)

12. Paul Patton, 'Introduction' in Paul Patton, ed., *Deleuze: A Critical Reader*, p. 3.
13. See Tournier, *Le Vent paraclet*, pp. 151–2.
14. Alain Badiou, 'The Fold: Leibniz and the Baroque', in Constantin V. Boundas and Dorothea Olkowski, eds, *Gilles*

Deleuze and the Theater of Philosophy (London: Routledge, 1994), pp. 51–69: 'When you read Deleuze, you never know exactly who is speaking, nor who assures what is said, or declares himself to be certain of it. Is it Leibniz? Deleuze? The well-intentioned reader? The passing artist?' (p. 64).

15. See *L'Abécédaire de Gilles Deleuze*, 'P comme professeur'.
16. Paul Auster, *The Art of Hunger: Essays, Prefaces, Interviews and The Red Notebook* (Harmondsworth: Penguin, 1993), p. 309.
17. See Daniel W. Smith, 'Deleuze's Theory of Sensation: Overcoming the Kantian Duality', in Paul Patton, ed., *Deleuze: A Critical Reader*, p. 41:

    > Modern art and modern philosophy converged on a similar problem: both renounced the domain of representation and instead took the *conditions* of representation as their object. Paul Klee's famous phrase echoes through Deleuze's writings on the arts like a kind of motif: *not to render the visible, but to render visible.* (p. 40)

18. See Gilles Deleuze, *L'Abécédaire de Gilles Deleuze*, 'O comme opéra'. See also FB, pp. 39–40.
19. See Michel Foucault, *The Order of Things: An Archaeology of the Human Sciences*, trans. Alan Sheridan (London: Tavistock, 1971): 'Nietzsche indicated the turning-point from a long way off, it is not so much the death of God that is affirmed as the end of man [...]' (p. 385).
20. See Félix Guattari, *Chaosmosis*, translated by Paul Bains and Julian Pefanis (Bloomington & Indianapolis: Indiana University Press, 1995). Guattari rejects charges of anti-humanism directed at Deleuze and Foucault, pointing out that they concentrate on the 'non-human pre-personal part of subjectivity' (p. 9).
21. See Gilles Deleuze, *L'Abécédaire de Gilles Deleuze*, 'G comme gauche'.
22. Deleuze, 'Literature and Life', p. 226.
23. Gilles Deleuze, 'Immanence: une vie ...', *Philosophie*, no. 47 (septembre 1995), pp. 3–7. Published in English as 'Immanence: a life ...', *Theory, Culture and Society* (May 1997).
24. Ibid., p. 3.
25. Ibid., p. 4.
26. Ibid., p. 5.
27. Deleuze, 'Literature and Life', p. 228.
28. Philip Goodchild, *Gilles Deleuze and the Question of Philosophy* (London: Associated University Presses, 1996), p. 19.
29. Mireille Buydens, *Sahara: l'esthétique de Gilles Deleuze* (Paris: Vrin, 1990). In a brief letter to the author, used as a preface

to the book, Deleuze cautiously agrees that Buydens has located 'ce qui est l'essentiel pour moi, ce "vitalisme" ou une conception de la vie comme puissance non-organique.'

30. Ibid., p. 169. As will be shown in the following chapter, other commentators have noted this connection, particularly in relation to Deleuze's work on Bergson.
31. See Petra Perry, 'Deleuze's Nietzsche', *boundary 2*, vol. 20, no. 1 (1993), pp. 174–91.
32. Todd May, 'The Politics of Life in the Thought of Gilles Deleuze', *SubStance*, no. 66 (1991), p. 31.
33. Deleuze, 'Immanence: a life ...', p. 5.
34. See Buydens, p. 167. Mireille Buydens also claims that 'le devenir' is the guiding theme of Deleuze's work.
35. Deleuze, 'Immanence: a life ...', p. 3.
36. See Michel Foucault, *L'Archéologie du savoir* (Paris: Gallimard, 1969). Translated by A.M. Sheridan-Smith as *The Archaeology of Knowledge* (London: Tavistock, 1972).
37. The concept of the unhistorical and the untimely is linked to the principle of becoming which is so important to Deleuze's philosophy. A truly creative act is unhistorical, or, as Nietzsche expresses it, untimely:

    > There is no act of creation which is not transhistorical and does not come up from behind or proceed by way of a liberated line. Nietzsche opposes history not to the eternal but to the subhistorical or superhistorical: the Untimely, which is another name for haecceity, becoming, the innocence of becoming (in other words, forgetting as opposed to memory, geography as opposed to history, the map as opposed to the tracing, the rhizome as opposed to arborescence). (TP, 296)

38. Daniel W. Smith, 'Deleuze's Theory of Sensation', p. 30.
39. Ibid., p. 31.
40. Ibid., pp. 32–3.
41. See Gilles Deleuze, *L'Abécédaire de Gilles Deleuze*, 'F comme fidélité'.
42. Ibid., 'F comme fidélité'.
43. Deleuze, 'Immanence: a life ...', p. 5.
44. See LS, 22: 'It is in this sense that it is an "event": *on the condition that the event is not confused with its spatio-temporal realization in a state of affairs.*'
45. Deleuze, 'Immanence: a life ...', p. 6.
46. See Gilles Deleuze, *L'Abécédaire de Gilles Deleuze*, 'H comme histoire de la philosophie'.
47. See Gilles Deleuze, *L'Abécédaire de Gilles Deleuze*, 'J comme joie'.

48. Jean-Jacques Lecercle, *Philosophy of Nonsense: The Intuitions of Victorian Nonsense Literature* (London: Routledge, 1994), p. 213.
49. Deleuze, 'Immanence, a life ...', p. 4.
50. See Philip Goodchild, *Deleuze and Guattari*, pp. 3–4.
51. See Jean-Clet Martin, *Variations: la philosophie de Gilles Deleuze* (Paris: Editions Payot et Rivage, 1993). For an explanation of the use of variation in Carmelo Bene's *Richard III* see 'One Manifesto Less'.
52. See Moira Gatens, 'Through a Spinozist Lens: Ethology, Difference, Power', in Paul Patton, ed., *Deleuze: A Critical Reader*, pp. 162–87. Gatens looks at Deleuze's reading of Spinoza, and emphasises the way in which Spinoza's 'modesty' concerning the knowledge we can have of the human body leads to an 'ethology' rather than a rule-based morality. Spinoza collapses distinctions between artifice and nature, human and non-human:

    > The collapse of these distinctions raises interesting questions concerning contemporary and future possibilities of hybrid life forms and body prostheses presented by technology. These new technologies present possibilities for making novel connections by producing assemblages capable of forging different extensive relations and new intensive capacities. (p. 167)

53. See Donna Haraway, *Primate Visions: Gender, Race and Nature in the Modern World of Science* (London: Routledge, 1989).
54. Rosi Braidotti, 'Toward a New Nomadism: Feminist Deleuzian Tracks; or, Metaphysics and Metabolism', in Constantin V. Boundas and Dorothea Olkowski, eds, *Gilles Deleuze and the Theater of Philosophy* (London: Routledge, 1994), p. 179.
55. Paul Virilio, Interview with Nicholas Zurbrugg, 'A Century of Hyper-Violence', *Economy and Society*, vol. 25, no. 1 (February 1996), p. 115.
56. Philip Goodchild, *Deleuze and Guattari: An Introduction to the Politics of Desire* (London: Sage, 1996), p. 218.
57. See N, pp. 184–5, translator's note 5:

    > The transcendent subject vanishes like a ghost into the unconscious machinery that produces (among other things) empirical subjects and their conscious ends. Desire is not rooted in a subject or its objectives or objects (not even in 'missing' Lacanian subjects and objects), but subjects and objects are produced by desiring machines.

Chapter 3

1. Although it is useful to consider Deleuze's work as divided into these three periods in terms of content, it would be wrong to impose a similar periodisation in terms of his theoretical development. Constantin V. Boundas, for example, proposes a theoretical progression which starts with an early interest, mediated through Hume, in the 'structure-Subject', followed by a dismantling of subjectivity influenced by May 1968, and finally a 'timid retrieval of the subject as folded interiority' (ES, Translator's Introduction, 12). However, Boundas also argues that a reading which divides Deleuze's work into distinct periods is ultimately unsatisfactory. It is more rewarding to consider Deleuze's work as a set of problems which coexist throughout his work. In this way, the questions posed by early work continue to resonate throughout his career.
2. See also *Dialogues*:

   > So I began with the history of philosophy – when it was still being prescribed. For my part, I could not see any way of extracting myself. I could not stand Descartes, the dualisms and the Cogito, or Hegel, the triad and the operation of the negation. But I liked writers who seemed to be part of the history of philosophy, but who escaped from it in one respect, or altogether: Lucretius, Spinoza, Hume, Nietzsche, Bergson. (D, 15)

3. Alain Badiou, *Deleuze: "La clameur de l'Etre"* (Paris: Hachette, 1997), p. 25–6.
4. See Michael Hardt, *Gilles Deleuze: An Apprenticeship in Philosophy* (London: UCL Press, 1993).
5. David Hume, *A Treatise of Human Nature* (Oxford: Oxford University Press, 1978), p. 253.
6. Philip Goodchild, *Deleuze and Guattari: An Introduction to the Politics of Desire* (London: Sage, 1996), p. 13.
7. See Marvin Minsky, *The Society of Mind* (London: Heinemann, 1987).
8. Alan D. Schrift, 'Nietzsche's French Legacy', in Bernd Magnus and Kathleen M. Turner, eds, *The Cambridge Companion to Nietzsche* ((Cambridge: Cambridge University Press, 1996).
9. Ibid., p. 326.
10. Ibid., p. 339.
11. Petra Perry, 'Deleuze's Nietzsche', *boundary 2*, vol. 20, no. 1 (1993), pp. 174–91.
12. Ibid., p. 178.
13. Ibid., p. 182.

14. Proceedings of the conference published as *Nietzsche: Cahiers de Royaumont*, Philosophie No. VI (Paris: Editions de Minuit, 1967).
15. The proceedings of the 1972 conference at Cérisy-la-Salle are published in the two volumes of *Nietzsche aujourd'hui* (Paris: 10/18, 1973). Deleuze's contribution appears in English as 'Nomad Thought', trans. D.B Allison, in *The New Nietzsche*, ed. David Allison (New York: Dell, 1977).
16. David Allison, ed., *The New Nietzsche* (New York: Dell, 1977).
17. Ibid., p. xiv.
18. Ibid., p. 43.
19. Ibid., p. xv.
20. For a useful discussion of Nietzsche's concept of genealogy, see Michel Foucault, 'Nietzsche, Freud, Marx', in Paul Rabinow, ed., *The Foucault Reader* (Harmondsworth: Penguin, 1984). Foucault shows how Nietzsche's 'genealogical' method eschews the idea of teleology, identity, or destiny in the historical process. Instead, history is a process of error and contingency:

    > Genealogy does not resemble the evolution of a species and does not map the destiny of a people. On the contrary, to follow the complex course of descent is to maintain passing events in their proper dispersion; it is to identify the accidents, the minute deviations – or conversely, the complete reversals – the errors, the false appraisals, and the faulty calculations that give birth to those things that continue to exist and have value for us [...]. (p. 81)

21. Alan D. Schrift, 'Putting Nietzsche to Work: The Case of Gilles Deleuze', in Peter R. Sedgwick, ed., *Nietzsche: A Critical Reader* (Oxford: Blackwell, 1995), pp. 250–75.
22. Gilles Deleuze, 'Nomad Thought', in *The New Nietzsche*, pp. 142–9.
23. Ibid., p. 142.
24. Ibid., p. 143.
25. Ibid., p. 145.
26. In his preface to the English translation of *Spinoza: Practical Philosophy* Robert Hurley emphasises the kinship between Nietzsche and Spinoza that Deleuze perceives. Spinoza writes prior to the form Man, and Nietzsche sees beyond it, and they both share a philosophy of forces as explanations of form (p. i).
27. See Christopher Norris, *Spinoza and the Origins of Modern Critical Theory* (Oxford: Blackwell, 1991). Norris, who views Deleuze's work with some suspicion, claims that Deleuze's own book, *Spinoza: Practical Philosophy*, mirrors the structure of the *Ethics* by working on at least two levels: logical rigour combined with 'diverse comments and local *aperçus*' (p. 62). Norris goes

further to claim that the dual nature of the *Ethics* has encouraged two very different readings of Spinoza amongst French postwar intellectuals. On the one hand, Spinoza exercised an important influence on the 'scientific' Marxism of Althusser, in whose hands Spinoza becomes one of the first 'theorists' of European thought. However, Spinoza also appeals to thinkers like Deleuze and Guattari, whom Norris describes as 'anti-theorists'. In one way, Spinoza's work represents what Norris calls a 'high theoreticist position', with the notion of 'adequate ideas' being equated to Marxist science. However, Norris also argues that Spinoza has links with the 'anti-theory' tradition represented by Deleuze:

> [...] it lends support to the converse set of claims: that theory is a pointless and delusive behaviour, that concepts must always falsify the nature of lived experience, and that the only reality is that of the body as a complex ensemble of drives, impulses and 'desiring machines' that acknowledge no necessity save that of preserving their own, sheerly physical or sensuous mode of existence. (p. 60)

Norris even goes so far as to describe the fact that Spinoza's *Ethics* have inspired two such different projects as 'an irony perhaps without parallel in recent intellectual history'.

28. Pierre Macherey, 'The Encounter with Spinoza', in Paul Patton, ed., *Deleuze: A Critical Reader* (Oxford: Blackwell, 1996), p. 141.
29. Ibid., pp. 141–2.
30. Ibid., pp. 146–7.
31. Ibid., p. 147.
32. Virginia Woolf, *The Waves* (St. Albans: Granada, 1977), p. 159.
33. Macherey, 'The Encounter with Spinoza', pp. 148–9.
34. Badiou, *Deleuze*, p. 62. See also André Pierre Colombat, 'A Thousand Trails', *SubStance*, no. 66 (1991): 'Deleuze is Bergsonian on at least two fundamental points: in his conception of time and movement, and in his constant linking of science and the necessity for a new representation of reality in its perpetual metamorphosis' (p. 19).
35. See Constantin V. Boundas, 'Deleuze-Bergson: an Ontology of the Virtual', in *Deleuze: A Critical Reader*, pp. 90–1.
36. See Frederick Burwick and Paul Douglass, eds, *The Crisis in Modernism: Bergson and the Vitalist Controversy* (Cambridge: Cambridge University Press, 1992), p. 371.
37. Ibid., p. 1.
38. Ibid., p. 2.
39. Ibid., p. 5.

40. Ibid., p. 4.
41. See Constantin V. Boundas, 'Deleuze-Bergson: an Ontology of the Virtual'. Boundas argues that Deleuze, through his reading of Bergson, denounces a whole series of transcendental illusions:

> Put in a nutshell, the transcendental illusion that Deleuze denounces is the result of our exclusive preoccupation with extended magnitudes in space at the expense of intensities in time. It is the result of our exclusive preoccupation with discrete manifolds at the expense of continua, differences of degree at the expense of differences of nature, space at the expense of time, with things at the expense of processes, with solutions at the the expense of problems, with sedimented culture at the expense of learning, with recognition at the expense of fundamental encounters, with results at the expense of tendencies. (p. 85)

42. Henri Bergson, *Creative Evolution*, translated by A. Mitchell (New York: Henry Holt, 1911), p. ix.
43. Ibid., p. xiii.
44. Henri Bergson, *Introduction to Metaphysics*, translated by T.E. Hulme (London: Macmillan, 1910), p. 55.
45. Burwick and Douglass, *The Crisis in Modernism*, p. 370.
46. Ibid., p. 5.
47. Ibid., p. 4.
48. See also Gilles Deleuze, 'What is a dispositif?' in Timothy Armstrong, ed., *Michel Foucault Philosopher* (Brighton: Harvester Wheatsheaf, 1992), pp. 159–68. Originally published in French as 'Qu'est-ce qu'un dispositif?' *Michel Foucault philosophe, rencontre internationale Paris 9, 10, 11 janvier 1988* (Paris: Seuil, 1989), pp. 185–95.
49. See Gilles Deleuze, *L'Abécédaire de Gilles Deleuze* (Paris: Editions Montparnasse, 1997), 'K comme Kant'.
50. This preface was published in revised form in *Critique et clinique*.
51. Alain Badiou, 'Gilles Deleuze, *The Fold: Leibniz and the Baroque*', in Constantin V. Boundas and Dorothea Olkowski, eds, *Gilles Deleuze and the Theater of Philosophy* (London: Routledge, 1994), pp. 51–69.
52. Ibid., p. 55.
53. See Gilles Deleuze, 'Leibniz, le pli, et le baroque: le point de vue', Département de philosophie Paris VIII (Novembre 1986). A video recording held at the Bibliothèque Nationale de France.

Chapter 4

1. Michel Foucault, 'Theatrum philosophicum', *Critique*, no. 282 (1970), pp. 885–908. Translated as 'Intellectuals and Power', in *Michel Foucault: Language, Counter-Memory, Practice*, edited by Donald F. Bouchard, translated by Donald F. Bouchard and Sherry Simon (Ithaca: Cornell University Press, 1977), p. 165.
2. Ibid., p. 168.
3. Ibid., p. 172.
4. Paul Patton, 'Anti-Platonism and Art', in Constantin V. Boundas and Dorothea Olkowski, eds, *Gilles Deleuze and the Theater of Philosophy* (London: Routledge, 1994), pp. 141–56.
5. Ibid., p. 152.
6. Foucault, 'Theatrum philosophicum', p. 170.
7. Ibid., p. 173.
8. Ibid., p. 186.
9. Ibid., p. 182.
10. Ibid., p. 189.
11. Ibid., p. 190. Interestingly, Deleuze adds a footnote to Foucault's drug reference, asking coyly: 'What will people think of us?'
12. See Maurice Merleau-Ponty, *The Phenomenology of Perception*, translated by Colin Smith (London: Routledge & Kegan Paul, 1962).
13. Foucault, 'Theatrum philosophicum', p. 192.
14. Todd May, 'Difference and Unity in Gilles Deleuze', in *Gilles Deleuze and the Theater of Philosophy*, pp. 33–50.
15. Ibid., p. 47.
16. Ibid., p. 43.
17. See Bruce Baugh, 'Deleuze and Empiricism', *Journal of the British Society for Phenomenology*, vol. 24, no. 1 (January 1993), pp. 15–31. Baugh presents a clear and detailed analysis of Deleuze's empiricism.
18. Ibid., p. 15.
19. See Daniel W. Smith, 'Deleuze's Theory of Sensation: Overcoming the Kantian Duality', in Paul Patton, ed., *Deleuze: A Critical Reader* (Oxford: Blackwell, 1996), pp. 29–56.
20. Baugh, 'Deleuze and Empiricism', p. 17.
21. Ibid., p. 17: 'Contrary to Kantianism or Hegelian Idealism, it is the empirical which explains the conceptual and the abstract conditions of all possible experience, not the reverse.'
22. Ibid., p. 15.
23. Ibid., p. 25.
24. Ibid., p. 26.

25. Constantin V. Boundas, 'Deleuze-Bergson: an Ontology of the Virtual', in Paul Patton, ed., *Deleuze: A Critical Reader* (Oxford: Blackwell, 1996):

    Bergsonian intuition is a method for dividing the mixture according to tendencies, that is, according to real differences. Viewed in this light, Bergson's intuition is identical with Deleuze's transcendental empiricism. It is true that whenever Deleuze names allies and forerunners of his brand of empiricism he comes up with Schelling who defined his philosophy as a quest for the conditions of real experience. Nevertheless he continues to praise Bergson for having endowed philosophy with the means for creating concepts fine-tuned to the point of merging with percepts. (p. 87)

26. 'Introduction', to Émile Zola, *La Bête humaine*, in *Oeuvres complètes*, tome 6 (Paris: Cercle du livre précieux, 1967), pp. 13–21. Reprinted in revised form in *The Logic of Sense* and as the 'préface' to a later edition of Émile Zola, *La Bête humaine* (Paris: Gallimard, 1977), pp. 7–24.
27. Gilles Deleuze, 'Immanence: une vie ...', *Philosophie*, no. 47 (septembre 1995), pp. 3–7. Published in English as 'Immanence: a life ...', *Theory, Culture and Society* (May 1997).

Chapter 5

1. Deleuze and Guattari's use of the term 'universal' is certainly ironic. Universal history is undoubtedly Nietzschean in inspiration, being a history of contingencies rather than necessity, and ruptures rather than continuity: 'In a word, universal history is not only retrospective, it is also contingent, singular, ironic, and critical' (AO, 140).
2. See Mireille Buydens, *Sahara: l'esthétique de Gilles Deleuze* (Paris: Vrin, 1990). Buydens regards the events of '68 as crucial for Deleuze, in that they represent a practical experiment in 'becoming' which remains relevant despite the fact that the '68 movement arguably had only minor political impact (p. 168).
3. Critics have been swift to condemn Deleuze and Guattari for this perceived celebration of the schizophrenic. See, for example, Peter Hallward, 'Deleuze and the Redemption from Interest', *Radical Philosophy*, no. 81 (Jan–February 1997): 'The artist-schizophrenic has absolutely nothing to learn *from* the world. There is nowhere the artist has not already been.'
4. See Brian Massumi, *A User's Guide to Capitalism and Schizophrenia: Deviations from Deleuze and Guattari* (London: MIT Press, 1992), p. 3.

5. See Ronald Bogue, *Deleuze and Guattari* (London: Routledge, 1989):

> [...] their vociferations against the Oedipus complex, no doubt timely in France in 1972, and perhaps proportionate in vehemence to their opponents' strength, seem at times excessive and redundant, once removed from that context. One wonders, in fact whether the dominance of French psychoanalysis did not lead Deleuze and Guattari to accord the Oedipus complex too important a role in the modern psyche [...]. (p. 104)

6. See Michel Foucault, 'A verdade e as formas juridicas' ['La Vérité et les formes juridiques'], in Michel Foucault, *Dits et écrits 1954–1988*, vol II: 1970–75 (Paris: Gallimard, 1994), pp. 538–645.
7. Ibid., pp. 570.
8. Ibid., pp. 554–5.
9. Philip Goodchild, *Deleuze and Guattari: An Introduction to the Politics of Desire* (London: Sage, 1996), p. 99.
10. Arthur Miller, *Timebends: A Life* (London: Methuen, 1987), p. 184.
11. Foucault, 'A verdade es as formas juridicas', p. 624.
12. Brian Massumi, *A User's Guide ...*, p. 92.
13. See Michel Foucault, *The Order of Things*, trans. Alan Sheridan (London: Tavistock, 1971). Foucault acknowledges the influence of Borges' imaginary Chinese encyclopedia, which suggests that a classificatory system which seems disphasic to Western culture may be perfectly reasonable for another culture.
14. Jean-François Lyotard, 'Capitalisme énergumène', *Critique*, no. 306 (1972), pp. 923–56. Translated as 'Energumen Capitalism', in *Semiotext(e)*, vol. 2, no. 3 (1977), pp. 11–26.
15. Bogue, *Deleuze and Guattari*, p. 94.
16. See Gilles Deleuze, 'Le "je me souviens" de Gilles Deleuze', *Le Nouvel Observateur*, no. 1619 (16–22 novembre 1995), pp. 50–1. Deleuze considered this book to be his greatest achievement (p. 50).
17. Jean-Jacques Lecercle, *The Violence of Language* (London: Routledge, 1990).
18. Ibid., pp. 41–2.
19. Ibid., pp. 45–6. See also Ronald Bogue, *Deleuze and Guattari* (Routledge: London, 1989), pp. 137–8.
20. Lecercle, *The Violence of Language*, p. 47.
21. Brian Massumi, *A User's Guide ...*, pp. 41–6.
22. Ibid., p. 31.
23. Ibid., p. 33.

24. On Dos Passos' 'cinematic' technique, see *Cinema 2*, p. 182.
25. For a discussion of Bakhtin and 'polyphonic' subjectivity, see Félix Guattari, *Chaosmosis*, trans. Paul Bains and Julian Pefanis (Bloomington & Indianapolis: Indiana University Press, 1995), pp. 13–18.
26. Don DeLillo, *Libra* (London: Penguin, 1988), p. 202.

Chapter 6

1. Pierre Klossowski, 'Digression à partir d'un portrait apocryphe', *L'Arc*, 49 (1972), p. 11.
2. See Michel Foucault, 'Les Rapports du pouvoir passent à l'intérieur du corps', interview with Lucette Finas, *La Quinzaine littéraire*, no. 247 (1–15 January 1977), p. 6. Translated as 'The History of Sexuality', in Colin Gordon, ed., *Power/Knowledge: Selected Interviews and Other Writings, 1972–1977*, translated by Leo Marshall (Brighton: Harvester, 1980), pp. 183–93.
3. Didier Eribon, *Foucault*, translated by Betsy Wing (London: Faber & Faber, 1992), p. 62.
4. Ibid., pp. 136–8. It perhaps gives some insight into the political climate of the time that Deleuze was apparently the unanimous choice of Foucault and his colleagues to succeed Jules Vuillemin in the philosophy department at Clermont. However, the post went to Roger Garaudy, a member of the political bureau of the Communist party. It was rumoured that Georges Pompidou requested the appointment of Garaudy, who subsequently bore the brunt of Foucault's anger throughout his time at Clermont. See also David Macey, *The Lives of Michel Foucault* (London: Hutchinson, 1993), pp. 109–10.
5. See Macey, *The Lives of Michel Foucault*, pp. 152–3. The papers of Deleuze and Foucault were both published in the conference proceedings: Gilles Deleuze, 'Conclusions: Sur la volonté de puissance et l'éternel retour', in *Cahiers de Royaumont: Philosophie # VI: Nietzsche* (Paris: Minuit, 1967), pp. 275–7; Michel Foucault, 'Nietzsche, Freud, Marx', in *Cahiers de Royaumont: Philosophie # VI: Nietzsche* (Paris: Minuit, 1967), pp. 183–220.
6. See Macey, *The Lives of Michel Foucault*, pp. 153–4. Deleuze and Foucault were the general editors of the French side of a joint French-Italian-Dutch project based on research in the Weimar archive. On the subject of this project, see Interview with Claude Jannoud, 'Michel Foucault et Gilles Deleuze veulent rendre à Nietzsche son vrai visage', *Le Figaro littéraire* (15 septembre 1966), p. 7.

7. Gilles Deleuze and Michel Foucault, 'Introduction générale', Friedrich Nietzsche, *Le Gai savoir, et fragments posthumes*, translated by Pierre Klossowski (Paris: Gallimard, 1967), pp. i–iv.
8. See Gilles Deleuze, 'The Intellectual and Politics: Foucault and the Prison', Interview with Paul Rabinow and Keith Gandal, *History of the Present* 2 (Spring 1986), pp. 1–2.
9. See Gilles Deleuze and Michel Foucault, 'Les intellectuels et le pouvoir', *L'Arc* 49: *Deleuze* (1972), pp. 3–10. Translated as 'Intellectuals and Power', in *Michel Foucault: Language, Counter-Memory, Practice*, edited by Donald F. Bouchard, translated by Donald F. Bouchard and Sherry Simon (Ithaca: Cornell University Press, 1977), pp. 205–17. Also published in *Telos*, no. 16 (Summer 1973), pp. 103–9. See also Didier Eribon, *Foucault*, pp. 258–9.
10. David Macey, 'Gilles Deleuze, mille Deleuze', *Radical Philosophy* (March/April 1996), p. 6.
11. Macey, *The Lives of Michel Foucault*, p. 392.
12. See Michel Foucault, 'Va-t-on extrader Klaus Croissant?' *Le Nouvel Observateur*, no. 678 (14 novembre 1977), pp. 62–3.
13. See Eribon, *Foucault*, pp. 260–1. Eribon refers to Claude Mauriac, *Le Temps immobile*, vol. IX: *Mauriac et fils* (Paris: Grasset, 1986), p. 388.
14. See Gilles Deleuze, 'Gilles Deleuze contre les "nouveaux philosophes"', *Le Monde* (19–20 juin 1977), p. 19. Reprinted in Sylvie Bouscasse and Denis Bourgeois, eds, *Faut-il brûler les nouveaux philosophes?* (Paris: Nouvelles Editions Oswald, 1978), pp. 186–94.
15. When questioned directly about the concepts that he 'shared' with Foucault, Deleuze suggests several possibilities (see N, 89–90). He thinks that Foucault may have been influenced by *Difference and Repetition*, and that the concept of 'l'agencement' may have had some influence on Foucault's concept of 'le dispositif'. As for Foucault's influence on Deleuze, the latter admits to being struck by the 'new pragmatics of language' implied by the concept of 'l'énoncé' (the 'statement').
16. Michel Foucault, 'Entretien avec Roger-Pol Droit', *Le Monde* (16 September 1986). Translated by Alan Sheridan as 'The Functions of Literature', in Lawrence D. Kritzman, ed., *Philosophy, Politics, Culture: Interviews and Other Writings 1977–84* (London: Routledge, 1988), p. 312.
17. Michel Foucault, 'Le Retour de la Morale', interview with Gilles Barbedette and André Scala, *Les Nouvelles* (28 June – 5 July 1984), pp. 36–41. Translated by Thomas Levin and Isabelle

Lorenz as 'The Return of Morality', in *Philosophy, Politics, and Culture*, p. 251.

18. Michel Foucault, 'A verdade e as formas juridicas' ['La Vérité et les formes juridiques'], in Michel Foucault, *Dits et écrits 1954–1988*, vol II: 1970–1975 (Paris: Gallimard, 1994), pp. 554–5.
19. For a useful discussion of the importance of Nietzsche in Foucault's work, see Keith Ansell-Pearson, 'The Significance of Michel Foucault's Reading of Nietzsche', in Peter R. Sedgwick, ed., *Nietzsche: A Critical Reader* (Oxford: Blackwell, 1995), pp. 13–30.
20. Ibid., p. 17.
21. See Michel Foucault, *Power/Knowledge: Selected Interviews and Other Writings*, Colin Gordon, ed. (Brighton: Harvester Press, 1980), p. 95.
22. Ansell-Pearson, 'The Significance of Michel Foucault's Reading of Nietzsche', p. 18.
23. Michel Foucault, 'Theatrum philosophicum', *Critique*, no. 282 (1970), pp. 885–908. Translated as 'Intellectuals and Power,' in *Michel Foucault: Language, Counter-Memory, Practice*, edited by Donald F. Bouchard, translated by Donald F. Bouchard and Sherry Simon (Ithaca: Cornell University Press, 1977), pp. 165–96.
24. Judith Revel, 'Foucault lecteur de Deleuze: de l'écart à la différence', *Critique*, nos. 591–2 (août–septembre 1996), pp. 727–35.
25. Revel claims that in *Madness and Civilisation, The Order of Things* and *The Archaeology of Knowledge* Foucault remained, perhaps despite himself, trapped within a dialectical framework in which he looks at the way in which reason defines itself by the careful management of difference.
26. Foucault, 'Theatrum philosophicum', p. 185.
27. See Michel Foucault, *L'Usage des plaisirs* (Paris, 1984). Translated by Robert Hurley as *The Use of Pleasure* (Harmondsworth: Penguin, 1985).
28. Michel Foucault, 'Réponse à une question', *Esprit*, 371 (1968), 850–74. Translated as 'Politics and the Study of Discourse', translated by Colin Gordon in Graham Burchell, Colin Gordon and Peter Miller, eds, *The Foucault Effect: Studies in Governmentality* (Hemel Hempstead: Harvester, 1991), pp. 53–72.
29. Michel Foucault, *Surveiller et punir: naissance de la prison* (Paris: Gallimard, 1975). Translated by A.M. Sheridan-Smith as *The Birth of the Prison* (Harmondsworth: Penguin, 1977).
30. Michel Foucault, *Histoire de la sexualité*, vol. 1: *La Volonté de savoir* (Paris: Gallimard, 1976). Translated by Robert Hurley

as *The History of Sexuality: An Introduction* (Harmondsworth: Penguin, 1978).

31. Gilles Deleuze, 'Désir et plaisir', *Magazine littéraire*, no. 325 (octobre 1994), pp. 57–65. (Includes a short introduction by François Ewald.)
32. Ibid., p. 59.
33. For a useful discussion of the translation and meaning of Foucault's 'dispositifs' and Deleuze's 'agencements' see Martin Joughin's Translator's Notes in *Negotiations* (pp. 196–7 no. 9.). Joughin considers 'dispositif' to be more 'mechanical' than 'agencement'.
34. Deleuze, 'Désir et plaisir', p. 60.
35. Ibid., p. 63.
36. Ibid., p. 64.
37. In *Negotiations* Deleuze points to the fact that Foucault's 'crisis' was most probably the result of various factors:

    [...] the eventual failure of the prison movement; on another level, the collapse of more recent hopes, Iran, Poland; the way Foucault became ever more dissatisfied with French social and cultural life; in his work, the feeling of growing misunderstandings about the first volume of *The History of Sexuality* [...] a feeling that he had himself reached an impasse, that he needed solitude and strength to deal with something relating not only to his thought but also to his life. (p. 109)

38. See David Macey, *The Lives of Michel Foucault*, pp. 387–9. Macey refers to a conversation between Claude Mauriac and Foucault in 1977, reported in the former's memoirs. Foucault felt that his generation had been 'cowardly' in tacitly accepting the Gulag Archipelago, and he also thought that it was now 'too late' to retrieve anything useful from Marxism. Macey sums up Foucault's position at this time:

    Foucault's political evolution was intersecting with that of the new philosophers. His own 'leftist' period was over, his disillusionment with marxism was complete and he was moving into a political arena dominated by dissidence and human rights. The political constellation in which he moved was also changing. It was widely claimed that his work, and particularly the theory of power elaborated in *Surveiller et punir*, had prepared the ground for the new philosophers. (p. 388)

39. Michel Foucault, 'La Vie des hommes infâmes', *Cahiers du chemin*, no. 29 (15 janvier 1977), pp. 19–29. Translated by Paul Foss and Meaghan Morris as 'The Life of Infamous

Men', in Foss and Morris, eds, *Power, Truth, Strategy* (Sydney: Feral, 1979), pp. 76–91.
40. Michel Foucault, *The Use of Pleasure*, pp. 8–9.

Chapter 7

1. Samuel Beckett, *Disjecta: Miscellaneous Writings and a Dramatic Fragment*, edited by Ruby Cohn (London: John Calder, 1983), p. 172.
2. Gilles Deleuze, 'Literature and Life', translated by Daniel W. Smith and Michael A. Greco, *Critical Enquiry*, vol. 23 (Winter 1997), p. 229.
3. See Gilles Deleuze, *L'Abécédaire de Gilles Deleuze* (Editions Montparnasse, 1997), 'S comme style'.
4. Jack Kerouac, *Big Sur* (London: Flamingo, 1993), p. 165.
5. Deleuze, 'Literature and Life', p. 225.
6. See Deleuze, 'Literature and Life', p. 226. See also Gilles Deleuze, 'The Exhausted', translated by Christian Kerslake, *Parallax*, no. 3 (September, 1996), pp. 113–35. Here, in a piece written as an accompaniment to Samuel Beckett's plays for television, Deleuze draws directly on Beckett's comments on language in *Disjecta*. In some ways, the very use of words mediates against this force of the impersonal, which lends itself more to art-forms such as music. Language must be dissolved so that the void is visible, so that the statement becomes impersonal, indirect:

   > It is not only that words are liars; they are so marked with calculations and significations, not to mention with intentions, personal memories and old habits which have cemented, that if a breach does occur in their surface it closes up again immediately. It congeals. It imprisons and suffocates us. Music manages to transform the death of a young girl into *a young girl dies*, it effects an extreme determination of the indefinite as a pure intensity which pierces the surface, as in [Berg's] 'Concerto to the memory of an angel'. (p. 131)

7. See Deleuze 'Literature and Life', pp. 227–9.
8. Ibid., p. 228.
9. Ibid., p. 227.
10. Ibid., p. 228.
11. Louis Wolfson, *Le Schizo et les langues* (Paris: Gallimard, 1971). Deleuze's preface also appears in revised form in *Critique et clinique*.
12. See Jean-Philippe Mathy, *Extrême-Occident: French Intellectuals and America* (University of Chicago Press, 1993), pp. 187–91.

13. Paul Auster, *The Art of Hunger: Essays, Prefaces, Interviews and The Red Notebook* (Harmondsworth: Penguin, 1993), p. 271.
14. Deleuze, 'Literature and Life', p. 228.
15. Jack Kerouac, *On the Road* (Harmondsworth: Penguin, 1972), p. 20.
16. Leslie Fiedler, *The Return of the Vanishing American* (London: Jonathan Cape, 1968).
17. See TP, '[...] the West, however, played the role of a line of flight combining travel, hallucination, madness, the Indians, perceptive and mental experimentation, the shifting of frontiers, the rhizome (Ken Kesey and his "fog machine," the beat generation, etc.)' (p. 520 n. 18).
18. Deleuze changed the title of *Marcel Proust et les signes* to *Proust et les signes* for the second and third editions – the English translation is based on the second edition – and made two major additions to the original book. For the second edition in 1970 he added five chapters which constitute a second part entitled 'La Machine littéraire', and in 1976 he added a conclusion, 'Présence et fonction de la folie, l'Arraignée'.
19. See Arnaud Villani, 'Méthode et théorie dans l'œuvre de Gilles Deleuze', *Les Temps modernes*, no. 586 (jan.–fèv. 1996), p. 151–2. Villani quotes from a letter written to him by Deleuze.
20. Ronald Bogue, *Deleuze and Guattari* (London: Routledge, 1989), p. 54.
21. Deleuze first published an article on Tournier's *Vendredi* in the 1960s: 'Une Théorie d'autrui (autrui, Robinson et le pervers)', *Critique*, no. 241 (1967), pp. 503–25. This appeared in English as 'Michel Tournier and the World without Others', trans. Graham Burchell, *Economy and Society*, vol. 13, no. 1 (1984), pp. 257–83. The essay was also published in revised form as an appendix to *The Logic of Sense* and as a 'postface' to a later edition of Michel Tournier, *Vendredi ou les limbes du pacifique* (Paris: Gallimard, 1972), pp. 257–83.
22. Moira Gatens, 'Through a Spinozist Lens: Ethology, Difference, Power', in Paul Patton, ed., *Deleuze: A Critical Reader* (Oxford: Blackwell, 1996), pp. 162–85.

Chapter 8

1. Gilles Deleuze, 'Portrait du philosophe en spectateur', Interview with Hervé Guibert, *Le Monde* (6 octobre 1983), pp. 1, 17.
2. Richard Dienst, *Still Life in Real Time: Theory after Television* (Durham and London: Duke University Press, 1994), p. 145.
3. Deleuze, 'Portrait du philosophe en spectateur', p. 17.

4. Paul Patton, 'Review of *Cinema 1* & *Cinema 2*', *Screen*, vol. 32, no. 2 (Summer 1991), p. 239.
5. The work of Charles Sanders Peirce informs much of Deleuze's work on cinema, but it is also generally important for an understanding of Deleuze's general approach to signs, semiotics and language. Peirce's rather enigmatic career would apparently make him ideally suited to be incorporated into Deleuze's alternative 'canon' of untimely philosophers. His work was largely neglected during his own life, and he spent the last twenty years of his life in a reduced state of poverty and neglect. Peirce, who was a member of the 'Metaphysical Club' with William James at Harvard in the 1870s, is sometimes thought of as the father of semiotics. He is also closely associated with the so-called New England pragmatist school of the late nineteenth century. Deleuze's interest in, and use of, Peirce's work centres on his non-linguistic conception of semiotics. Rather than opt for a linguistic approach, Peirce attempts to show how signs work at the heart of all human activity, particularly in the domain of thought itself. According to Peirce's triadic structure, signification is never the product of a simple relation between that sign and that which it signifies. It is rather the case that a sign is a function of an object and an 'interpretant'. The fact that the elements of this triadic structure may refer to other signs, and so on, means that meaning can never be finally fixed. Interpretation, the search to attribute meaning, becomes, therefore, an infinite process. In this way, Peirce can be considered as a poststructuralist *avant la lettre*.
6. See Alison Butler, 'New Film Histories and the Politics of Location', *Screen*, vol. 33, no. 4 (Winter 1992), pp. 413–27. Butler accuses Deleuze of basing his historical framework on a European, if not French, view of the postwar world. The periodisation of American cinema is consequently vague.
7. Deleuze, 'Portrait du philosophe en spectateur', p. 17.
8. Henri Bergson, *Creative Evolution*, p. 306.
9. In *Cinema 2* Deleuze extends these three categories to six: perception-image, affection-image, impulse-image, action-image, reflection-image, relation-image (C2, 32).
10. Eric Rohmer and Claude Chabrol, *Hitchcock* (Paris: Éditions d'aujourd'hui, 1957).
11. Andrey Tarkovsky, *Sculpting in Time: Reflections on the Cinema*, translated by Kitty Hunter-Blair (London: Faber & Faber, 1989).
12. Ibid., p. 62.
13. See Michel Chion, 'La maison où il pleut', *Cahiers du cinéma*, no. 358 (avril 1984), pp. 37–43.

14. Marcel Proust, *In Search of Lost Time: 6 Time Regained*, translated by C.K. Scott Montcrieff and Terence Kilmartin, revised by D.J. Enright (Vintage: London, 1992), pp. 290–1.
15. Tarkovsky, 'Sculpting in Time', p. 83.
16. Ibid., pp. 117–18.
17. Pier Paolo Pasolini, 'The Cinema of Poetry', in *Movies and Methods: Volume 1* (London: University of California Press, 1976), pp. 542–58.
18. Dienst, *Still Life in Real Time*, p. 150.
19. Ibid., p. 148.
20. Ibid., p. 148.
21. See François Zourabichvili, 'Six Notes on the Percept', in Paul Patton, ed., *Deleuze: A Critical Reader* (Oxford: Blackwell, 1996), p. 201 188–216. See also François Zourabichvili, *Deleuze: Une Philosophie de l'Événement* (Paris: P.U.F., 1994), pp. 5–6 and 116–26.
22. On the perception-image and indirect discourse, see Chapter 5 of *Cinema 1*, 'The perception-image'.
23. Patton, 'Review of *Cinema 1* & *Cinema 2*', p. 238.
24. Peter Hallward, 'Gilles Deleuze and the Redemption from Interest', *Radical Philosophy*, no. 81 (January–February 1997), pp. 6–21. Although it appears in the context of an article which raises generally critical questions with regard to Deleuze's work, Peter Hallward's summary of *Cinema 1* and *Cinema 2* captures something of the philosophical importance of cinema for Deleuze. Hallward argues that Deleuze conceives of cinema as a *literal* form: 'There is no more "in-between" art and life' (p. 15).

Conclusion

1. Gilles Deleuze, 'Le "je me souviens" de Gilles Deleuze', *Le Nouvel Observateur*, no. 1619 (16–22 novembre 1995), pp. 50–1.
2. See Philip Goodchild, 'Deleuzean Ethics', *Theory, Culture and Society*, vol. 14, no. 2 (May 1997), pp. 39–50. As Goodchild argues, Deleuze's ethical philosophy of the event is a theory of 'what we do, not what we are' (p. 39).
3. See Arnaud Villani, 'Méthode et théorie dans l'œuvre de Gilles Deleuze', *Les Temps modernes*, no. 586 (janvier–février 1996), pp. 142–153. Villani argues that Deleuze's philosophy of the event is developed from a 'method' of difference, and that *Difference and Repetition* is the foundation for Deleuze's entire œuvre.

4. Nick Millett, 'The Trick of Singularity', *Theory, Culture and Society*, vol. 14, no. 2 (May 1997), pp. 51–66.
5. Ibid., p. 55.
6. Ibid. Ultimately, Millett argues that the singularity of Deleuze was to extend the practice of free indirect discourse to his life as a thinker. He preferred self-effacement to self-promotion, and became the 'Gulliver' of French philosophy. Millett quotes from Deleuze's fortnightly television appearances on *L'Abécédaire de Gilles Deleuze*: 'what is wonderful about old age is that people leave you alone, society drops you; what bliss! the joy of being dropped by society' (p. 62). *L'Abécédaire de Gilles Deleuze* consisted a series of discussions with Claire Parnet filmed in 1988. The programmes were shown fortnightly from 15 January 1995 on the Franco-German channel *Arte*.
7. Ibid. Millett talks of:

   > [...] the *practice* of 'free indirect discourse' that Deleuze is entranced by in all of his books. This is a strange schizoid mimicry, where allied to the indefinite article is the indefinite third person or the 'fourth person singular', the impersonal instance of an anonymous collectivity of voices which transpire behind an erased subject of the enunciation. (p. 62)

8. Alain Badiou, 'The Fold: Leibniz and the Baroque', in Constantin V. Boundas and Dorothea Olkowski, eds, *Gilles Deleuze and the Theater of Philosophy* (London: Routledge, 1994), p. 64.
9. Kenneth Surin, 'The "Epochality" of Deleuzean Thought', *Theory, Culture and Society*, vol. 14, no. 2 (May 1997), pp. 9–21.
10. Ibid., p. 13.
11. Ibid., p. 15.
12. Jonathan Ree, 'Philosophy for Philosophy's Sake', *New Left Review*, no. 211 (May/June 1995), pp. 105–11.
13. Ibid., p. 105–6.
14. Ibid., p. 111. For a vigorous defence of *What is Philosophy?* as a mature statement of poststructuralist philosophy, see Iain MacKenzie, 'Poststructuralism and Radical Politics', in Iain Hampsher-Monk and Jeffrey Stanyer, eds, *Contemporary Political Studies*, vol. 2 (PSA, 1996), pp. 1234–41. For MacKenzie, Deleuze and Guattari perpetuate a form of post-structuralism which depends not upon relativism but rather 'perspectivism'. By combining the Nietzschean belief that thought is creative with Spinoza's image of thought as 'immanent to itself', and Bergson's 'vitalist ontology of movement as the substance of being', they do not so much deny truth as highlight its irreducible complexity (pp. 1240–1).

15. Peter Hallward, 'Gilles Deleuze and the Redemption from Interest', *Radical Philosophy*, no. 81 (January–February 1997), pp. 6–21.
16. Ibid., p. 6.
17. Ibid., p. 13.
18. Ibid., p. 6.
19. Ibid., p. 10.
20. Ibid., p. 9.
21. Ibid., p. 8.
22. Ibid., p. 12.
23. Ibid., p. 13.
24. Ibid., p. 8.
25. Ibid., p. 18.
26. Alain Badiou, *Deleuze: "La clameur de l'Etre"* (Paris: Hachette, 1997). Beyond the specific question of Deleuze's treatment of the univocity of being, Badiou's intention is, in part at least, to demonstrate that Deleuze produced work which was abstract and 'aristocratic', which modifies the received wisdom of Deleuze as a sort of a vaguely anarchistic thinker. As Badiou puts it, Deleuze's ideal of subjectivity is the philosophical figure, the 'conceptual persona' as it were, of the spiritual automaton, rather than the 'bearded sixty-eighters' who are sometimes seen as Deleuze's audience.
27. Ibid., p. 30.
28. Ibid., p. 42.
29. Paul Patton, 'One of the saints', *Radical Philosophy*, no. 76 (March/April 1996), p. 2.

Bibliography

Books and Articles by Gilles Deleuze

Publications are listed here in order of publication date in the original language. Translations appear immediately after the original publication regardless of publication date.

Empirisme et subjectivité: Essai sur la Nature humaine selon Hume (Paris: Presses Universitaires de France, 1953).

English translation: *Empiricism and Subjectivity: An Essay on Hume's Theory of Human Nature* (Oxford: Columbia University Press, 1991) by Constantin V. Boundas.

'La conception de la différence chez Bergson', *Les Etudes Bergsoniennes*, vol. 4 (1956), pp. 77–112.

Nietzsche et la philosophie (Paris: Presses Universitaires de France, 1962).

English translation: *Nietzsche and Philosophy* (London: Athlone, 1983) by Hugh Tomlinson.

La Philosophie critique de Kant: Doctrine des facultés (Paris: Presses Universitaires de France, 1963).

English translation: *Kant's Critical Philosophy: The Doctrine of the Faculties* (London: Athlone, 1984) by Hugh Tomlinson and Barbara Habberjam.

Marcel Proust et les signes (Paris: Presses Universitaires de France, 1964). Second edition (1970) changes title to *Proust et les signes* and adds a chapter entitled 'La Machine littéraire'. Third edition (1977) adds a chapter entitled 'Présence et fonction de la folie, l'Arraignée'.

English translation: *Proust and Signs* (New York: George Braziller, 1972) by Richard Howard.

'Il a été mon maître' (on Sartre), *Arts* (28 octobre – 3 novembre 1964), pp. 8–9. Reprinted in Jean-Jacques Brochier, *Pour Sartre* (Paris: Éditions Jean-Claude Lattès, 1995), pp. 82–8.

Nietzsche (Paris: Presses Universitaires de France, 1965).

Le Bergsonisme (Paris: Presses Universitaires de France, 1966).

English translation: *Bergsonism* (New York: Zone Books, 1988) by Hugh Tomlinson and Barbara Habberjam.

'L'homme, une existence douteuse' (book review of Foucault's *Les Mots et les choses*), *Le Nouvel Observateur* (1 juin 1966), pp. 32–4.

'Conclusions: Sur la volonté de puissance et l'éternel retour' *Cahiers de Royaumont: Philosophie* #VI: Nietzsche (Paris: Editions de Minuit, 1967), pp. 275–87.

Présentation de Sacher-Masoch (Paris: Editions de Minuit, 1967). Contains 'Le froid et le cruel' by Deleuze and 'Venus à la fourrure' by Sacher-Masoch. Reprinted by 10/18 (Paris, 1974).

English translation: *Masochism* (New York: Zone Books, 1989) by Jean McNeil.

'Une Théorie d'autrui (Autrui, Robinson et le pervers)' (on Michel Tournier's *Vendredi*), *Critique*, no. 241 (1967), pp. 503–25. Reprinted in revised form as an appendix to *Logique du sens* and as a postface to Tournier's *Vendredi ou les limbes du Pacifique* (Paris: Gallimard, 1972), pp. 257–83. Reprinted in *Critique*, nos. 591–2 (août–septembre 1996), pp. 675–97.

'Introduction' to Émile Zola, *La Bête humaine* in *Oeuvres complètes* tome sixième (Paris: Cercle du livre précieux, 1967), edited by Henri Mitterrand, pp. 13–21. Reprinted in revised form as an appendix to *Logique du sens*, and as the préface to the Gallimard edition of *La Bête humaine* (Paris, 1977), pp. 7–24.

With Michel Foucault: 'Introduction générale', to F. Nietzsche, *Le Gai Savoir, et fragments posthumes* (Paris: Gallimard, 1967), pp. i–iv. Nietzsche texts edited by Giorgio Colli and Massimo Montinari and translated by Pierre Klossowski.

'La Méthode de Dramatisation', *Bulletin de la Société française de Philosophie*, vol. 61, no. 3 (juillet–septembre 1967), pp. 89–118. Reprinted in revised form in *Différence et répétition*.

Différence et répétition (Paris: Presses Universitaires de France, 1968).

English translation: *Difference and Repetition* (London: Athlone, 1994) by Paul Patton.

Spinoza et le problème de l'expression (Paris: Editions de Minuit, 1968).

English translation: *Expressionism in Philosophy: Spinoza* (New York: Zone Books, 1990) by Martin Joughin.

Logique du sens (Paris: Editions de Minuit, 1969). Reprinted by 10/18 (Paris, 1973).

English translation: *The Logic of Sense* (London: Athlone, 1990) by Mark Lester with Charles Stivale.

Spinoza: textes choisis (Paris: Presses Universitaires de France, 1970).

'Schizologie'. Preface to Louis Wolfson, *Le Schizo et les langues* (Paris: Gallimard, 1970) pp. 5–23.

With Félix Guattari: *Capitalisme et schizophrénie tome 1: l'Anti-Oedipe* (Paris: Editions de Minuit, 1972). Second edition (1973) adds 'Bilan-programme pour machines-désirantes' as an appendix.

English translation: *Anti-Oedipus: Capitalism and Schizophrenia* (London: Athlone, 1984) by Robert Hurley, Mark Seem and Helen R. Lane. Preface by Michel Foucault.

'A quoi reconnait-on le structuralisme?' in François Châtelet, ed., *Histoire de la philosophie tome 8: Le XXe siècle* (Paris: Hachette, 1972), pp. 299–335.

With Michel Foucault: 'Les Intellectuals et le pouvoir', *L'Arc*, no. 49: *Deleuze* (1972), pp. 3–10. Reprinted in 1980.

English translation: 'Intellectuals and Power', in Foucault, *Language, Counter-Memory, Practice* (Ithaca: Cornell University Press, 1977) edited by Donald F. Bouchard, translated by Donald F. Bouchard and Sherry Simon, pp. 205–17. Also published in *Telos*, no. 16 (Summer 1973), pp. 103–9.

'Ce que les prisonniers attendent de nous ...' (on the Groupe d'Information sur les Prisons), *Le Nouvel Observateur* (31 janvier, 1972), p. 24.

'Pensée nomade' (with discussion), in *Nietzsche aujourd'hui? tome 1: Intensités* (Paris: 10/18, 1973), pp. 105–21, 159–90.

English translation: 'Nomad Thought' (without discussion) in David B. Allison, ed., *The New Nietzsche: Contemporary Styles of Interpretation* (New York: Dell, 1977) by David B. Allison, pp. 142–9. Also published in *Semiotext(e)* 3:1 (1978), pp. 12–20.

Preface to Guy Hocquenghem, *L'Après-Mai des Faunes* (Paris: Grasset, 1974), pp. 7–17.

With Félix Guattari: *Kafka: Pour une littérature mineure* (Paris: Editions de Minuit, 1975).

English translation: *Kafka: Toward a Minor Literature* (Minneapolis: University of Minnesota Press, 1986) by Dana Polan. Foreword by Réda Bensmaïa.

With Félix Guattari: *Rhizome: Introduction* (Paris: Editions de Minuit, 1976). Reprinted in revised form in *Capitalisme et schizophrenie tome 2: Mille plateaux* (1980).

English translation: 'Rhizome', *Ideology and Consciousness*, no. 8 (Spring 1981) by Paul Foss and Paul Patton. Also translated by John Johnston in Deleuze and Guattari, *On the Line* (New York: *Semiotext(e)*, 1983).

With Claire Parnet: *Dialogues* (Paris: Flammarion, 1977).

English translation: *Dialogues* (London: Athlone, 1987) by Hugh Tomlinson and Barbara Habberjam.

'Gilles Deleuze contre les "nouveaux philosophes"', (interview) in *Le Monde* (19–20 juin 1977), p. 19. Reprinted in *Faut-il brûler les nouveaux philosophes?* (Paris: Nouvelles Editions Oswald, 1978), pp. 186–94, as 'A propos des nouveaux philosophes et d'un problème plus général'.

With Félix Guattari: 'Le pire moyen de faire l'Europe' (on Klaus Croissant and the Baader-Meinhof group), *Le Monde* (2 novembre 1977), p. 6.

With Carmelo Bene: *Superpositions* (Paris: Editions de Minuit, 1979). Contains 'Un manifeste de moins' by Deleuze, pp. 85–131.

English translation: 'One Manifesto Less', in C.V. Boundas, ed., *The Deleuze Reader* (New York & Oxford: Columbia University Press, 1993), pp. 204–22. By Alan Orenstein.

With Fanny Deleuze: 'Nietzsche et Paulus, Lawrence et Jean de Patmos', preface to D.H. Lawrence, *Apocalypse* (Paris: Balland, 1978), pp. 7–37. Lawrence text translated by Fanny Deleuze. Reprinted in revised form in *Critique et clinique* (1993).

'Philosophie et Minorité', *Critique*, vol. 34, no. 369 (février 1978), pp. 154–55.

With Félix Guattari: *Capitalisme et schizophrénie tome 2: Mille plateaux* (Paris: Editions de Minuit, 1980).

English translation: *A Thousand Plateaus: Capitalism and Schizophrenia* (Minneapolis: University of Minnesota Press, 1987) by Brian Massumi.

Spinoza: Philosophie pratique (Paris: Editions de Minuit, 1981). Expanded reprint of *Spinoza: textes choisis* (1970)

English translation: *Spinoza: Practical Philosophy* (San Francisco: City Lights, 1988) by Robert Hurley.

Francis Bacon: Logique de la Sensation (Paris: Editions de la Différence, 1981). The first volume contains Deleuze's text; the second contains reproductions of Bacon's paintings.

Forthcoming English translation: *Francis Bacon: The Logic of Sensation* (publisher uncertain) by Daniel W. Smith.

'La peinture enflamme l'écriture' (interview by Hervé Guibert), *Le Monde* (3 décembre 1981), p. 15.

English translation: 'What counts is the scream', *The Guardian* (January 10, 1982).

Preface to Antonio Negri, *L'Anomalie sauvage: Puissance et pouvoir chez Spinoza* (Paris: Presses Universitaires de France, 1982), pp. 9–12.

Cinéma-1: L'Image-mouvement (Paris: Editions de Minuit, 1983).

English translation: *Cinema 1: The Movement-Image* (London: Athlone, 1986) by Hugh Tomlinson and Barbara Habberjam.

'Cinéma-1, première' (interview by Serge Daney), and 'Le Philosophe menuisier' (interview by Didier Eribon), *Libération* (3 octobre 1983), pp. 30–1.

'Portrait du philosophe en spectateur' (interview by Hervé Guibert), *Le Monde* (6 octobre 1983), pp. 1, 17.

With François Châtelet and Félix Guattari: 'Pour un droit d'asile politique un et indivisible', *Le Nouvel Observateur*, no. 1041 (octobre 1984), p. 18.

Cinéma-2: L'Image-temps (Paris: Editions de Minuit, 1985).
English translation: *Cinema 2: The Time-Image* (London: Athlone, 1989) by Hugh Tomlinson and Robert Galeta.
'Il etait une étoile de groupe' (on François Châtelet's death), *Libération* (27 décembre 1985), pp. 21–2.
Foucault (Paris: Editions de Minuit, 1986).
English translation: *Foucault* (Minneapolis: University of Minnesota Press, 1988) by Seán Hand. Foreword by Paul Bové.
'Le cerveau, c'est l'écran' (interview by A. Bergala, Pascal Bonitzer, M. Chevrie, Jean Narboni, C. Tesson and S. Toubiana), *Cahiers du cinéma*, no. 380 (February 1986), pp. 25–32.
'The Intellectual and Politics: Foucault and the Prison' (interview by Paul Rabinow and Keith Gandal), *History of the Present*, vol. 2 (Spring 1986), pp. 1–2, 20–1.
Le Pli: Leibniz et le Baroque (Paris: Editions de Minuit, 1988).
English translation: *The Fold: Leibniz and the Baroque* (Minneapolis: University of Minnesota Press, 1993). Foreword and translation by Tom Conley.
Périclès et Verdi: La philosophie de François Châtelet (Paris: Editions de Minuit, 1988).
'A Philosophical Concept ...', *Topoi*, vol. 7, no. 2 (September 1988), p. 111–12. Reprinted in E. Cadava, ed., *Who Comes After the Subject?* (New York: Routledge, 1991). Translated by Julien Deleuze.
'Qu'est-ce qu'un dispositif?' in *Michel Foucault philosophe, Rencontre internationale Paris 9, 10, 11 janvier 1988* (Paris: Seuil, 1989), pp. 185–95.
English translation: 'What is a dispositif?' in *Michel Foucault Philosopher* (New York: Routledge, 1992) by Timothy J. Armstrong, pp. 159–68.
Pourparlers 1972–1990 (Paris: Editions de Minuit, 1990).
English translation: *Negotiations 1972–1990* (New York: Columbia University Press, 1995) by Martin Joughin.
With Pierre Bourdieu, Jérôme Lindon and Pierre Vidal-Naquet: 'Adresse au gouvernement français' (on Operation Desert Shield), *Libération* (5 septembre 1990), p. 6.
With René Scherer: 'La guerre immonde' (on the Persian Gulf War), *Libération* (4 mars 1991), p. 11.
With Félix Guattari: *Qu'est-ce que la philosophie?* (Paris: Editions de Minuit, 1991).
English translation: *What is Philosophy?* (London: Verso, 1994) by Hugh Tomlinson and Graham Burchell.
With Félix Guattari: 'Secret de fabrication: Deleuze-Guattari: Nous Deux' (interview by Robert Maggiori), *Libération* (12 septembre 1991), pp. 17–19. Reprinted in Maggiori, *La Philosophie au jour le jour* (Paris: Flammarion, 1994), pp. 374–81.

With Félix Guattari: 'Nous avons inventé la ritornelle' (interview by Didier Eribon), in *Le Nouvel Observateur* (12–18 septembre 1991), pp. 109–10.

Quad et autre pièces pour la télévision, suivi de L'Epuisé (Paris: Editions de Minuit, 1992). Contains four pieces by Beckett and 'L'Epuisé' by Deleuze, pp. 55–112.

English translation: 'The Exhausted', with an introduction by Christian Kerslake, *parallax*, no. 3 (September 1996). Also translated by Anthony Uhlmann in *SubStance*, no. 78 (1995), pp. 3–28.

'Lettre-préface', to Jean-Clet Martin, *Variations: La Philosophie de Gilles Deleuze* (Paris: Editions Payot, 1993) pp. 7–9.

Critique et clinique (Paris: Editions de Minuit, 1993).

'Désir et plaisir', *Magazine littéraire*, no. 325 (octobre 1994), pp. 59–65. A series of notes on Foucault's *La Volonté de savoir.*

'L'immanence: une vie ...', *Philosophie*, no. 47 (septembre 1995), pp. 3–7.

'Le "Je me souviens" de Gilles Deleuze', interview with Didier Eribon, *Le Nouvel Observateur*, no. 1619 (16–22 novembre 1995), pp. 50–51.

'Fragment d'un texte inédit', *Cahiers du Cinéma*, no. 497 (décembre 1995), p. 28.

'L'Actuel et le virtuel', appendix to second edition of Deleuze and Parnet, *Dialogues* (Paris: Flammarion, 1996) pp. 177–85.

Gilles Deleuze and Claire Parnet, *L'Abécédaire de Gilles Deleuze* (Paris: Editions de Montparnasse, 1997).

Other Sources

Allison, David, ed., *The New Nietzsche* (New York: Dell, 1977).

Auster, Paul, *The Red Notebook: Essays, Prefaces, Interviews and The Red Notebook* (Harmondsworth: Penguin, 1993).

Badiou, Alain, *Deleuze: "La clameur de l'Etre"* (Paris: Hachette, 1997).

Baugh, Bruce, 'Deleuze and Empiricism', *Journal of the British Society for Phenomenology*, vol. 24, no. 1 (January 1993), pp. 15–31.

Beckett, Samuel, *Disjecta: Miscellaneous Writings and a Dramatic Fragment*, edited by Ruby Cohn (London: John Calder, 1983).

Bergson, Henri, *Introduction to Metaphysics*, translated by T.E. Hulme (London: Macmillan, 1910).

——, *Creative Evolution*, translated by A. Mitchell (New York: Henry Holt, 1911).

Bogue, Ronald, *Deleuze and Guattari* (London: Routledge, 1989).

Boundas, Constantin V. and Dorothea Olkowski, eds, *Gilles Deleuze and the Theater of Philosophy* (London: Routledge, 1994).

Burchell, Graham, Colin Gordon and Peter Miller, eds, *The Foucault Effect: Studies in Governmentality. With Two Lectures and an Interview with Michel Foucault* (London: Harvester Wheatsheaf, 1991).

Burwick Frederick, and Paul Douglass, eds, *The Crisis in Modernism: Bergson and the Vitalist Controversy* (Cambridge: Cambridge University Press, 1992).

Butler, Alison, 'New Film Histories and the Politics of Location', *Screen*, vol. 33, no. 4 (Winter 1992), pp. 413–27.

Buydens, Mireille, *Sahara: l'esthétique de Gilles Deleuze* (Paris: Vrin, 1990).

Chabrol, Claude and Rohmer, Eric, *Hitchcock* (Paris: Editions d'aujourd'hui, 1957).

Chion, Michel, 'La maison où il pleut', *Cahiers du Cinéma* no. 358 (avril 1984), pp. 37–43.

Colombat, André Pierre,'A Thousand Trails', *SubStance*, no. 66 (1991).

Cressole, Michel, *Deleuze* (Paris: Editions Universitaires, 1973).

DeLillo, Don, *Libra* (London: Penguin, 1988).

Derrida, Jacques, *Spectres de Marx* (Paris: Editions Galilée, 1993). *Specters of Marx: The State of Debt, the Work of Mourning, & the New International*, translated by Peggy Kamuf (London: Routledge, 1994).

Deschamps, Christian, et al., 'Dossier: Gilles Deleuze', *La Quinzaine littéraire* (1–15 février 1996), pp. 16–24.

Descombes, Vincent, *Le Même et l'autre: quarante-cinq ans de philosophie française* (Paris: Minuit, 1979). *Modern French Philosophy*, translated by L. Scott-Fox and J.M. Harding (Cambridge: Cambridge University Press, 1980).

Dienst, Richard, *Still Life in Real Time: Theory after Television* (Durham and London: Duke University Press, 1994).

Engel, Pascal, 'La philosophie analytique peut-elle être française?', *Magazine littéraire*, no. 339 (janvier 1996), pp. 47–51.

Eribon, Didier, *Michel Foucault* (Paris: Flammarion, 1989). *Michel Foucault*, translated by Betsy Wing (London: Faber & Faber, 1992).

Fiedler, Leslie, *The Return of the Vanishing American* (London: Jonathan Cape, 1968).

Foucault, Michel, *Les Mots et les choses: une archéologie des sciences humaines* (Paris: Gallimard, 1966). *The Order of Things*, no translator identified (London: Tavistock, 1970).

——, 'Nietzsche, Freud, Marx', *Cahiers de Royaumont 6: Nietzsche* (Paris: Minuit, 1967), pp. 183–207.

——, *L'Archéologie du savoir* (Paris: Gallimard, 1969). *The Archaeology of Knowledge*, translated by A.M. Sheridan-Smith (London: Tavistock, 1972)

——, *L'Ordre du discours* (Paris: Gallimard, 1971). 'The Order of Discourse', translated by Ian McLeod, in R. Young, ed., *Untying the Text: A Poststructuralist Reader* (London: Routledge, 1981), pp. 48–78.

——, *Surveiller et punir: naissance de la prison* (Paris: Gallimard, 1975). *Discipline and Punish: The Birth of the Prison* (Harmondsworth: Penguin, 1977).

——, *Language, Counter-Memory, Practice*, edited by Donald F. Bouchard, translated by Donald F. Bouchard and Sherry Simon (Ithaca: Cornell University Press, 1977).

——, 'Va-t-on extrader Klaus Croissant?' *Le Nouvel Observateur*, no. 678 (14 novembre 1977), pp. 62–3.

——, *Power, Truth, Strategy* (Sydney: Feral, 1979).

——, *Power Knowledge: Selected Interviews and Other Writings, 1972–1977*, edited by Colin Gordon (Brighton: Harvester, 1980).

——, *Histoire de la sexualité*, vol. 2: *L'Usage des plaisirs* (Paris: Gallimard, 1984). *The Use of Pleasure*, translated by Robert Hurley (Harmondsworth: Penguin, 1985).

——, *Philosophy, Politics, Culture: Interviews and other Writings 1977–84*, edited with an introduction by Lawrence D. Kritzman (London: Routledge, 1988).

——, 'A verdade e as formas juridicas' ['La Vérité et les formes juridiques'], in Michel Foucault, *Dits et écrits 1954–1988*, vol. II: 1970–1975 (Paris: Gallimard, 1994), pp. 538–645.

George, Michael, 'Marx's Hegelianism', in David Lamb, ed., *Hegel and Modern Philosophy* (Beckenham: Croom Helm, 1987), pp. 119–42.

Goodchild, Philip, *Deleuze and Guattari: An Introduction to the Politics of Desire* (London: Sage Publications, 1996).

Goodchild, Philip, *Gilles Deleuze: And the Question of Philosophy* (London: Associated University Presses, 1996).

——, 'Deleuzean Ethics', *Theory, Culture and Society*, vol. 14, no. 2 (May 1977), pp. 39–50.

Guattari, Félix, *Chaosmose* (Paris: Galilée, 1992). *Chaosmosis: an Ethico-Aesthetic Paradigm*, translated by Paul Bains and Julian Pefanis (Bloomington and Indianapolis: Indiana University Press, 1995).

Hallward, Peter, 'Deleuze and the Redemption from Interest', *Radical Philosophy*, no. 81 (January–February 1997), pp. 6–21.

Haraway, Donna, *Primate Visions: Gender, Race and Nature in the Modern World of Science* (London: Routledge, 1989).

Hardt, Michael, *Gilles Deleuze: An Apprenticeship in Philosophy* (London: UCL Press, 1993).

Hume, David, *A Treatise of Human Nature* (Oxford: Oxford University Press, 1978).

Kerouac, Jack, *On the Road* (Harmondsworth: Penguin, 1972).

——, *Big Sur* (London: Flamingo, 1993).

Klossowski, Pierre, 'Digression à partir d'un portrait apocryphe', *L'Arc* 49 (1972), pp. 11–14.

Kojève, Alexandre, *Introduction à la lecture de Hegel: Leçons sur 'La Phénoménologie de l'Esprit'* (Paris: Gallimard, 1947).

Lecercle, Jean-Jacques, *The Violence of Language* (London: Routledge, 1990).

——, *The Philosophy of Nonsense: The Intuitions of Victorian Nonsense Literature* (London: Routledge, 1994).

——, 'The Pedagogy of Philosophy', *Radical Philosophy*, no. 75 (January-February 1996), pp. 44–6.

Lyotard, Jean-François, 'Capitalisme énergumène', *Critique*, no. 306 (1972), pp. 923–56. 'Energumen Capitalism', *Semiotext(e)*, vol. 2, no. 3 (1977), pp. 11–26.

——, et al., 'À Gilles Deleuze, l'inventeur, l'innocent, le fugueur: l'adieu des philosophes', *Libération* (7 novembre 1995), pp. 36–8.

Macey, David, *The Lives of Michel Foucault* (London: Hutchinson, 1993).

Magnus, Bernd and Kathleen M. Higgins, eds, *The Cambridge Companion to Nietzsche* (Cambridge: Cambridge University Press, 1996).

Martin, Jean-Clet, *Variations: la philosophie de Gilles Deleuze* (Paris: Editions Payot et Rivage, 1993).

Massumi, Brian, *A User's Guide to Capitalism and Schizophrenia: Deviations from Deleuze and Guattari* (London: MIT Press, 1992).

Mathy, Jean-Philippe, *Extrême-Occident: French Intellectuals and America* (University of Chicago Press, 1993).

Mauriac, Claude, *Le Temps immobile*, vol. IX: *Mauriac et fils* (Paris: Grasset, 1986).

Todd May, 'The Politics of Life in the thought of Gilles Deleuze' *Substance*, no. 66 (1991) pp. 24–35.

Merleau-Ponty, Maurice, *La Phénoménologie de la perception* (Paris: Gallimard, 1945). *The Phenomenology of Perception*, translated by Colin Smith (London: Routledge & Kegan Paul, 1962).

Miller, Arthur, *Timebends: A Life* (London: Methuen, 1987).

Miller, James, *The Passion of Michel Foucault* (London: Simon & Schuster, 1993).

Millett, Nick, 'The Trick of Singularity', *Theory, Culture and Society*, vol. 14, no. 2 (May 1997), pp. 51–66.

Minsky, Marvin, *The Society of the Mind* (London: Heinemann, 1987).

Nietzsche, Friedrich, *Beyond Good and Evil*, translated by R.J. Hollingdale (Harmondsworth: Penguin, 1973).

——, *Untimely Meditations*, translated by R.J. Hollingdale (Cambridge: Cambridge University Press, 1983).

Norris, Christopher, *Spinoza and the Origins of Modern Critical Theory* (Oxford: Blackwell, 1991).
Pasolini, Pier Paolo, 'The Cinema of Poetry' in *Movies and Methods: Volume 1* (London: University of California Press, 1976), pp. 542–8.
Patton, Paul, 'Review of *Cinema 1* & *Cinema 2*', *Screen*, vol. 32, no. 2 (Summer 1991), pp. 238–43.
Patton, Paul, ed., *Deleuze: A Critical Reader* (Oxford: Blackwell, 1996).
Patton, Paul, et al., 'Symposium: Gilles Deleuze, 1925–1995', *Radical Philosophy* (March/April 1996), pp. 2–6.
Perry, Petra,'Deleuze's Nietzsche', *boundary 2*, vol. 20, no. 1 (1993), pp. 174–91.
Proust, Marcel, *In Search of Lost Time: 6 Time Regained*, translated by C.K. Scott Moutcrieff and Terence Kilmartin, revised by D.J. Enright (Vintage: London, 1992).
Ree, Jonathan, 'Philosophy for Philosophy's Sake', *New Left Review*, no. 211 (May/June 1995), pp. 105–11.
Revel, Judith,'Foucault lecteur de Deleuze: de l'écart à la différence', *Critique*, nos 591–2 (août–septembre 1996), pp. 727–35.
Rorty, Richard, *Contingency, irony, and solidarity* (Cambridge: Cambridge University Press, 1989).
Sedgwick, Peter R., ed., *Nietzsche: A Critical Reader* (Oxford: Blackwell, 1995).
Surin, Kenneth,'The "Epochality" of Deleuzean Thought', *Theory, Culture and Society*, vol. 14, no. 2 (May 1997), pp. 9–21.
Tarkovsky, Andrey, Sculpting in *Time: Reflections on the cinema*, translated by Kitty Hunter-Blair (London: Faber & Faber, 1989).
Tournier, Michel, *Le Vent paraclet* (Paris: Gallimard, 1977).
——, 'Gilles Deleuze', *Critique*, nos 591–2 (août–septembre 1996), pp. 725–6.
Villani, Arnaud, 'Méthode et théorie dans l'œuvre de Gilles Deleuze', *Les Temps modernes*, no. 586 (janvier–février 1996), pp. 142–53.
Virilio, Paul, interview with Nicholas Zurbrugg, 'A Century of Hyper-Violence', *Economy and Society*, vol. 25, no. 1 (February 1996), pp. 112–26.
Wolfson, Louis, *Le Schizo et les langues* (Paris: Gallimard, 1971).
Woolf, Virginia, *The Waves* (St. Albans: Granada, 1977).
Zourabichivili, François, *Deleuze: Une Philosophie de L'Evénement*, (Paris: P.U.F. 1994).

Index